GOOD
SEXUAL
CITIZENSHIP

GOOD SEXUAL CITIZENSHIP

HOW TO CREATE A (SEXUALLY) SAFER WORLD

ELLEN FRIEDRICHS

CLEiS
PRESS

Published in the United States by Cleis Press, an imprint of Start Midnight, LLC, 101 Hudson Street, Thirty-Seventh Floor, Suite 3705, Jersey City, New Jersey 07302.

Printed in the United States.

Cover design: Emily Mahon
Jacket Design: Allyson Fields
Text design: Frank Wiedemann

First Edition.
10 9 8 7 6 5 4 3 2 1

Trade paper ISBN: 978-1-62778-287-6
E-book ISBN: 978-1-62778-501-3

To my students,
who have also been wonderful teachers.

CONTENTS

• • • • •

GOOD SEXUAL CITIZENSHIP —WHAT'S THAT ALL ABOUT?

There's no way around it: a lot of folks are having a lot of bad experiences with sex. Maybe they live or work in hostile sexual climates or have survived harassment or sexual assault. Maybe they are victims of misogyny, "toxic" masculinity, stifling gender expectations, or trans- or homophobia. Maybe the sex they are having is consensual but decidedly unsatisfying. Or maybe they just feel like something about their sexual experience is off, but they can't quite pinpoint what that is.

To be sure, things are different than they once were. A lot of people feel that gender roles are relaxing, that there is more space for noncishet* experiences, and that we aren't bound by the sexual conventions and morals of previous generations.

---

* The term *cishet* describes a person who is both cisgender and heterosexual. People are cishet if they are cisgender, meaning they identify with their assigned-at-birth gender, as well as heterosexual, or primarily experience cross-gender attraction.

Nevertheless, in recent years, laws and policies that restrict access to reproductive health care and that roll back recently won LGBTQ+† rights and protections have gained traction. Today's girls and women continue to be policed for how they dress, act, and experience sex, and today's boys and men continue to be fed a poisonous stew of messages urging them to hide emotions, pursue women for sex at all costs, and constantly guard against the charge that they might appear in any way feminine. And for trans, nonbinary, and gender-nonconforming folks, well, in a lot of places it can be a struggle just to find a place to pee, let alone to move safely through the world.

The result is that despite many important legal and social advances, some pretty powerful forces seem intent on turning back the clock. This can be exhausting for those of us who are trying not only to hold on to what we've got, but also to move the dial forward. Consequently, while there may be some times when we feel fired up and ready to act, there will also be plenty of others when we might just want to close our eyes to the enormity of the situation around us. Culture can feel too big to challenge, and interpersonal dynamics too, well, personal.

---

† I choose to use the acronym *LGBTQ+* instead of a longer acronyms like LGBTQIA or LGBTQQIP2SAA since I believe it simply and clearly identifies important aspects of a diverse group, and with the "+" aims to welcome and recognize the full spectrum of sexual orientations and gender identities. I also use the word *queer* throughout the book. In many ways I prefer this term to LGBTQ+, since it is widely inclusive and lacks any sense of hierarchy. I do understand that for some people *queer* retains the sting of an insult. However, I embrace it as a long-standing term of self-identification and one that, as historian George Chauncey explains in his book *Gay New York*[1] has been used in positive ways by the LGBTQ+ community since early in the twentieth century.

But one of the first ways to weaken hostile sexual climates is to ask ourselves where we, as individuals, might subconsciously support them in our personal lives. After that, it will be a lot easier to take on the political and social forces that sustain them. Tackling the power of these two components—the personal and the political, if you will—can allow us to strive for something that I like to think of as *good sexual citizenship.*‡

In this context, citizenship isn't about nationality, and it's not some kind of McCarthy-era ideal of conformity or purity. This is a modern citizenship, which means being honest, inclusive, compassionate, respectful, and responsible. It is one that means being courageous both in our intimate relationships and as people moving through the larger world around us.

Ultimately, this view of citizenship brings these ideals into the sexual arena and envisions working toward the creation of communities where every member feels safe and respected regardless of their involvement, or lack of personal involvement, in sexual activity. In this vision, people of all gender identities and sexual orientations, of all abilities, ages, and ethnicities, of all races and religions, of all social classes, geographic locations, and national origins are treated as humans deserving of respect. If we believe that freedom is fundamental to human dignity, then how hard is it to allow for freedom in the sexual realm as well?

---

‡ The term *sexual citizenship* can have a few different meanings. For example, it has been used to refer to the lack of rights afforded LGBTQ+ individuals and to discuss the sexual rights of youth. I am using it in a different context here, to refer to the responsibilities individuals have to themselves and others in the sexual realm.

At its heart, good sexual citizenship espouses a very basic idea: all sex should be wanted by all parties and enjoyed by all parties. This concept is essentially a simple one. And yet we so often stumble and fall so far from what should be an achievable goal. I mean, why is it that we still blame victims of sexual assaults for the attacks they have suffered? Can it truly be the case that the male orgasm is still frequently the expected end to cross-gender hookups, while the female orgasm is seen as a nice bonus, if that? Are we really still labeling people's identities based on the kind of sex they do or don't have? Why on earth are we still questioning if sex is consensual when someone has passed out after a night of drinking? Or whether or not they have the right to change their mind midway through? Or even if they should have the ability to make decisions about their own bodies at all?

Understanding why these situations are so common and developing strategies for change are the best ways to break the dangerous patterns in which so many of us are stuck. Then we can move toward a place where taking care of ourselves and others sexually is neither complicated nor confusing.

Good Sexual Citizenship connects important historical events to the current struggles that a lot of people are facing. It challenges the idea that we should be happy with what we've got, since when we consider the not-too-distant past, we've got so much. It also provides tools to navigate an increasingly complicated swirl of modern messages and lingering stereotypes about what kinds of behaviors are appropriate for whom.

This book is a guide to examining your own beliefs. It is a plan for action that can help you dismantle the social structures that sustain sexual hostility, like the myths we believe, the media we consume, and the policies we support. And it is map for anyone—educators, parents, everyday people in the world—who has looked around and wondered, in the face of so much sexual trauma and so little guidance, just what they could personally do to help.

I know that for years, I'd find myself in situations where someone would make an off-putting sexual comment or joke, or say something borderline homophobic or sexist. I'd titter uncomfortably, roll my eyes, maybe mumble, "That's kind of weird . . ." Or I'd make an excuse to leave. But I often wasn't sure how to respond beyond that, and then I would feel unsettled and guilty about my inaction. I also know there were plenty of times when I blamed folks—including myself—for predicaments where we should have shown a lot more compassion. Or when I wished I had the language to name what I was seeing or feeling.

I've improved at dealing with situations like that, and I've also gotten better about cutting myself some slack when I still don't quite know what to do—or even when I decide the safest bet is not to do anything. These are things this book can help you with, too. It can also help the people who have made those jokes or crossed those lines understand why their actions were harmful.

Good Sexual Citizenship opens with Chapter 1: The Bases for Our Biases, which looks at how, despite extraordinary advances, gender disparities continue to color so many sexual interactions, and how people of all genders are negatively impacted as a result. Chapter 2: Standing Up for Sex dives into the demonization of sex and challenges us to divorce sexuality from the lifetime of shame so many

xiv | GOOD SEXUAL CITIZENSHIP

people carry. Chapter 3: Consent—(I Promise) It's Not That Complicated dissects the history of sexual violence and looks at how prevention efforts have evolved, where they have stalled, and what we can do about it. Chapter 4: Little Kids, Big Questions and Chapter 5: The Teen Sex Situation ask anyone who has children, anyone who works with them, or even anyone who just cares about young people to reassess everything we think we know about keeping young people safe and helping them grow up sexually healthy. The last chapter, Chapter 6: Getting to Good Sexual Citizenship, creates a model for sexual citizenship that uses concrete strategies and community engagement as a way to build positive sexual spaces and dismantle hostile ones.

There is no doubt that my background, as a white, Jewish, Canadian woman who has lived in New York for most of her adult life, shapes the lens through which I operate. What also shapes my lens is my almost two decades spent educating kids, teens, and college students, my role as a parent to three children, and my own experiences as someone who, like so many others, has faced her own fair share of sexual hostility. Ultimately, though, I am a teacher, so that is my main frame of reference in *Good Sexual Citizenship*. As such, I am so grateful to my students, who have taught me so well, and to the social scientists, historians, psychologists, feminist theorists, sexuality educators, and critical thinkers whose research undergirds my own. In this book, I have tried to build on their foundational work as a way to help us create sexual spaces that are safe, beautiful, and not all that complicated. So, let's get started . . .

CHAPTER 1

THE BASES FOR OUR BIASES

SET UP BY SEXISM

The summer after eleventh grade, I left my boyfriend Mike[§] at home in Canada and hopped on a plane with forty other kids. We were bound for Three Rivers, Michigan, to spend six weeks doing a leadership training program at a summer camp. One of our roles as budding leaders was to run activities for the younger campers. So once a week we were assigned partners and told to come up with a thought-provoking session.

At first, most of my activities involved goofy games or baking cookies. But then I was assigned to work with a girl named Lily. Lily wore green Doc Martens, came to Three Rivers armed with a stack of books by authors I had never heard of (William S. Burroughs! Charles Bukowski! Anaïs Nin!), and had a great idea for an activity: we would get the kids to analyze songs to see if they were sexist.

So we collected a bunch of songs, like Guns N' Roses' "Used to Love Her," the Beastie Boys' "Girls," and the

---

§ All names used anecdotally in the book have been changed.

Beatles' "Run for Your Life." Then we made a mixtape (this *was* the '90s, after all), got our assigned campers together, and pressed play. Afterward, we put on the punk band Fugazi's "Suggestion" (which is possibly still the most pointedly anti–sexual harassment anthem ever) to counter the messages of the previous songs.

Now, I don't know if the eight-year-olds we were working with actually got a lot out of our session. But I certainly did.

Though I had led Lily to believe I was as up on this issue as she was, the idea of listening to music for the message was actually pretty new to me, though it was something that I had been thinking about more and more. Mainly, that was because of a really uncomfortable experience I'd had at a concert the previous spring.

It was the Public Enemy/Anthrax show. I went with Mike and some of his guy friends. As the bands joined forces to belt out some early version of a rock/rap hybrid, three women came out on stage. They had big hair and were wearing thong bikinis and heels. They didn't sing or dance or play an instrument. Instead, they strutted around the stage as the bands encouraged the crowd to scream, "Pussy! Pussy! Pussy!"

I was sixteen, and aside from the models on stage, I felt like the only girl in the place. I didn't know where to look, and I wasn't sure what to do with my hands as the fist-pumping crowd around me, boyfriend included, chanted in unison.

That concert ended any interest I had in rock/rap.

However, it wasn't until Lily suggested that we dissect song lyrics that I realized just how prevalent sexism was in music and that it was possible to find bands I liked that didn't make me uncomfortable. It's not that I pored over lyric sheets before buying new music after that. But thinking about the issue definitely made me more conscious of what I listened to and which bands I wanted to support.

That event was one of my first *aha* moments about the very real role sexism played in my life, and in the lives of all the girls and women around me. But even though I became better and better at identifying the more blatant examples of it, like so many of us, I can still find it hard to get at the heart of what drives a lot of the more insidious, often subtle forms of gender-based discrimination that we find ourselves having to navigate as a culture.

And boy, do we still have a lot to navigate. At the same time, it can be tricky to unpack the less obvious forces driving gender bias without making people, particularly some men, feel defensive or under attack.

To a certain extent, I understand that response. I remember as a kid overhearing my mother's friend fretting about an experience at a women's rights march that she attended with her ten-year-old son: "He saw a sign that said, 'Stop raising boys to be rapists' and immediately asked if that meant he was going to grow up to be one."

Thirty years later, it's not just kids trying to figure this stuff out. There are plenty of men of all ages who still have trouble when they encounter statements that don't line up with how they see themselves and their place in the world. These might be comments about how men are statistically more likely to perpetuate violence than are other groups. Or references to male privilege. Or even ads that attempt to address men's roles in issues like bullying and violence and sexual harassment.

To some people, such statements feel an awful lot like individual indictments, rather than the critiques of culture that were intended. Think about it: if someone criticizes a group you belong to, it's a natural reaction to feel that person is, by implication, also criticizing you. And on the individual level, feeling defensive about such a criticism might make sense when we acknowledge that just because most violence is committed by men, that doesn't mean that most men are violent. Or that just because men tend to hold more power than women and gender minorities, practically speaking, most men aren't all that powerful.

So while we try to unpack the societal forces that uphold sexism, it can help to remember that condemning a cultural system is not the same as condemning an individual person. There is no question that individuals need to be held accountable for their actions. But we can hold individuals accountable when deserved, while also critiquing a culture that encourages hostile and discriminatory behavior. This chapter looks at how gender-based discrimination and gender bias are at the heart of so much sexual hostility, and it shows how dismantling these forces can help create an overall sexually safer world for everyone who inhabits it.

AREN'T WE JUST WIRED DIFFERENTLY?

Often-cited research has found different patterns of connectivity within and between the hemispheres of female and male brains.

As a result, some neuroscientific studies have been interpreted as saying that women are "wired" better for emotional intelligence, social skills, memory, and multitasking, while men are "naturally" better at perception and coordinated movement.

But even if it sounds like there is some science behind this view, we have to be careful before assuming it is fact.

Our interpretations of studies, as well as the interpretations by researchers and the media, may be influenced by gender stereotyping.

Plus, the brain adapts in the same way as a muscle: it gets larger with extra use. This means that it is possible that a woman's brain may become "wired" for multitasking simply because society expects that of her, and so she uses that part of her brain more often. And social rewiring starts early. Segregating the way children play—giving dolls to girls and cars to boys—could be changing how our brains develop! In other words, these interests might not be "natural" at all.

As psychologist Cordelia Fine writes in *Testosterone Rex: Myths of Sex, Science, and Society,*

> Sex isn't a biological dictator that sends gonadal hormones hurtling through the brain, uniformly masculinizing male brains, monstrously feminizing female brains. Sexual differentiation of the brain turns out to be an untidily interactive process, in which multiple factors—genetic, hormonal, environmental, and epigenetic . . .—all act and interact to affect how sex shapes the entire brain.[1]

The bottom line is that we still know remarkably little about how the brain works, so making claims about what is "hardwired" and what is behavior that responds to social conditions is risky, if not misleading. Additionally, such claims can tend to reinforce existing views about gender, many of which are problematic.

What we can do is continue to follow ongoing brain research with the full awareness that we're all subject to implicit bias (aka, the unconscious attribution of certain qualities to people based on their membership in a certain group) about gender norms and roles.

IT ALL OVERLAPS

With all this talk about gender, it probably pays to pause for a minute and be clear about what is typically meant by that term. Though *gender* is often used interchangeably with the word *sex*, the two have been defined somewhat differently, at least since the 1970s. Sex is generally understood to be the biological way we categorize people (typically as male, female, and intersex). Gender, on the other hand, refers to the social and psychological ways those designations translate.

While in reality there are endless possible genders, in a post-colonial society, the vast majority of people grow up in a culture that assumes sex and gender to be *binary*, and where the prevailing expectation is that they will identify as one of two genders: male or female. These categorizations are usually assigned at birth and are based solely on the appearance of someone's genitals and/or on their chromosome pattern. People with penises and XY chromosomes are typically assigned a male gender (sometimes called assigned male at birth, or AMAB). Folks with vaginas and XX chromosomes are usually assigned a female gender (sometimes called assigned female at birth, or AFAB). When these birth assignments line up with how a person identifies their own gender, we refer to that person as being *cisgender*. But when they don't, that person might identify as transgender, genderfluid, genderqueer, agender, or nonbinary, or two-spirit, for example. And when someone's physical body doesn't fit exactly into either the male or female categories (which happens in as many[2] as one in fifteen hundred births), they might identify as intersex.

One challenge in talking about sexual violence is that traditionally most research has been conducted on a male/female binary. This is something that Safe Passage, a Massachusetts-based anti–domestic violence group, covers in their guide to eliminating interpersonal violence. In the guide, they take on the fact that, while such research can provide valuable information, it can also erase people of other gender identities. This is a major problem. However, if we react to this problem by ignoring the findings of such research, we also lose the ability to disrupt the forces that support so many violent acts.

Safe Passage suggests a few ways to address this. For one thing, they suggest we work to integrate increasingly available research that covers a larger range of populations into our existing knowledge. For another, we need to accept the paradox of using information gleaned from a binary worldview to help dismantle violence that is often a product of that very system. As they write, "If we ignore the gendered nature of domestic and sexual violence, we would fail to define and understand the problem accurately . . . We would ignore the connection between cultural sexism and men's violence against women. But if we talk about violence in only [binary] gendered terms, using the inaccurate categories provided to us by social science, we risk erasing the experience of people of other genders, of male survivors, and of those who were harmed by female perpetrators."[3]

In large part, the fact that we are even able to have these conversations at all can be attributed to the foundational work of two African American women: legal scholar Kimberlé Crenshaw and feminist writer bell hooks. Crenshaw developed the theory of *intersectionality* back in the late 1980s to describe the overlapping nature of oppression. This theory introduced the idea that many people experience oppression not solely based on one quality, but rather they are marginalized by complex and interwoven factors. For example, the oppression of a queer Black woman cannot simply be seen through the lens of sexism without also understanding the role of homophobia and racism, and other individual factors, as well.

hooks's vast canon includes a phenomenon she identified as *the imperialist white supremacist capitalist patriarchy*. That phrase can sound overwhelming, but it is an important one, since what it describes are the interlocking structures that are the foundation of much of American identity, as well as American political and social makeups.

The idea of *imperialism* grew out of the "colonization" of indigenous populations by Europeans. Today we also use this term to refer to a dominant entity that imposes its way of life upon another culture. The concept of *white supremacy* can conjure up visions of the KKK or avowed

Nazis. However, white supremacy is much more than these extremes. It can also explain a system where white people and their institutions are seen as the norm and promoted at the expense of nonwhite people and nonwhite cultures. *Capitalism* is defined as an economic system of privately owned goods and services where owners are encouraged to compete for economic control, which can relegate those with fewer resources to lower economic strata. Finally, the term *patriarchy* describes a system where men hold the most power and dominate social and political life.

hooks's definition understands these terms as interconnected systems, and not as individual people or groups. So people can't be "the patriarchy," but they sure can facilitate, uphold, or perpetuate it. And people who uphold these systems can be of any race, gender, sexual orientation, or class. They can even be a member of a targeted group. Similarly, people who work to dismantle these systems can be from any group, including one that is privileged by this system. There are men, for example, who work against patriarchal systems and women who support them. Some people call this entire system working together the *kyriarchy*, a term that explains how all structures of power are actually interlocking forces.

Taken together, these systems can be seen as the backbone for what is often called "toxic masculinity." This refers to an idea of masculinity that requires men to be strong physically and emotionally and that tells them to be aggressive and stoic at all times. As writer Laurie Penny (who uses both she and they pronouns) explains in their book, *Unspeakable Things: Sex, Lies and Revolution*, "One of the saddest things about modern society is that it has made us understand masculinity as something toxic and violent, associated with domination, control and savagery, being hungry for power and money and acquisitive, abusive sex." But masculinity, in and of itself, is not defined by these things.

Penny also reminds us that while many people like to imagine a "golden age" of masculinity, pointing to any number of icons, from the founding fathers to the strong but silent screen heroes of 1950s cinema, this was more myth than anything. Penny continues, "There have always been men who were too poor, too queer, too sensitive, too disabled, too compassionate or simply too clever to fit in."[4]

As people have begun to try to dismantle the idea of toxic masculinity, there has been increasing alarm over a perceived attack on "traditional masculinity." In some ways, this is a reactionary outcry by men who fear losing power—even if they never really had power to begin with. But in other ways, there is a real sense of unmooring among some men who worry that everything they have learned about being male is now being called into question. Just think, if you had been raised to think that good, decent men protect women, are providers, and are strong and brave and stoic, it can feel like a real blow to think you're being told that your concept of being a decent person in the world is no longer valued, and rather is being deemed a threat. But that's thing: it is not the qualities of human decency that are being attacked. Critiquing "toxic masculinity" is *not* the same as critiquing masculinity in general, nor is it calling all traits associated with masculinity "toxic." For some people, this is a hard distinction to make.

On the flip side, for other folks, it can be hard to defend terms like *masculinity* or *femininity* at all. But I think that before we try to abolish them altogether, it is worth considering how redefining a word like *masculinity* could actually be really positive. Currently, a lot of the traits that our culture values, and then, as a result, rewards, are harsh ones that encourage violence. It doesn't have to be that way, and it isn't too hard to imagine valuing other traits that a lot of men already possess.

In reality, there are so many ways men can and do express positive sides of their gender. I think of my dad solemnly telling me, at age ten, why I should not be calling the school musical *gay* after I determined it to be overly schmaltzy. Or of my son and his classmates putting on a glamorous fashion show of found objects from a friend's closet. Or of the role my children's four uncles play in their lives. Or of my partner coparenting with me following the death of my older kids' father. Or of my former student coming back to talk to my high school classes about the importance of consent during sex. Sure, people of any gender could have done these things, but when boys and men do them, I also think we have an opportunity to amend our understanding of what it means to be *masculine*.

SEXISM: WHAT YOU MAY HAVE HEARD AND WHY THAT'S BS

WHAT YOU MAY HAVE HEARD:
Sexism is just not a problem like it used to be.

WHY THAT'S BS:
When women and girls still have to navigate the wage gap, beauty standards, sexual harassment and rape,

double standards, and internet trolls threatening violence at every turn, this is a pretty tough claim to make.

· · ·

WHAT YOU MAY HAVE HEARD:
Women have the same opportunities as men. Didn't that happen when they got the ability to vote?

WHY THAT'S BS:
Structural inequality, which gives certain groups of people unequal power in relation to other groups, continues to bar women from taking political power, and female candidates still face major hurdles that male candidates do not. Just think: even after the historic gains in the 2018 midterm elections, women still only held a little more than 20 percent of elected positions in the United States.

· · ·

WHAT YOU MAY HAVE HEARD:
If sexism is still a problem, why are more women currently graduating from college than men?

WHY THAT'S BS:
Once they graduate, women still face workplace discrimination. Women only hold 5 percent of Fortune 500 CEO positions, and they are more often funneled into lower-paying professions, like teaching and nursing, than are men. Or they become family practitioners instead of surgeons, or do public interest

law instead of corporate—all great options, but all ones that command significantly lower salaries.

• • •

WHAT YOU MAY HAVE HEARD:
I know lots of women who: make more money than men, have husbands who stay home with the kids, don't take any crap . . . etc.

WHY THAT'S BS:
The problem with sexism is that it is part of a larger system that holds all women down and hurts people of all genders in the process.

Everyone can think of examples of women who break the glass ceiling (Angela Merkel! Sheryl Sandberg! Oprah Winfrey!), and men who defy stereotypes by staying home with kids or who have been the victims of sexual harassment. But when these are exceptions rather than the rule, the fact is, sexism is alive and well.

CAN BOYS AND MEN BE VICTIMS OF SEXISM?

It is pretty clear that much of what we call *toxic* masculinity is born of a system that views girls and women as inferior to boys and men. The manifestation of this system is typically called *sexism*, and the views that drive it are sometimes referred to as *misogyny*. Even though we might not use the term *sexism* to describe actions that disenfranchise or marginalize boys and men, it is important to understand how they can also be harmed in such environments.

The threat of being called "too feminine" is often used as a way to control men's actions. For example, for a lot of boys and men, being called *gay* (and its far more hostile F-word synonym) remains the most powerful way to keep them in line. And this line is reinforced a thousand times a day in a thousand subtle and not-so-subtle ways. Think about it: in many communities, if a woman tells her friend she looks hot in a new outfit, or if two girls watching a movie play with each other's hair or share a bed at a sleepover, no one thinks anything of it. Sometimes, if girls or women hook up sexually with each other, it isn't even seen as a big deal, or as an indication of their sexual orientation.

Now flip the script. Imagine two male friends snuggling on the couch while they watch TV. Or one guy saying to another, "Wow, that bathing suit is really sexy." Or kissing at a party one night. It's not a stretch to say that in plenty of places, these kinds of things would find guys on the receiving end of a slur.

That isn't to say nothing has changed in recent years. We now live in a world where a gay teen can come out to his peers by changing his social media status and then can aim to go to an LGBTQ+-friendly college, and if he wants, get legally married and have a family; where transgender celebrities like Laverne Cox are not only household names but are seen as public role models and inspirations; and where Cover Girl can cause great excitement by naming a popular male YouTuber as a spokesperson.

These are big advances from my experiences in the '90s, when the fight for gay marriage was in its earliest days, and when the only time trans folks were seen in media was as a punch line (think: *Ace Ventura: Pet*

Detective), or as a talk-show curiosity. And it is a world far different from the one folks grew up in during the 1950s and '60s, where a boy who carried his books wrong (never hugged to the chest, only tucked under one arm and propped on a hip!), was committing social suicide, and where girls were literally banned from wearing pants to school.

In light of these changes, young people often get the message that they are living in a world of gender equality and acceptance for the LGBTQ+ community. That is a real positive. So one would have hoped that over the past decade there would have been a lot less gender scrutinizing. But as many of us know, we have a long way to go. Plenty of boys still suffer at the hands of assumptions that keep them on a fairly short leash and that make them police their actions and emotions at every turn. And what does this policing offer protection from? Well, for a long time it was protecting them from being called a sissy. Today, we all know that was just code for something else. But that *something else* still remains a powerful threat today.

Much of this has to do with the very real forces of misogyny, homophobia, and misinformation in our society. Many people still hold the mistaken view that lesbians want to be men and gay men want to be women. Since we live in a world that is both patriarchal and homophobic, and that doesn't understand the difference between sexual orientation (who you are attracted to) and gender (identifying as male, female, trans, or nonbinary, for example), this baffles folks who perceive gay men as *wanting* to be the *lesser* gender. This belief justifies homophobia with the rationale that gay men have chosen to be inferior, and so deserve any condemnation they encounter.

This belief is also why the use of the word *gay* as a slur is so effective. For heterosexual men and boys, this threat of being perceived as the *lesser* gender is held over them to make sure they conform to stereotypically masculine ways of behaving. For some men, this constant checking of oneself and others for signs of transgression can result in the feeling that they need to live up to unrealistic expectations of masculinity. This can negatively affect relationships with women, and it can make it hard for a lot of men and boys to form close, intimate, same-gender relationships because they're wary of the implications of those connections.

It's not that girls and women are off the hook. Being mislabeled a lesbian is still an effective tool of controlling women. But girls and women are more commonly kept in line by another set of unwritten rules that police their sexual behaviors and that dangle the threat of sexual violence over their heads at all times. So they are monitored and their actions scrutinized, but just with a slightly different emphasis. (That's something I'll cover in much more depth in chapters 2 and 3.)

The forces of sexism create an environment that can be negative for people of all genders. But why are we so set on monitoring the actions of others in the first place? There are a few reasons. Social psychologists view the need to belong as an intrinsic human motivation. But when we combine this motivation with another common human emotion—namely, insecurity—things can get messy. Many people worry that any action on their part will be questioned and will single them out as being different. In order to deflect attention from what they're doing and direct it toward someone else, it can be tempting to name-call, almost as a protective measure. This becomes even more severe when the people involved are also working under the premise that difference is scary and change is threatening.

IT'S NOT ALWAYS OBVIOUS

Of course, while some of the harms of sexism are obvious, others are much more subtle.

For example, a few years ago I was teaching my college class. We were talking about sexual assault and the role of alcohol. One of the male students was trying to make the point that sometimes women get drunk as an excuse to hook up, and then they can't really call it rape if they decide things went further than they wanted.

A lot of the other students immediately spoke up and challenged this logic. For example, one explained that having sex with a drunk person was illegal. Another pointed out that it was up to the person trying to move things further along to really be sure that the other person was into it. A third added that just because something didn't fit the "stranger in the alley" rape model, that didn't mean that an incident wasn't an assault. All the comments seemed to fall on deaf ears until a last guy said, "Just think about if that happened to your sister." Finally, the first student began to back down, and you could feel the energy in the room change.

But I couldn't let that reasoning sit. So I jumped in. "I appreciate how you're trying to get a classmate on board. The thing is, no woman should be raped, whether or not she's related to a man." All of a sudden the mood changed again, and I knew I was in for another round.

That "what if it was your sister" rationale is a pretty good example of benevolent sexism. This is a kind of discrimination that is presented in positive ways and often expresses admiration for women or a sense that women need to be protected and cared for, or promotes the idea that women should be celebrated if they have qualities that are traditionally seen as feminine, such as being nurturing, peaceful, or loving.

Sounds nice, right? Unfortunately, the impact of benevolent sexism is significant. For example, studies have found that in many ways, benevolent sexism is more likely to reinforce women's acceptance of gender inequality than is overt hostile sexism, which is easier to criticize.[5] It has also been shown that the more people are exposed to benevolent sexism, the more likely they are to justify discrimination, and the less likely they are to actively fight against it.[6]

And fighting against this type of subtle sexism can be tough because a lot of people are so used to the gender dynamics that underpin it. These dynamics include things like men paying on dates, women staying home with the kids, and people working in fields that are still viewed in gendered terms, like nursing or construction. Plus, since so much benevolent sexism seems complimentary, pointing out how it is harmful can feel petty. For example, many of us are familiar with the idea that women are just kinder and gentler. That sounds like a good thing, but the result is that women who are outspoken or who are more confrontational are often judged in a particularly harsh light.

Similarly, when we accept a premise like one that says women are more natural parents or are better caregivers, women who don't adopt those roles are seen as betraying their gender, and men who do adopt those roles are either looked at with suspicion or lauded as examples of exemplary behavior for something that women are simply expected to do. As another example, think about someone who was raised to believe that "good girls say no." What does that make a woman who says yes to sex? Even if she is your partner? What does that say about you, if you are the women now saying yes? Even in the context of a socially sanctioned marriage, this message can result in a lot of baggage.

If you wonder how benevolent sexism might play out in your life, ask yourself if you agree with any of these statements:

▸ Women are naturally sensitive and nurturing.
▸ Men are naturally less emotional.
▸ It's a little weird for men to ask women for help with a physical task.
▸ Women are simply better parents than men.
▸ Women are more peaceful.
▸ Men are more aggressive. It's probably all the testosterone.
▸ It's a man's role to take care of and protect women.
▸ It's just polite for men to open doors for women or offer them a seat.
▸ It's a sign of respect if men initiate dates, make the first move, or pay for food and drinks in cross-gender relationships. Plus, how else would you know they were interested in more than just being friends?

I know that I can buy into some of these views and that some, like expecting a guy to pay on a first date, are pretty hard for a lot of people to give up! But I also know that it is always worth examining our assumptions and asking if our behaviors are motivated by being kind, helpful, or generous, or if they are motivated by a gendered sense of how we think the world should operate.

WHAT YOU CAN DO TO FIGHT SEXUALLY HOSTILE CLIMATES

Consider your responses:

▸ Don't excuse sexist behavior as being natural, or normal, or "just the way things are."

▸ Don't tolerate sexist jokes or comments. Address them, or leave when you hear them.

▸ If you have or work with kids, don't blame them for provoking harassment. Stand up for them and be the adult voice they need to fight for change.

▸ Same thing for anyone in your life. Give the person telling you about their experience the benefit of the doubt. If that isn't your first instinct, ask yourself why you'd assume a potential harasser has more credibility than someone who felt you were close enough to them to be a confidant.

▸ Stand up for other people when you see them being harassed. This will help change your community's atmosphere and make harassment and hostile behavior seem less acceptable.

Be aware of your options:

▸ Telling someone to stop bothering you may be all it takes. Sometimes people don't realize that their behavior is unwanted.

▸ If you do decide to confront a harasser, bring a friend (or, if you are a teen, bring an adult) along to back you up and to be a witness.

▸ Text or email the harasser and keep a copy for yourself and tell them to stop. (Keep in mind the harasser might show this to other people.)

▸ If confronting a harasser doesn't work, or if you don't feel comfortable doing so, figure out if there is someone higher up in the chain of command whom you can loop in (say, school officials or employers).

▸ Keep a record of everything that happens. This doesn't mean you have to secretly record every comment you hear, but jot down when and where things occur.

▸ Be aware you have the legal right to complain to your school, college, or employer anonymously.

▶ When necessary, take legal action. This is obviously a huge step and will require getting other supportive folks involved. But if you are subject to a persistent hostile environment, it might be what you choose to do.

Address your larger communities:

▶ Find out what your campus, school, or employer's policy on harassment is. If there isn't a policy about harassment or sex discrimination, ask for one to be created.
▶ Advocate for your school or workplace to implement a program on sexual harassment, consent, and sexual assault that goes beyond a twenty-year-old movie where a boss pinches his secretary's butt.
▶ Reach out to folks of all genders and sexual orientations in your advocacy work.
▶ If you are connected to a school or college, run a peer training, or have other students, educate your community, since research shows that some of the most effective education comes from people you can relate to.

THE IMPACT OF THE STANDARD SEX MESSAGE

One of the places where gendered views are often the most deeply entrenched is in regard to sex, and like many people, I first started getting messages about this subject at home. I remember an early conversation with my mom, when I was maybe seven or eight, after a girl from my school was molested by her neighbor. "Do you know what sex is?" my mom had asked.

"Um, yeah?" I'd told her.

I mean, I knew that when I had asked my dad if a woman could get pregnant in jail, I got some confusing information about eggs and sperm. I also knew about the word *humping*, which my friend Tanya had explained in hushed tones meant when a boy lay on top of a girl and pushed his penis between her legs. And I knew what was inside the covers of the *Playboy* magazines my friend Jill's dad kept in their basement. All that was sex.

But this was the first time my mom had broached the subject with me, and what I was about to add to my roster of sex knowledge was the fact that sex was also something grown men could do to children, and that this was a very, very bad thing from which a girl might never recover. Ostensibly, the conversation was supposed to give me warnings and rules designed to keep me safe. Yet far from being empowering, my mom's message was terrifying.

It was also regularly reinforced at every turn: by the outdated reel-to-reel stranger-danger films shown to the girls, but not to the boys, in my fourth-grade class; by a complicated formula of whom to go to for help in public spaces (first police, then women with children in tow, followed by women without kids); by suggestions about whom to avoid sitting next to on the bus (men, basically in any way, shape, or form); and by the rules that my parents had for me, but not for my brothers, about coming home after dark.

Of course, I wasn't only getting messages about avoiding rape at this age. I was also learning what sex was supposed to look like and what was considered sexy. Those messages could be subtle, dribbled out in the comments of classmates about who was or wasn't hot, or via the media's endless and interchangeable barrage of skinny, pretty, big-boobed white girls. And they could be overt, like the first porn video I ever saw, shown to me at thirteen by the adult tenant who lived in my friend's basement suite, who'd asked if we wanted to watch a movie. The movie, it turned out, was of the triple-X variety, and I sat in frozen shock as he gave a running commentary: "Yeah, this one's got a great ass. This girl's not as hot. Her boobs are too small. This one's okay—she's better at blow jobs."

The messages also came from the girls I wanted to befriend and who teased me for being a virgin until I wasn't one anymore. They came from the books I read, the TV I watched (oh, what I learned from *Married With Children*), and from the fashion magazines whose tips I alternately mocked and devoured.

However, in the grand scheme of things, I was spared a lot of the worst messaging.

I didn't have abstinence education that taught us that a girl's virginity was to be prized above all else, and that those who could not claim this title were tarnished.

I wasn't part of a religious institution that told me I was going to hell for being queer.

I didn't live with parents who celebrated my brothers' sexual conquests while punishing any expression on my part.

I also wasn't getting the same messages as a lot of the boys around me. I might have been learning that I should avoid getting raped while still looking attractive to men.

But as I later discovered, boys were learning that sex with a girl was an initiation and the ultimate display of hetero-sexual masculinity.

In many ways, the environment I grew up in was really different one than the world today's teens are navigating. I feel relieved that when I tell my students about the stuff that passed as normal when I was in high school (like clear incidents of rape or harassment that we never labeled, blatantly homophobic comments made by teachers, or the fact that not a single person was out in my high school), they seem surprised. That surprise is a good reminder that there has been progress. This can be easy to forget, since the fact that we are openly talking about these issues so much more today can make it seem like we are living in a more dangerous time than ever. That isn't the case, and this is important to keep in perspective.

However, we're talking about these issues more frequently today precisely because there are still deeply problematic prevailing cultural messages that Americans get about sex. These messages tend to be contradictory, confusing, and reinforced at every turn. One of the most enduring for women is that their worth as people is directly correlated to how sexually desirable men find them. Another common one is related to the importance of women's sexual purity and chastity. So, unless it is in a very limited setting (at the extreme, solely in a cishet marriage), these combined messages boil down to *look sexy but don't have sex*.

In some ways, this is less confusing than the messages that boys and men hear from day one. A lot of men grow up hearing that they should never hit a girl and that they should protect women. Though these views are forms of benevolent sexism, since they default to the notion that men are strong and women weak, they are also in direct contradiction to another set of messages many boys hear: that sex is something they are owed and need to pursue at all costs, and that any girl who resists is either frigid, playing hard to get, or a lesbian. This can translate into: *Never take no for an answer. Oh, not interested? What are you, a wimp? Gay?* Boys and men are then generally left to sort out which messages to listen to on their own.

But if they listen to the sex "pursuit and pressure" script, they may think that women are supposed to play hard to get and will only acquiesce to sex after much negotiation. As a result, plenty of women have had the exhausting experience of dealing with a guy who just won't take no for an answer. His persistence may be the result of his belief that a woman really wants to have sex and is just playing coy, or it might come of thinking he is a really good guy and she just needs to be convinced of this fact. This behavior is seen at totally acceptable in our culture. For example, in movies like *Say Anything*; *Crazy, Stupid, Love*; and *500 Days of Summer*, characters who basically meet the legal definition of stalkers are presented as romantic leads. Then there is the "promposal" trend, where teens try to outdo each other with over-the-top, public, and sometimes humiliating or scary (think fake kidnappings) invitations to a school dance.

Why is this a big deal? For some people, the results of this collective narrative can be deadly. Take, for example, the fact that according to the Justice Department, most domestic assaults and murders that are reported are committed by men against women and take place *after* a couple breaks up.[7] Writer Jessica Valenti calls these "rejection killings," and while they often impact women who were in a relationship with the assailant, they have also been committed by near, or total, strangers. Examples include murders by boys whose prom invitations were declined and by men who were turned down on the dance floor or who were called out for sexual harassment, just to name a few.[8] This chilling phenomenon is, of course, in part driven by misogyny—those same messages that tell men that sex is owed to them, and that women who reject them are frigid or coy. These beliefs, at their extreme, allow men to see women as personal property and then to adopt an attitude of "if I can't have you, nobody can."

Another troubling outcome of this environment is the creation of *incels* (self-proclaimed "involuntary celibates") who justify violence, whether real or imaginary, against women on the basis that these women have rejected their advances, and MRAs, or men's rights activists. Incels tend to feel intense resentment and anger over the fact that they aren't having the sex they think they deserve. Though incels have existed for some time, it has only been in recent years—following horrifying events like the 2014 California rampage by self-proclaimed incel Elliot Rodger, which left six people dead and fourteen injured, or the 2018 van massacre in Toronto by another self-proclaimed incel named Alek Minassian, which saw ten people killed and another sixteen critically injured— that the issue began to attract more national attention.

MRAs, on the other hand, have been in the public consciousness a little longer. In comparison to incels, they can seem less terrifying. But while this movement has not been punctuated by as much intense violence, it is still troubling. MRAs are often focused on issues of, well, men's rights, particularly surrounding fathers' custody fights, often challenging what they see as antimale double standards. They also rally around issues social safety nets for women, which they feel discriminate against men.

Yet nothing seems to collectively upset them as much as the idea of feminism, which MRAs tend to blame for any problem men might have. As Anne Thériault writes in *HuffPost Canada*, "They do things like starting the Don't Be That Girl campaign, a campaign that accuses women of making false rape reports. They attend feminist events in order to bully and intimidate women, they flood online feminist spaces with threatening messages, and they regularly use smear campaigns and scare tactics to make the women who don't back down afraid for their physical safety."[9] These are really terrifying actions, and what makes them ever more worrisome is the fact that such views, which can lead to and then justify extreme actions, are not exclusively held by outspoken incels or MRAs.

Some research has found that there is a prevailing cultural belief that sex should be pursued by men at all costs.[10] The impact of this was demonstrated in a paper published in the *Journal of Sex Research* that looked at the tactics of sexual coercion. In the study, over 40 percent of the women interviewed said they had experienced pressure for sex by men, yet many didn't see this as a problem. In fact, many of the study participants even understood it as a positive method of achieving sex! As the authors write:

> Our study raises an interesting question about the disparity between the relatively large number of participants who reported being receivers of sexual

persistence and the much smaller number who reported being perpetrators. [One] explanation is that participants did not perceive their behaviors as tactics of sexual persistence. Many of our participant perpetrators qualified their behaviors as playful or beneficial, indicating that the behaviors were intended to improve their relationships.[11]

This study is a reminder that while some men blatantly think that they are owed sex and need to chase it at all costs, others assume the pressure role under the guise of flirting. And it isn't men alone who buy into this script. Women often do as well. This is troubling. But given all the messages that normalize the idea that men shouldn't take no for an answer, it isn't really surprising.

LEGISLATING AGAINST SEXISM

The term *sexism* was only coined in the 1960s, but the fight against gender-based discrimination began well before that and has continued long after. Here are some highlights:

1920: With the passage of the Nineteenth Amendment, suffragettes win the right for women to vote. This is an important accomplishment but one which, in practice, really only guarantees the vote for white women.

1947: The Supreme Court rules that women are allowed to serve on juries.

1963, 1964: Taken together, the Equal Pay Act of 1963 and Title VII of the Civil Rights Act of 1964 prohibit employment discrimination on the basis of race, color, religion, sex, pregnancy, and national origin.

1965, 1972: *Griswold v. Connecticut* is ruled on in 1965, legalizing contraceptives for married couples. With *Eisenstadt v. Baird* in 1972, the *Griswold* ruling was extended to allow unmarried people to use birth control as well.

1972: Title IX passed, banning sex discrimination and harassment in schools.

1973: In *Roe v. Wade*, the Supreme Court legalizes abortion on the basis that women have a constitutional right to privacy with their doctors.

1993: The Family and Medical Leave Act (FMLA) guarantees eligible employees twelve weeks of unpaid leave each year to care for a newborn or newly adopted child or seriously ill family member, or to recover from their own serious health conditions.

1994: The Violence Against Women Act passes. This provides funding for services for victims of rape and domestic violence.

2009: The Lilly Ledbetter Fair Pay Act allows victims of pay discrimination to file a complaint with the government against their employer.

2010: The Affordable Care Act (ACA) passes. This covers maternity care, eliminates preexisting condition exemptions, and prevents health plans from charging women more than men for the same coverage. The ACA also covers well-woman preventive health services (contraceptives, mammograms, cancer screenings, prenatal care, and counseling for domestic violence) as basic health care for women at no additional cost and includes the first federal ban on sex discrimination in health-care programs and activities.

There have also been a lot of significant losses. Some of these include the erosion of existing protections, like attacks on *Roe v. Wade*, which have resulted in the passage of countless laws limiting access to abortion and making this legal medical procedure functionally unobtainable for countless people. Or the chipping away at the Violence Against Women Act, which has resulted in LGBTQ+, indigenous women, and undocumented immigrants losing protections over the years. Or the deliberate undercutting of the Affordable Care Act (Obamacare) and the constant threats to dismantle the program altogether.

Other losses relate to legislation that never passed in the first place. One of the most notable examples of this is something called the Equal Rights Amendment. The ERA was a proposed amendment to the United States Constitution that was designed to guarantee equal rights for women. Originally written by suffragettes Alice Paul and Crystal Eastman, it was introduced in Congress in 1923. For years it was defeated. But in 1972, the ERA was finally passed by Congress and sent to the states for ratification. Yet even so, it did not achieve the required thirty-eight states needed to be successful. So despite being reintroduced annually, at the time of this writing, this most basic of gender safeguards has yet to pass.

BUT THE GIRLS LIKE IT WHEN OTHER GUYS DO THE SAME THING!

Have you ever heard someone joke that the difference between sexual harassment and flirting is whether the guy is attractive? I hate that one, but it makes me think about an experience I had early in my career when I worked for a gap-year program. One day, a few of the girls called me. "You have to kick Louis off the program," they said. They explained he creeped them out, looking at them while they were changing and making comments about wanting to touch them when they were sleeping.

When I talked to Louis, he was utterly confused. He felt like he wasn't doing anything different than the other guys in the group, and he couldn't understand why the other boys' comments were met with giggles, while his were met with hostility. It fell to me to explain to Louis that the difference between his actions and those of the other boys was that Louis's behavior was unwanted. That just because a girl enjoyed attention from another boy, it didn't mean she enjoyed the same thing when Louis did it.

Ultimately, we asked Louis to leave the program, but I felt bad about the situation. The group was living together in close quarters and sharing all of their personal space. A fairly visible number of the participants talked casually about sex and hooked up with each other freely.

I could see how this could be confusing to someone like Louis, having grown up in a world where boys learn that these type of cues mean that a woman is sexually available to all comers. That's why we need to teach boys from day one that this just isn't the case. Louis had been taught different rules, and kicking him out felt complicated. But being sexually respectful isn't about ensuring everyone gets a piece of the sex pie. No one is entitled to sex, no matter how hungry for it they are. If behavior isn't wanted, it is just never okay.

After Louis left, we held an open forum for the group to discuss the situation and ran a workshop on respect, and the year ended without any other major incidents. Still, I felt that we had failed everyone, since ideally there should have been a way to prevent the situation from ever occurring in the first place.

SEXUAL HARASSMENT: WHAT YOU MAY HAVE HEARD AND WHY THAT'S BS

WHAT YOU MAY HAVE HEARD:
These days, anything a guy does can be called sexual harassment.

WHY THAT'S BS:
Just because there is more awareness today, that

doesn't mean people are "too sensitive." What it means is that a lot of people were getting away with an awful lot of bad behavior in the past.

• • •

WHAT YOU MAY HAVE HEARD:
All these rules about sexual harassment mean that people will get in trouble for flirting.

WHY THAT'S BS:
Flirting is mutual and both people enjoy it. Sexual harassment might make one person feel good, but it is upsetting to the other. Flirting is simply not possible when your actions are unwanted and when that behavior is not reciprocated.

• • •

WHAT YOU MAY HAVE HEARD:
What do you expect if you dress like that?

WHY THAT'S BS:
People dress in all manner of ways that have nothing to do with suffering *unwanted* attention. Maybe someone wants to be fashionable, or likes the outfit they picked. Maybe they feel sexy and confident. Really, who cares! Telling someone they were "asking for it" is just another way we blame victims and let harassers off the hook.

SEXUALITY SPOTLIGHT:
HOSTILE SEXUAL CLIMATES

Tom Edwards. He was the kid in high school who could say anything to girls and get away with it. Tom was the guy who cornered me in the library in front of all his friends and asked if I had bowed legs because I'd been having sex with Mr. Wainwright, our science teacher; who informed Mandy Lee that she would be giving him a blow job as soon as her braces came off; who crowded Gillian Sands into her locker as he breathed into her face, telling her what he was going to do to her when no one was around.

Looking back, it seems clear to me that this was sexual harassment. But as teenagers, it never occurred to us to call it that. As girls, we knew boys could humiliate you, and make you feel scared and uncomfortable, but doing something about it was not an option anyone considered. The way it worked where I went to school, in the Vancouver of the 1990s, was that there was a certain kind of boy who made comments to girls all the time. Your job as a girl was to come up with a quick reply that kept those guys in their place. It was almost expected that boys would make sexual remarks and that girls would be able to shrug them off. Only prudes were openly offended.

Sadly, in a lot of places, that hostile environment remains.

A number of years ago, I asked a group of high school girls I worked with at an after-school program if they felt like their school was sexually safe. At first everyone said of course. "It's not like some guy is going to jump out of his locker and attack me," laughed one.

But after a little while, they started talking. "Well,

sometimes the guys make jokes about sex stuff," I heard from one.

"Yeah, but that's not really a big deal. They don't mean it," offered another.

"That's just flirting," said a third.

"Well," I asked, "when a guy makes a comment like that, does it make you feel good or bad?"

"I don't know. It's stupid," said one.

"Yeah," added another, "it's annoying, but it's not like they're doing anything. They just don't know how to flirt."

Now, the boys might not have known how to flirt, but the girls also didn't seem to know how to name the behavior that they were actually experiencing, and those "jokes" are often a gateway to sexually hostile environments. So calling sexual harassment what it is can be the first step toward eradicating something that has been found to cause even more damage than bullying.[12]

What's the Background?

The #MeToo movement first emerged in 2006 when an African American woman named Tarana Burke began using the phrase *Me Too* in her work as a community organizer to highlight just how common sexual assault and sexual harassment were. The movement gained steam in October 2017, shortly after sexual abuse allegations against movie producer Harvey Weinstein became increasingly public, and celebrities started using the phrase as a hashtag on social media.

Since then, the impact of #MeToo has grown significantly, and today it can be hard to remember that there was a time before the phrase *sexual harassment* even existed.

We now understand that term to refer to a wide range of unwanted or coercive behaviors of a sexual nature. These include inappropriate sexual comments or touching; invasion of privacy; unwelcome sexual emails, texts, or calls; sexual bribery; coercion; unwelcome overt requests for sex; persistent requests for a date; or the creation of hostile environments where such behaviors are treated as the norm. That's a long list, but we have really only been collectively naming these forms of aggression as sexual harassment for the past few decades, even if attempts to tackle it started long before.

Even though slaves and domestic servants had long endured sexual abuse, the coordinated nationwide fight against harassment only began in the late nineteenth and early twentieth centuries, as more and more middle-class white women entered the workforce and, as a result, more of these women were traveling through public spaces unaccompanied by men. Suffragettes began to advise women to learn self-defense as a way to deal with "mashers" (a slang term used to describe men we would now call street harassers). The Woman's Christian Temperance Union, a group whose main goal was the prohibition of alcohol, then raised the alarms about sexual improprieties on the job, and by the 1920s, guidebooks were being published to tell women how to handle unwanted advances in the workplace. These tended to advise quitting if women were unable to ward off lecherous coworkers.

Then, as the numbers of working women grew, more attention was given to their daily conditions, and in 1964 the first law was passed to prohibit sex discrimination in the workplace. But probably the most important change came in 1972, with the passage of Title IX. This bill is now credited with everything from prohibiting sex discrimination in school sports to challenging campus sexual assault. It also made what we now call sexual harassment illegal in any schools that received federal funding, and its passage provided the first legal regulation in this area.

The term *sexual harassment* was first coined in 1975 by Cornell University activists. But it only came into wider usage in 1991 during the Anita Hill/Clarence Thomas case. Hill, a law professor, had alleged that Supreme Court justice nominee Thomas had sexually harassed her when they worked together. During Hill's powerful testimony to an all-male Senate, she was asked if she got her ideas from *The Exorcist*, was called delusional and a scorned woman, and was made to recount, in detail, the graphic nature of the comments she endured. In the press she was called "a little bit nutty and a little bit slutty."

So it wasn't shocking when, in that climate, the Senate confirmed Thomas's nomination. Hill's case did usher in some changes, and following Thomas's confirmation, the Civil Rights Act was amended to allow a jury trial for victims of sexual harassment. Since then, more and more schools, colleges, and workplaces have adopted policies specifically prohibiting sexual harassment. Needless to say, we all know these don't ensure that every academic and professional environment is a safe one. And we know that the more marginalized one is, the fewer protections from sexual hostility there are. Plus, following the 2018 confirmation of Brett Kavanaugh to the Supreme Court, despite accusations of sexual violence, many people wondered how much things had actually changed.

Why It's a Problem

It can be really hard to define sexual harassment, partly because harassing behaviors are so normalized in our society. Many people also fear the outcomes of labeling an experience "sexual harassment," especially since it is often perpetuated by a person closely known to the victim. Plus, if you name what has happened to you *sexual harassment* and you aren't believed, there is the very real possibility of being accused of lying. And even if you are believed, the chance that someone will blame you for provoking the situation looms large. Additionally, people often minimize the harm of sexual harassment with the rationalization, "Well, it's not like I was raped."

But not being raped doesn't mean the harm from sexual harassment is minimal. The impact can be devastating and can result in issues like anxiety, loss of self-esteem, PTSD, and even suicidal ideation. We also know that victims can feel helpless and trapped.[13] That can be exacerbated for young victims and LGBTQ+ folks who are already disenfranchised and tend to have the fewest resources to seek help or to make a situation stop.

Where We're at Now

It still blows my mind to realize that if a woman told me she'd never encountered a sexually hostile climate, I'd be surprised.

That's because, not only is this stuff everywhere, but it just starts so damn early. Every year, I teach about sexual harassment in my eighth-grade classes. We look at the school's sexual harassment policy and we talk about actions kids can take if they feel like they are experiencing a hostile environment. And every year, it becomes apparent that an awful lot of these twelve- and thirteen-year-olds have already experienced street harassment.

They talk about hearing comments when they are out alone, and they talk about hearing comments when they are with their moms. They mention creepy men sitting next to them on near-empty subways, and even security guards they dread walking by when coming home from school.

And I tell them stories from my youth, about the men who sat next to me on near-empty buses and tried to strike up a conversation, or who leered at me, muttering something undecipherable under their breath as I passed by. Or who, conversely, called out loud comments about my height or my body as they drove by in cars. And I tell them I didn't know what to do then.

But I also tell them what I think they can do now when it happens out in the world.

"You can respond or not. But if you do respond, make it firm and just keep walking. Don't do that if responding makes you feel unsafe, since your safety is the number one thing you need to think about."

"You can film them if you think you can do it secretly."

"You can walk into a store or you can find someone who you think can help."

I also tell them to move or to change seats. "No adult, and no older teen, should ever sit next to a lone girl on public transit when there are empty seats around. Not in this climate. Not when doing so could make her feel uncomfortable. And no man should ever try to strike up a conversation with a kid who is out by themselves. And they sure shouldn't comment on their appearance or on their body."

Some of my advice is identical to that which I got back when I was a kid, and I wonder how far we've really come. But if my advice sounds regressive and gendered, that's partly because we do not live in a world that has advanced to a point where this is no longer needed. And it's because these kids don't always move away from creeps, or because they often answer lecherous questions politely. Their reasons are often the same as mine as an adult: they don't want to provoke an angry response. They don't want to assume romantic or sexual intent. They don't want to hurt anyone's feelings. They don't want things to be awkward.

The election of an American president who won despite numerous accusations of sexual harassment helped usher in a climate which saw an explosion of people—mostly women—coming forward about sexual harassment. And things are changing fast, both in our understanding of this crime and in what we're doing to combat it. But there is no doubt that we still have a long way to go, and there is no doubt that a lot of today's girls and women, a lot of today's LGBTQ+ folks of all genders, and yes, plenty of cishet men and boys, too, still have to navigate sexually hostile climates at every turn.

BEFORE TITLE IX

Ever thought about whether or not there should be girls' or women's sports offered at schools or colleges? Or if kids should be able to walk down the halls at school free from sexual harassment? Or even if a student should be allowed to attend school at all if they are pregnant or a teen mom? If you haven't had to think about those things, you can thank 1972's Title IX.

For example, before its passage:

> ▸ It was perfectly legal to spend all of a school's money on boys' sports without putting a penny into girls' programs. That literal playing field sure isn't leveled yet, but for a lot of female athletes, the ability to play sports today is a direct result of Title IX.
> ▸ Sexual harassment at school was not a crime. In fact, many students knew that reporting harassment was likely to get them in more trouble for allegedly provoking the situation than the harasser would get in for their actions.
> ▸ From middle school through college, educational institutions were allowed to kick a girl out for getting pregnant or having a baby. Pregnant girls in high school were typically put on "medical suspension" until after their babies were born, then banned from returning to their original schools afterward. Thousands of girls were sent, often by court order, to shelters or to attend "special" schools.
> ▸ Although the law impacted other aspects of women's educational experiences, it was not uniformly applied to cases of sexual assault until 2011 when something called the Dear

Colleague letter was sent to colleges from the Department of Education's Office for Civil Rights. The letter declared that "The sexual harassment of students, including sexual violence, interferes with students' right to receive an education free from discrimination and, in the case of sexual violence, is a crime." This allowed students to file Title IX complaints when their cases were not handled properly by their college or university.

Obviously, Title IX has not eliminated discrimination based on sex. In a world where the general public is only just starting to acknowledge sexual violence, where female athletes can hope for only a fraction of the college scholarship money that male athletes qualify for, and where women still only earn two-thirds, or less, of what men do, we can't pretend that the fight for equality is over. But one can only imagine how much more dire things would be if we never had any Title IX protections.

WHAT IT ALL COMES DOWN TO

Sexism shows up in plenty of ways, wearing plenty of different disguises. Sometimes it is immediately recognizable, say, when I endured the Anthrax/Public Enemy "pussy" rallying cry. Other times, it's less so—for example, childhood messages about what behaviors are and are not acceptable for boys or girls. Then there are the beliefs that come with legitimate-sounding—benevolent—justifications that can be hard to refute offhand. Justifications that sound like, "Women are just better caretakers! Men are just better breadwinners!"

It's also common to see discrimination against women and girls dismissed as a thing of the past, or not a personal problem, or, if it's an issue, no different than "reverse sexism" against boys and men. People hold these views for many reasons, but a complicating factor is that we have evolved to overcome some of the most obvious forms of sexism (women got the vote, girls can wear pants to school, we passed laws against sexual violence).

However it appears, though, sexism is the product of an unjust social system that is often made up of social, political, and/or economic mechanisms designed to promote (cis) male dominance over all other genders. And while women and sexual and gender minorities are the main targets of such thinking, when we tell men they're expected to be sex-driven, violent, dominant, and emotionless, and punish them when they don't live up to those rigid expectations, we are just encouraging divided gender roles that ultimately hurt us all.

HOW COMFORTABLE ARE YOU?

Even those of us who believe in gender equality can find ourselves slipping into some gendered behavior that is worth examining. So on a scale of one to five, with one being the least comfortable and five being the most, ask yourself how comfortable you are with these situations.

1) How comfortable are you with a woman asking a man out on a date?

1   2   3   4   5

If you are less comfortable, what is your concern?

....
....
....
....
....
....

2) How comfortable are you with a woman paying when she is on a date with a man, especially a first date?

1   2   3   4   5

If you are less comfortable, what is your concern?

....
....
....
....
....
....

3) How comfortable are you with a woman initiating sex with a male partner?

1 2 3 4 5

If you are less comfortable, what is your concern?

....
....
....
....
....

4) How comfortable are you with a woman readily agreeing to sex on a first date without having to be talked into it?

1 2 3 4 5

If you are less comfortable, what is your concern?

....
....
....
....
....

5) How comfortable are you with a man turning down sex with a woman who is interested in having sex with him?

1 2 3 4 5

If you are less comfortable, what is your concern?

....
....
....
....

6) How comfortable are you with a man crying?

1 2 3 4 5

If you are less comfortable, what is your concern?

....

....

....

....

....

....

Did any of your answers make you rethink how you navigate sexual spaces? Or how you perceive the ways other people do? If so, is that something you want to consider challenging?

Everyone has their own boundaries and comfort levels, and there is absolutely nothing wrong with men paying for dates or initiating sex, for example. But if you feel like you are reliant on specific sexual roles for men and for women to help guide your choices, you may want to ask yourself if you are living in a way that feels authentic or satisfying.

CHAPTER 2

STANDING UP FOR SEX

MIXED MESSAGES, CLEAR DAMAGE

When it comes to sex, we are living in a world of messy contradictions. Young women are highly sexualized then punished for actually having sex. Young men are encouraged to be sexual aggressors but often don't learn about the ethical (or even legal) consequences of their actions. Parents of young children are not given a support system, yet we heavily regulate birth control, emergency contraception, and abortion. We deny children sex education then tell adults that they are supposed to be proficient and knowledgeable lovers.

For a lot of folks, the idea of talking about sexual desires, limits, and concerns with partners can seem really unfamiliar. As a result, it's common for people to default to assumptions about what is or is not sexually healthy, *normal*, and socially acceptable. Tackling these assumptions at their core is one of the best ways to challenge them. But to do that, one has to also understand where they come from. So throughout this chapter we are going to explore where we learn about sex, ask why so many of us accept a double standard about men's and women's sexual experiences, and look at how the double standard allows us to create a hierarchy of pleasure in which women and gender and sexual minorities often learn to tolerate distinctly intolerable experiences.

WHERE WE LEARN ABOUT THAT THING CALLED SEXUALITY

Whenever I teach Human Sexuality, I ask my college students to complete an assignment called "My Sex Education." I always offer the ones who don't want to share personally the option to write a formal essay on the history of American sex education. But I have to say, the majority choose the first assignment, and I don't think it's just because they don't want to worry about citations.

For the paper, I ask the class to reflect on how and where they learned about sex. I explain that this can include everything from a formal sex-education class to conversations with a family member or something they saw on TV. Then I give them the following questions:

▸ Did you feel like the experience was positive?
▸ Was the information you received accurate?
▸ Do you think you first learned about sex at the appropriate age?
▸ Do you think people should learn about sex the way you did?

The answers I have received over the years have been powerful. Students write about walking in on parents having sex, about discovering porn, about awkward sex talks over dinner. They share stories of sexual abuse, health class, and church. They reflect on conversations that left them with even more questions, and on those that came long after they would have been useful. Every paper is unique. But what a lot of them have in common is that so many of my students wish they had learned about sex in a different way.

So, I will ask you to do the same thing. Think about how you learned about sex. Then go a little further and also think about how your early experiences may have impacted you and how that could translate into the current experiences you are having.

Consider:

▸ What is your earliest memory of sex? Is it positive or negative?
▸ Growing up, did you ever get in trouble for expressing your sexuality?
▸ Did you get different messages from your family about sex than your siblings of another gender?
▸ What messages did you get about the role of gender in sex?
▸ What messages did you get about things like masturbation, birth control, reproductive rights, or sex outside of marriage?
▸ What messages did you get from your family about sexual orientations and gender identities?
▸ Could you get questions about sex answered by people you trusted growing up?
▸ What were some of the informal messages you learned about sex from your peers?
▸ What were some of the informal messages you learned about sex from the media?

▸ How do you feel about your earliest experiences with sex? Do you think about them fondly? If not, what about them was negative?

▸ Did you feel sexually safe at home? What about at school or out in the world?

▸ Have you been impacted by sexual trauma? By nonsexual trauma?

▸ Do you have any regrets about your sexual experiences? If so, what would you change if you could?

▸ Do you have any regrets about how you have treated others sexually? If so, what would you do differently in the future?

▸ If you are currently sexually active with a partner, what aspects of your experience do you feel are the most positive? Are there any things you'd like to change?

So many of us default to some deep-rooted views about sexuality without ever contemplating the origin stories of these views. But considering if those origin stories still hold up can help us determine if the views they support do as well.

TACKLING YOUR OWN VIEWS

Now that you have thought about how you learned about sex, you can think about your opinions on sex. That is something researchers have long tried to study. In the 1940s and 1950s, a zoologist named Alfred Kinsey undertook a massive project designed to document sexual attitudes and behaviors. In it, he asked his subjects questions about things like masturbation and same-gender experiences, topics that were considered taboo at the time. Then, in the 1960s, gynecologist William Masters and therapist Virginia Johnson began to examine the human sexual response system in a laboratory setting. Since then, sex research has exploded, with one new study or another appearing every day. Not all studies are of equal value, of course, but the breadth of available knowledge has grown exponentially, and those of us who work in the field now have a sense of the general outlooks and practices of a range of different populations.

Yet it isn't only researchers and educators who can benefit from an increase in information. The more individuals can make sense of their own experiences, the better. Though plenty of people are well aware of their sexual motivations and understand the roots of their desires, for many others, questions remain. If you fall into this second camp, it can be helpful to contemplate where you stand on key issues and why. Self-reflecting about your sexual values and beliefs can help you determine whether you want to modify your behavior or not.

In the late 1980s, researchers Clyde and Susan Hendrick developed the Sexual Attitudes Scale, which was designed to compare sexual attitudes with sexual experiences. Consider your position on the following questions, some of which were inspired by their work:

▸ People have more sexual freedom today than they did in the past.
▸ In sexual encounters between men and women, it is up to the man to initiate sex.
▸ Sex is primarily about physical pleasure.

- Sex is best when you let yourself go and focus on your own pleasure.
- My partner's pleasure is of more or equal importance to my own.
- The main purpose of sex is to enjoy oneself.
- The main purpose of sex is for reproduction.
- Sometimes people get so turned on they can't stop.
- It is okay to change your mind once you've started sexual activity and decide to stop.
- During sex between men and women, there is usually equal attention to both partners' pleasure.
- Sexual harassment and rape are bigger problems today than they were in the past.
- Some people cry rape after they regret sex.
- It's so hard to know if you have consent for sex these days.
- Sexual harassment isn't as common as people make it out to be.
- Casual sex is okay as long as both people are comfortable with it.
- Casual sex is okay for men.
- Casual sex is okay for women.
- I think it's easier to hook up with someone after drinking or using other substances.
- I think people who carry condoms are probably promiscuous.
- I think using birth control is part of responsible sexuality if unwanted pregnancy is possible.
- I think abortion should be available on demand.
- I think LGBTQ+ people should have equal rights.

> ‣ I think LGBTQ+ people have gained equal rights.
> ‣ I think transphobia is a problem.
> ‣ I think homophobia is a problem.
> ‣ A lot of gay men are promiscuous.
> ‣ A lot of lesbians aren't that interested in sex.
> ‣ It's fine to look at porn whether you are single or in a relationship.
> ‣ Most porn is misogynistic.
> ‣ A woman who is sexually active is less likely to be considered a desirable partner.
> ‣ Women who dress in sexy clothes usually want to have sex.
> ‣ Women often say no to sex even if they mean yes.
> ‣ If a woman doesn't appear interested in a man, he should just try harder.

Reflect on your answers. Did any surprise you? Did any upset you? Did any stand out? Are there any statements you wished you felt differently about? Are you curious why you hold some of your beliefs? Now think about where your attitudes might have come from. Can you link any to the previous exercise that asked about your sex education? We're going to examine these commonly held assumptions about sexuality throughout the following chapters. I encourage you to revisit this list after you have finished the book, to see if your reactions have changed in any way.

Understanding that your attitudes and actions may be related to a core set of unexamined beliefs can help explain your behaviors and guide your choices. And if there are things you want to reevaluate or change, or patterns you want to break, making those adjustments will be far easier if you have a sense of where your drives have come from.

Additionally, getting a handle on where you're coming from can also help you explain some potentially uncomfortable experiences. It can make it easier to understand why you may have crossed someone's boundaries. Or it can allow you to sort through why you may have blamed yourself or diminished the harm of harassment or abuse you were subjected to.

Reflecting on your history and values around sex can also shed light on why you may believe one thing but then act in a completely contradictory way. Perhaps you have been placing more stock in what you think is socially acceptable, or in what you think others want from you, than in what you want for yourself or what you actually believe is the most decent course of action.

Or you might decide that you failed to act in accordance with your core beliefs out of impulsiveness (for example, you may really believe in using condoms, but if one wasn't available, you might have just skipped it), as a defense mechanism (for example, you may have thought no one would know you're gay if you made fun of someone else's feminine mannerisms), or because there was a short-term benefit to contradicting your beliefs that outweighed the deeper values you hold (for example, you care about supporting reproductive rights but let others do the work of speaking out).

Understandably, most of us do not live value-driven lives at all times. But while not speaking up about one off-color joke might not be the end of the world, having sex with someone who might not have wanted sex, because it was too hard or time-consuming to figure that out, is a different story altogether.

NOT HELPED BY THE NOSTALGIA MYTH

A lot of our beliefs about sex are the product of assumptions about "how things have always been." These ideas are perpetuated by something called the *nostalgia myth*, which holds that present generations are always inferior to past ones, a claim that is commonly believed and far from accurate. In fact, in some ways, we could argue that "morals" were lower in the past when blatant sexism, racism, domestic violence, bullying, transphobia, and homophobia were both unnamed and also widely accepted.

Just think about the fact that until the landmark 1967 *Loving v. Virginia* ruling, there were still state laws banning interracial marriage. Or that before rape shield laws began to pass in the late 1970s and early 1980s, it was perfectly legal to use information about a victim's past sexual history to discredit her rape claims in court. Or that marital rape was not a crime in all fifty states until 1993. Or that it was only in 2003 that the United States repealed sodomy laws, which had disproportionally been used to criminalize gay men and sex workers. Or that federal marriage equality only passed in 2015.

Yet we are living in a time when the nostalgia myth holds more sway than ever. Historian Stephanie Coontz writes in the *Harvard Business Review* that historically, the pervasive view was one that envisioned the future as a time of opportunity and progress. However, in recent years, what has become more prominent is people clinging to an idealized version of the past. This, she explains, has some pretty serious consequences. "When people are collectively nostalgic about their past experiences as members of a group or as inhabitants of an era, rather than individually nostalgic for their personal experiences, they start to identify more intensely with their own group and to judge members of other groups more negatively. They become less optimistic about their ability to forge new connections—and more hostile to people perceived as outsiders. When such nostalgia gets politicized, it can lead to delusions about a mythical, magical Golden Age of the homeland, supposedly ruined by interlopers."[1]

That's important to keep in mind when it comes to sex. Really, it is not the internet, weakening values, or an increasingly permissive culture that we should fear. It's the sanctimonious preaching dressed up in new clothes and the recycled claims about the dangers of sex that continue to pose the greatest threats to our sexual health.

And those threats are pretty significant.

REPRODUCTIVE RIGHTS: FROM FREE LOVERS TO *ROE V. WADE*

When we think about women's sexual emancipation, many of us imagine that the fight for equality began sometime in the last fifty years, when second-wave feminism opened our eyes to the ubiquity of sexual double standards. But the groundwork had actually been laid a hundred years earlier by a group of Victorians who called themselves *free lovers*.

The free love movement of the 1860s and '70s supported ideas that even some people today would find shocking. These folks saw sex as important for both men and women, advocated for sexual relationships outside of marriage, and called for the ability to end those marriages through divorce if need be. Some of the more radical argued that children need not be born in wedlock, or in the case of siblings, even to the same father, and many promoted an idea called "voluntary motherhood." Initially, this referred to sexual abstinence within a marriage as a form of contraception. Eventually, it lead to a call for the ability to separate reproduction from sex—something many people today just take for granted.

Nevertheless, much of the credit for modern birth control can go to Margaret Sanger, an often controversial New Yorker who came to prominence in the early 1900s. Sanger was the daughter of Irish immigrants who watched her mother endure as many as eighteen pregnancies in as many years before dying of TB and cervical cancer at age fifty.

This experience, and Sanger's later career as a nurse and midwife, led to a lifelong crusade to give women the ability to protect themselves from pregnancy without needing male involvement or permission. As a result, she was called depraved and indecent, attacked in her day for contributing to "race suicide," and remembered in some communities after her death for being a eugenicist. Her legacy includes the birth control pill and the founding of the reproductive health organization Planned Parenthood.

Yet long before these accomplishments came to fruition, Sanger not only had to endure criticisms, but also jail time, after being found guilty in 1913 of breaking the notorious Comstock laws for opening a family planning clinic that didn't even distribute birth control, but simply gave out information about it.

Passed in the United States in 1873, the Comstock laws were named after their architect, a Civil War vet named Anthony Comstock, whose personal mission was to rid New York City of *vice*. His definition of this included alcohol consumption, gambling, prostitution, reading "dirty books," and anything related to contraception or abortion.

It took twenty years before another case involving Sanger ended up lifting the federal ban on birth control, and it wasn't until a 1965 court case known as *Griswold v. Connecticut* that the last state law banning birth control (tellingly, in Comstock's home state) was finally overturned. Following this, it would take an additional eight years until the Supreme Court overturned the federal ban on abortion in 1973's landmark *Roe v. Wade* case.

Yet even as some women, often those who were white and middle class, were fighting for the ability to make motherhood voluntary, it is important to remember that others were fighting for their basic right to be mothers or to raise their children. For example, there has been a long history in North America of children being removed from indigenous families. In Canada this was marked notably by the horrors of residential boarding schools that lasted from the 1870s through the 1990s, which were designed to assimilate indigenous children into white society, largely by cutting ties between children and their families.[2] And in the United States, programs of eugenics and forced sterilization were used to control "undesirable" populations, which were often defined as people of color, immigrants, unmarried mothers, and people with disabilities.[3]

So while I would argue that the development of birth control and the legalization of abortion mark milestones for reproductive choice, they sure don't mean we have achieved reproductive justice.

STILL TRYING TO CONTROL FEMALE SEXUALITY

It goes without saying that the issues we currently face didn't just materialize out of the blue. Many of them are simply the most recent iterations of the long-standing understanding of female sexuality as a uniquely dangerous force that is to blame for a range of societal ills not attributed to men—a belief that has resulted in countless societies throughout history enacting unequal rules about sexual behaviors.

Evolutionary psychologists have theorized that these rules emerged out of paternity anxiety. Supposedly, this fear—that a child was not biologically a man's own—drove nervous fathers and husbands to all sorts of desperate actions designed to prevent women from having sex with anyone other than the man to whom they were wed. Others have posited that some of this control is actually employed by other women, since sex is a limited resource that women use to gain power with men. So the less sex there is to spare, the more women are privileged.

Many others have claimed that rules about sex are not about controlling women, but rather are about offering them protection from men.

Whatever the real motivation (and to be sure, these can differ between time and place), the results have included everything from menstrual taboos to female genital cutting, coverture laws (which in colonial America meant a married woman was not legally considered a person), different drinking ages for men and women, college dorms with female-only curfews, and the jailing of rape victims for everything from out-of-wedlock pregnancy to adultery.

In the recent history of the United States, controlling women's sexuality has played out in a few ways. Many people are aware that until the late 1960s, it was common practice for unmarried pregnant girls and women to be shipped away to homes for wayward mothers, sent to live with far-off relatives, or cordoned off in special high schools. But what is less known is that deep into the twentieth century, women could also be held in asylums for *promiscuous* behavior, and until the 1970s, sexually active teen girls could find themselves sentenced to time at a reform school.

Reform schools, which were essentially kid jails, emerged around the turn of the twentieth century. These schools were seen as an alternative to the previous method of dealing with child criminals, which was simply to lock them up in adult prisons. Both boys and girls were sent to reform schools, but the reasons for incarceration often differed. As Lisa Pasko writes in *The Journal of Criminal Law & Criminology*, many of the girls who found themselves in these institutions were immigrants, girls of color, or poor white girls who were (or who were suspected of being) sexually active and who caught the eye of moral reformers (primarily middle-class white women), or the courts.[4] One of the most famous inmates? Jazz legend Ella Fitzgerald, who at age sixteen was sent to the New York State Training School for Girls for being deemed "ungovernable"!

This practice began to shift in the 1970s with the emergence of the idea that juveniles had rights. So while reform schools began to close down and fewer girls saw themselves locked up by the state for having sex, something else was poised to fill this void. A spate of troubled teen programs, often in the form of "boot camps," began to emerge in the 1980s. These gained support with liberals for being an alternative to prison, and with conservatives for being tough on crime. Needless to say, some of these programs became the scenes of horrible abuse. After a rash of revelations, many were shut down or forced to operate with increased oversight. But problems continue. Some of these boot camps remain open today, and "promiscuity" alone can still be a criterion for a girl's enrollment.

To be sure, much has changed in how sexually active women and girls are treated. But some things remain the same, and one of the most enduring and cross-cultural methods of control is through the use of shame.

Legal scholars Shulamit Almog and Karin Carmit Yefet have suggested that even today, society employs a "humiliation scale" to sustain the control of female sexuality. Under this scale, the greatest humiliation is directed at sex workers, and the least is directed toward married women who only have sex with their husbands. According to Almog and Yefet, so long as there is widespread acceptance for the scale's hierarchy, the policing of female sexuality is able to continue.[5]

This policing was most famously studied by the French philosopher Michel Foucault, who coined the term *biopolitics* to explain how power is used to control populations. According to Foucault, one of the most effective ways to maintain order is through the regulation of sex. This regulation can still be seen in some of the modern forces used to keep today's girls and women in line, including something as seemingly innocuous as school dress codes. When we remember that dress codes are rationalized by the need for girls to hide the fact of having a female body lest they tempt or distract boys, we can see their clear connection to the control of sexuality.

Additionally, there are still countless laws on the books that penalize women in different ways than they do men. These include restrictions on abortion and reproductive health services. They include the fact that there is no federally mandated maternity leave. And they include laws, in at least seven states, that allow rapists to fight their victims for custody over a baby conceived from a sexual assault.[6] Women in these situations may even be required to obtain consent from the assailant before doing an adoption. These laws gained more attention in 2017 after a convicted sex offender in Michigan, who had raped a woman when she was only twelve, was granted joint custody of his victim's eight-year-old son.[7]

Whether it is justified as a means to curb promiscuity, sold as a protective measure, or written into law, attempts to control women's sexuality are still prevalent and show little sign of letting up. In our punishment-hungry society, despite all the conflicting information sent our way, we tend to throw the book at anyone (from consensual teen sexters, to miscarriers, to folks who just want to buy a vibrator in Texas) who missteps. Considering that we still live in a time when even birth control, something that over 99 percent of American women have used at some point in their lives,[8] can come under attack, it should be little surprise when other aspects of sexual expression meet the same fate.

CRIMES AGAINST NATURE

Until 2003, America had sodomy laws that banned a variety of different types of nonprocreative sex. That year, a case known as *Lawrence v. Texas* was brought to court by a gay couple who had been charged with a crime for having consensual anal sex in one of the men's own homes.

Following a victory in *Lawrence*, sodomy laws were declared unconstitutional by the United States Supreme Court and repealed.

You would think that this would have been the end of the story. But in some places around the country, that hasn't been the case. One issue is that despite *Lawrence v. Texas*, a number of states still have what are called "crimes against nature" laws on the books. These make it illegal to have sex that is not considered "natural." So what isn't natural? Well, bestiality, necrophilia, incest, and prostitution are usually on the list. But often, so too are *homosexual* sex acts, anal sex, and occasionally even oral sex.

Though most states understood that after the

passage of *Lawrence v. Texas*, crimes against nature laws could no longer be used to regulate sexual conduct between consenting adults, nine states kept such laws on the books. Why? Doing so would allow them to return to using them if *Lawrence* was ever overturned by the courts.

That's upsetting enough, but what is even more concerning is that in some of these states, people (disproportionately gay men and sex workers) have still found themselves charged under crimes against nature laws.[9] Prosecutors typically know they can't actually gain convictions by using these laws, yet in a culture of discriminatory sex policing, they continue to be used as a tool of intimidation and control.

THE SEXUAL DOUBLE STANDARD

Along with the control of female sexuality comes a double standard that punishes women for sex far more than it does men. This double standard is evident in every *she's a slut/he's a stud* dichotomy around, and it is reinforced every time we hear that if we don't want women to wantonly sleep with everyone they see, we need to crack down on their sexual freedom and reproductive rights.

Now I hate to even mention this, since the existence of these studies is yet another example of the double standard that assumes there is something wrong with sexually active women, but just in case you're wondering if these claims have any merit, everyone from the American Medical Association to the American Association of Pediatrics and the American Psychological Association confirm that making reproductive health care available does not lead to an increase in sexual activity for girls and women.[10] Yet even though the claims are without merit, repeating them serves to reinforce the long-standing view that there are two sets of rules when it comes to sex: those for cishet men and those for everyone else.

Win the right to an abortion? Soon enough, antiabortion activists will begin working to make getting one functionally impossible, citing, among other rationalizations, the fear that this medical procedure "promotes female sexual promiscuity." Want to get your HPV vaccine, emergency contraception, or condom? Well, you might have to wade through the barriers imposed by critics warning that their availability will encourage young girls to have sex.

Misunderstandings and biases about sexual promiscuity in women aren't benign beliefs with no real-world impact. Such views are the foundation for myriad legal and social disparities that can have a devastating effect on everything from job prospects to personal lives and mental health. For example, slut shaming, which one study found affected almost 50 percent of American girls,[11] has been linked to disordered eating, self-harm, and substance use, among other issues. Or think about the fact that a study out of Cornell University found that college-aged women judge female peers who are labeled as "promiscuous" more negatively than female peers they see as "chaste" and are less likely to befriend them![12]

The double standard can also take credit for the casual acceptance of seemingly contradictory ideas (like the notion that a man who pursues a woman is considered persistent, while a woman who does the same is seen as a "stalker"), for the treatment of every doubted or blamed rape survivor, and for the fact that women's reputations can still be destroyed simply by the implication that their sexual choices are somehow untoward.

Many people accept the idea that women should fundamentally be held to different sexual standards than men. Solid research to the contrary simply cannot counter our existing assumptions: if a woman claims to be unhurt by sex, and especially by sex outside of a monogamous relationship with a man, then she must be lying, unethical, or, at the very least, deluded. Contemporary research shows that even for today's young Americans, a lot of old beliefs about sexual double standards remain. For example, sociologists Derek A. Kreager and Jeremy Staff have demonstrated that having a greater number of sexual partners is positively correlated with boys' peer acceptance, but negatively correlated with girls' peer acceptance.[13]

That isn't to say that nothing has changed. In plenty of social circles, sexually active girls and women are, if not celebrated, at least considered a nonissue. But when women are still asked what they did to provoke a sexual assault, when revenge porn is a thing, and when women can still find themselves socially ostracized for actual or perceived sexual activity, we can't presume to be living in a brand-new sexual world.

THE PLEASURE PART

One of the effects of the double standard is that we can view pleasure as a hierarchy where male gratification tends to rank highest. One reason for this is that our understanding of sex is often really limited in a way that advantages certain bodies (often those that are cisgender, male, and able-bodied) over others. As a result, women and gender minorities are often expected to put the sexual pleasure of male partners above their own needs.

But just what exactly do we mean when we talk about *sex*? While the LGBTQ+ community has long had a broader understanding of what it means to *have sex* (a fact that is intuitive to many, but which was also confirmed by a 2016 study out of the University of Utah[14]), for a lot of cishet people, *having sex* typically refers exclusively to penis-in-vagina intercourse (PIV) that is often considered completed when the penis ejaculates.

In fact, a University of Indiana study from 2017 found that while almost 95 percent of respondents agreed that vaginal intercourse "counted" as sex, 11 percent of respondents did not consider it sex if the man did not orgasm, and almost 20 percent of men over sixty-five did not consider PIV to be sex if a condom was used.[15] In a different study, psychologists at the University of Utah asked heterosexual college students if twenty-one different physically intimate behaviors were included in their understanding of what it meant to have sex. Respondents overwhelmingly identified PIV as sex. But their views on other behaviors varied greatly. As the researchers explained, anal sex was more likely to "count" as sex than were other non-PIV acts. Oral sex was more likely to be seen as sex when it led to orgasms than when it didn't. Manual stimulation, on the other hand, was rarely counted as sex, whether or not orgasm happened.[16]

Such views are common and unsurprising. But the impacts are significant, since beliefs like these contribute to the perception that vaginal intercourse is the gold standard. This means that a lot of the acts that "rank" lower are those that are more likely to lead to female orgasm. Now, it's not that people with vaginas aren't enjoying vaginal intercourse. Nor does it mean that sex without orgasm can't be good sex. But for a lot of people, male orgasm is an assumed outcome or goal of sex, while female orgasm, if it occurs at all, is just a nice addition.

That notion is also reinforced by a disproportionate cultural focus on male pleasure—as demonstrated by how much more it is seen on screen (both in porn and beyond), discussed in casual conversation, and even taught in sex education, where puberty is typically announced by a period in girls and a wet dream in boys. These factors are then compounded by a general lack of knowledge about how other types of bodies (say, those that are female, trans, intersex, or that live with a disability) actually work. For such bodies, that can result in little regard for things like arousal (or even the role of the clitoris!).

The impact of this is notable. A study published in *Sexuality & Culture* in 2018 found that nine out of ten women surveyed had engaged in unwanted sexual acts just to please their partner and that eight out of ten women prioritized their partner's pleasure over their own. (The same study also found that those women who saw their own pleasure as equal to their partner's tended to be the ones who had not experienced unwanted sexual acts!)[17] Another study, this one published in *The Canadian Journal of Human Sexuality*, found that heterosexual women are more likely to give oral sex to their male partners than to receive it, even though many of these women reported that they often did not particularly enjoy performing the act.[18] Additionally, a study in the *Journal of Sex Research* found that both men and women think giving oral sex to a woman is more difficult and more unpleasant than giving it to a man.[19]

Then consider the sexual climate on many college campuses discussed by journalist Rebecca Traister in *New York Magazine*. Traister found that while modern college women may feel freer to have casual sex with their male peers than did their predecessors, in cishet situations, a lot of that sex just isn't all that good.

As she wrote, "Students I spoke to talked about 'male sexual entitlement,' the expectation that male sexual needs take priority . . . Male attention and approval remain the validating metric of female worth, and women are still (perhaps increasingly) expected to look and fuck like porn stars—plucked, smooth, their pleasure performed persuasively. Meanwhile, male climax remains the accepted finish of cishet encounters; a woman's orgasm is still the elusive, optional bonus round."[20]

Partly, this disparity is due to a perception that the male orgasm is just physically easier to achieve than the female orgasm. That might be the case for some couples, but it definitely isn't a universal truth. Take the fact that lesbian women with female partners have a significantly higher probability of orgasm than do heterosexual women with male partners.[21] Or think about the work of University of Pennsylvania professor Kristen R. Ghodsee, the author of *Why Women Have Better Sex Under Socialism: And Other Arguments for Economic Independence*, who found that the more egalitarian a society, the better the sexual experiences for women![22]

The sexual hierarchy is further reinforced by an outdated understanding of virginity. Many people continue to define virginity as something tangible that is "lost" following PIV sex. In large part, this idea emerged out of a misplaced emphasis on the hymen. The hymen is the thin piece of skin that partially covers the opening of the vagina a few inches into the body. Contrary to popular belief, the hymen isn't a steel drum that needs to be forcefully smashed through by a ramrod penis in order to "pop" or "break." It actually has natural perforations in it. How else would menstrual fluid leave the body before this event occurred?

The hymen stretches when something is inserted into the vagina—sometimes tearing and bleeding a small amount, but sometimes not. Though it can be stretched during vaginal sex, the hymen can also be stretched while masturbating, participating in other types of sex play, doing gymnastics, riding a bike, riding a horse, or even using a tampon. So using the hymen as a measure of virginity is not accurate. Also, defining virginity based on the presence of an "unbroken hymen" means that a cisgender man could never lose his virginity, or that people of all genders and sexual orientations would be lifelong virgins if they didn't have vaginal sex.

Really, virginity is a social construct and not a physical fact. While many people do believe that you can only lose your virginity through vaginal sex, plenty of others think that other sex acts, like oral or anal sex, are also ways to "lose virginity." Unfortunately, since virginity is still prized in girls and women far more than it is in boys and men, girls and women have a greater investment in not calling their behaviors "sex." That can involve some pretty complicated mental gymnastics.

The result of all of these factors (and many others) is a "pleasure gap" that affects much more than the physical experience of sex alone. To be sure, this gap has become so normalized that many women believe that what should give them the most pleasure is not their own physical or psychological response to sex, but rather feeling desired by someone else and helping that (usually male) someone feel pleasure. In many ways, this is reinforced by what Peggy Orenstein described in her book *Girls & Sex* as a culture that sees female sexuality simply as a performance piece designed to win male approval.[23]

Accepting this gap not only positions male pleasure as more important than female pleasure, it can also lead to situations where men think they have the right to obtain pleasure regardless of the cost to their female partners. This then makes it acceptable for all genders to expect or tolerate encounters where one person feels sexually gratified regardless of the price to another person, and it contributes to a range of poor outcomes, from sex being less enjoyable to sex being downright coercive.

THE INCREDIBLE LENGTHENING VAGINA!

When people get aroused, more blood flows into the genitals than flows out. In folks with penises, this can cause erections. In folks with vaginas, this causes the vulva and clitoris to swell and become more sensitive, thickens of the walls of the vagina, and increases vaginal lubrication.

But something else also happens.

In a nonaroused state, the vagina is about four inches long, and the walls on either side lie flat against

---

each other. These walls contain muscular folds called rugae. The top of the vagina—the cervix—is also the bottom of the uterus. As a person becomes sexually excited, the uterus tips back. This stretches out the rugae, pulls the cervix up, and allows the vagina to grow both longer and wider, making more room for penetration. If this does not happen, sex can hurt no matter how wet a person is, despite the use of artificial lube, and regardless of whether people go slow and try to be sensitive to their body's needs.

The takeaway? Though it might take a while, waiting for physical arousal before attempting penetration will make things feel a lot better!

THE PAIN PART

One of the costs of a hierarchy of pleasure is that a lot of sex actually causes pain. The authors of a paper published in the *Journal of Sex Research* explain that while prevalence rates vary by age group and culture, one consistent theme is that women experience pain a whole lot more than men.[24] A 2015 study published in the journal *Sexual Medicine* found that 30 percent of women report regular pain during vaginal sex, and 72 percent report pain during anal sex. Notably, the same study found that a comparatively low 7 percent of men experience regular pain with vaginal sex and 15 percent of men experience pain with anal sex.[25] Another study found that almost 75 percent of women have experienced pain with sex in their lifetimes,[26] and that between 7 to 22 percent of women experience it regularly.[27] Those numbers jump up to 45 percent for menopausal women[28] and 60 percent for cancer survivors.[29]

Yet even despite these numbers, a lot of painful sex goes unacknowledged.

Partly, that is because while it is common to assume that there will be pain as the receptive partner during first-time vaginal intercourse, and, at least among a lot of hetero folks, as the receptive partner during anal sex, other sources of pain are often ignored or stigmatized.

People with certain health issues or disabilities may learn that pain with sex is inevitable. This is particularly difficult for folks who feel their disabilities might make them less sexually desirable. Some may even feel that they should be grateful to potential partners for dating them.

For people who experience pain with sex after gender-confirmation surgery, an admission of discomfort can prompt doubts about the interventions, or it can open the door for others to challenge the need for medical procedures they might undergo as part of their transition.

Those who identify as intersex, or who have what are referred to medically as "conditions of sex differentiation," may have undergone surgeries that can make sex hurt, but which they are actually told are "normalizing." There has been a long tradition of secrecy surrounding intersex conditions, and many people had the truth about their medical histories withheld or were encouraged to hide their conditions in order to pass as their assigned gender. The result was that if something was painful, there could be a reluctance to speak up, for fear that doing so would reveal the truth about their bodies.

Sometimes medical issues like fibroids, pelvic inflammatory disease, endometriosis (a condition of the uterine lining), vaginismus (involuntary contractions of the vaginal muscles), Peyronie's disease (which leaves scar tissue in the penis), phimosis (tight foreskin), and sexually transmitted infections cause pain with sex. These conditions typically have to be diagnosed by a health-care provider. This can be a hurdle in and of itself. The person experiencing pain first has to be able to talk about this stuff themself, which may mean overcoming shame and self-doubt. Then they have to find a health-care provider who is familiar with the issue. That can actually be pretty hard, particularly for women, since as James M. Weinberger, a physician in the Department of Urologic Surgery at UCLA, demonstrated in two papers published in 2018, treatment for female sexual dysfunction simply lags far behind the available treatment for male sexual dysfunction.[30][31] As a result, even well-meaning providers may just not have certain health issues on their radar, let alone the means to address them.

Nevertheless, it sure isn't only medical or physical concerns that cause pain. There are a variety of societal ideas that pressure women into having sex that feels painful. For example, people with penises may be aroused and ready to have PIV sex in a matter of minutes. But people with vaginas can take a whole lot longer to be ready for comfortable penetration. When we position female arousal in contrast to male arousal, and then assume that male desire must be satisfied immediately, the result is that a lot of women have sex before their bodies are ready for penetration, which can cause real discomfort or pain.

Underlying all these issues is an assumption that women should enjoy, or at least accept, sex despite pain, or that pain is part of the pleasurable experience. This idea comes from a range of places, including from a lot of mainstream porn where women typically wince and cry out in agony before they succumb to ecstasy. It's just pretty common to equate hot sex with rough, sometimes violent sex, where pain is overcome by passion. That isn't to say rough sex is problematic (or isn't hot). The problem lies with unwanted roughness, and with unwanted pain.

Plus, while many women have learned that sex is an unpleasant chore that is owed to a partner, others learn that their sex appeal is directly related to how sexually adventurous they can make themselves seem. Though these messages may seem to lie in opposition, in some ways they are a coordinated "recipe" of what it takes for women to earn the desire of men. The result is that women may feel they need to push themselves into new territories they aren't totally comfortable with, or embrace painful activities as a way to increase their sex appeal and to ensure male orgasm.

Conversely, many men are taught that sex is supposed to be a powerful expression of virility, which they should seek out at all costs, and that anything that challenges this script—say, admitting that a hand job hurts or that they'd rather make out than have intercourse—undermines their masculinity.

Religious or cultural views of sex can also impact how people interpret pain. For example, someone who is part of a community where genital cutting is performed might expect pain with sex. Another example would be someone who is part of a religion that suggests the only goal of sex should be pregnancy. In this case, the only legitimate sexual complaint is infertility.

For survivors of sexual assault, pain can be a particularly complicated issue. Chronic pelvic pain and conditions like dyspareunia (painful sex) and vaginismus are common in adult survivors of childhood sexual assault. Survivors, however, may not report the resulting pain, since doing so could also disclose an assault, or because they may associate pain with sex and assume it to be normal.

Age is another issue. For girls who haven't yet gone through puberty or whose vaginas are still prepubescent, vaginal sex might just always be painful. Conversely, acknowledging painful sex resulting from the normal vaginal changes that occur with menopause can brand someone as past their sexual prime or even as altogether too old for sex.

Just like there are many causes of painful sex, there are also many reasons that people aren't comfortable talking about it. These include people's understanding of what sex should look like, and societal expectations about what someone's relationship to sex should be. Depending on how you grew up, or on your cultural background, talking about sex at all might be a radical act in and of itself.

While a lot of people are really uncomfortable talking about sex, telling partners that something hurts or just doesn't feel very good is an important first step. It's also a good idea to figure out what feels better, what your own turn-ons are, and if you need to go slowly, use more lube, or take a break from sex for a while.

Plenty of people like intense sex, and many folks are into mixing pain with their pleasure. But that isn't the same as an unwanted raw, chafing, sandpaper, or stabbing feeling that a lot of people experience and that makes them just want to get sex over with.

WHAT WE GET WRONG ABOUT THE SEXUAL REVOLUTION OF THE '60S AND TODAY'S SEX POSITIVITY

Many of us who grew up after the sexual revolution of the 1960s imagine that time as one when people were finally freed from puritanical shackles that only allowed sex within a cishet marriage and when women were finally able to have sex on their own terms.

And while it is true that women's ability to control their own fertility changed sex in ways previously unimaginable, for a lot of women, the experience was by no means positive—it simply served to give men more freedom to access their bodies.

In fact, many women who had been raised under one set of rules (in which sex was dangerous and taboo) were then expected to have sex under another. What remained, however, was the idea that men were the authorities who called the shots. As Hera Cook explains in *The Long Sexual Revolution: English Women, Sex, and Contraception, 1800–1975*, changes to the traditional moral framework around sex left many people unmoored.

Women could no longer protest often-exploitative sex on the basis of morality, and the invention of the birth control pill meant they couldn't turn to the fear of pregnancy as an excuse to avoid sex, either. She writes, "By the early 1970s, men assumed fashionable young women were on the pill and statistics show that well over half actually were. For this generation of young single women, the widespread use of the pill did mean some men assumed that if women could not get pregnant they had no reason to say no. Women were brought up to accept, and prioritize, other people's needs, not to express their own feelings or desires. There was also a societal rejection of emotion as insufficient when opposed to rational argument. The fact that a woman did not feel desire was not an adequate argument—for or against anything. Women had no right to sexual autonomy."[32]

So when we remember the sexual revolution as a time of great freedom, it pays to note that for many women, the changing rules just opened the door to new forms of manipulation and coercion. Really, one of the sneakiest tricks of the history of sex has been to omit the impact of power imbalances between men and women and the role the sexual revolution played in reinforcing them.

This narrative might seem familiar to women today who often get the message that to really be emancipated, they also have to be sexually open and "sex positive." At its heart, the idea of sex positivity is that people should have the autonomy to freely make choices about their own sexual experiences, so long as those choices don't infringe on the ability of others to do so as well. But how this plays out in real life can unwittingly reinforce gendered assumptions about sex. For one thing, it can add to the pressure some women feel to have sex under the guise of proving their liberation.

That is especially problematic when what is considered sexually liberating in our society is often, at its most base level, just being sexually appealing to men. Think about the performative nature of some women's hookups with other women. They happen semipublicly and are driven less by the participants' desires and more because their hookups add to the sense that they are wild or open to anything. The men who encourage this behavior still see these actions as risqué or boundary crossing in a way that appeals to them but that doesn't actually challenge their sense of the sexual hierarchy. The female participants get the benefit of elevated sexual status, but only in the eyes of these men, a questionable station at best.

As Rafia Zakaria writes at *Dame* magazine, "With everything defined in the language of choice, there is little time or effort allotted to considering how the nature of choices themselves are not equal, and that a woman who 'chooses' to sleep with her new boss is less free to decide or deny than he may be. Young women enter college campuses and then workplaces schooled in the cool sex-positive feminism that has been adopted by popular culture but without the safe spaces and resources to discuss and report campus rapes and assaults."[33]

It can be almost impossible to separate our desires and actions from the messages we get from the world around us. But assuming that being sexually adventurous, open, or "freaky" is synonymous with being "sex positive" is as risky as not learning the history of the sexual revolution and erasing the negative experiences that women had during its epoch.

SEXUALITY SPOTLIGHT:
CASUAL SEX AND HOOKUP CULTURE

Depending on whom you ask, terms like *casual sex* and *hooking up* can refer to anything from a one-night stand to any sex outside of marriage. But whatever one's personal definition, even typically progressive folks can fall into the trap of nervously fretting about the consequences of sex without commitment.

Many of us can rattle off a list of the dangers associated with casual sex. We might blame it for everything from sexually transmitted infections, to unplanned pregnancy, depression, alcoholism, and even the breakdown of the nuclear family. And sure, sex can be risky. One in four people will contract an STI by the time they are twenty-five; American teen birth rates, while not what they were when they peaked in the 1950s, are still the highest in the Western world; and sexual violence continues to plague our communities. But these are problems of our health-care systems, poverty, culture, and sex education—not of a rampant casual sex epidemic.

Still, reactionary books with titles like *Hooked: New Science on How Casual Sex Is Affecting Our Children*; *The End of Sex: How Hookup Culture Is Leaving a Generation Unhappy, Sexually Unfulfilled, and Confused About Intimacy*; and even *Smart Sex: Finding Life-Long Love in a Hook-Up World* lament the dangers of casual sex. These are used to bolster the claim that people today are increasingly amoral and at risk, even if evidence doesn't actually support this idea.

Though people worry about the impact of casual sex on anyone who has it, a lot of the concern is specifically directed toward women, who are assumed to be more damaged by sex without commitment. There may be some truth to that, but like so much of what we have discussed in this book, most of that has to do with social stigmas more than any natural "female" response to casual sex.

What's the Background?

In recent history, there have been some real shifts in the understanding and experience of casual sex. For example, the General Social Survey (GSS), out of the University of Chicago, has asked about "premarital" sexual relations since the survey's advent in the early 1970s. Notably, in 1972, 45 percent of respondents described premarital sex as always or almost always wrong. In 2016 that number had dropped to 26 percent.[34] However, data from the GSS also tells us that attitudes don't always translate into action and that with 8.26 partners on average, today's millennials actually have fewer sex partners than their parents, who on average had 11.68.[35]

Though many find it hard to believe, in the United States, at least, sex outside of marriage has been around an awfully long time. In fact, a 2006 study found that 95 percent of Americans, including people born as far back as the 1940s, had had "premarital" sex.[36] That makes sense when we realize these folks were often coming of age in the 1960s during what is commonly called the sexual revolution. And while much of our understanding about the sexual revolution is mythologized, this was indeed a time of real change that saw increasing openness to the idea of sex outside of marriage.

Obviously, not everyone in the '60s and '70s was sleeping around freely or having wild orgies, and not everyone in the 1980s was embarking on cocaine-fueled office affairs. Plus, plenty of the premarital sex was in fact just that—sex with someone you would eventually marry. But these were pivotal years. Syphilis had long since been cured, morals were changing, the birth control pill was an option, abortion became legal, and until the '80s, few people even knew about the dangers of HIV/AIDS.

Today, those worried about the rise in promiscuity, hookup culture, or weakening values just need to take a glance at the past to see that, while the details may have changed, an awful lot about how casual sex happens remains the same.

Why It's a Problem

There are a lot of claims about the impact of casual sex. But how many of these are legitimate? Many studies have demonstrated a range of negative findings related to casual sex, like sexual regret, low self-esteem, and psychological distress, especially among women. Some research has found that while men regret the sexual opportunities they missed, women often regret some of the casual sex they did have.[37]

But those studies don't tell the whole story.

Think about the finding that women are less comfortable with casual sex, or tend to regret it more than do men. Now consider a study out of Durham University in the UK, which found that what upset women after casual sex was not the act itself, but rather it was being treated badly by their male sex partners![38] As the lead researcher explained, "What the women seemed to object to was not the briefness of the encounter but the fact that the man did not seem to appreciate her."[39]

This really resonates with me, because I often hear about a lot of poor treatment during or after hookups among the college and high school students I work with. The unwritten rules for how this plays out can lead to some truly unpleasant behavior. For example, in some circles it is considered weak, immature, or uncool to show any feelings for someone you have just been physically intimate with. Many girls know that texting a boy you were with last night, let alone trying to sit next to him at lunch, can leave you branded a stalker and mocked for thinking he might ever have been interested in you. It can happen the other way around, too, but there seems to be a bit more leeway given to a posthookup crushing boy than to a posthookup crushing girl.

I wonder, why is the idea that someone might actually feel something for another person a sign of emotional instability rather than an expected response to physical closeness? And why do we think the only way to make it clear that we don't want to date someone we've hooked up with is by freezing them out or by being cruel? Responding to someone's text, sitting next to them in class, or checking in to make sure they had a good time are not marriage proposals. But so many people are so worried about the implications of these basic acts of kindness that they do a complete one-eighty.

It shouldn't be all that hard to say, *that was fun. Thanks so much. I'm not interested in dating. But let's see a movie sometime.* We need to teach people from the outset that there are alternatives to ghosting or slandering, and that being direct is far kinder and far easier in the long run. Blaming sexual regret on the fact that someone had casual sex, and not on what is often its true cause—a lack of kindness and respect—just makes us overlook the real solutions that are needed. Doing this also makes people ashamed about their sexuality without doing anything to address the underlying problem of how they are being treated in their sexual encounters. When we combine the poor postsex treatment that so many people experience with the actual experience of sex itself, it becomes easier to understand what can make good casual sex so hard to achieve.

When it comes to women's experiences specifically, some recent research can shed a light on what's going wrong. For example, one Canadian study found that when women have "high-quality" sex, which is defined as sex that they enjoyed, they rarely regret a casual encounter.[40] We also know that not that many women are having this "high-quality" sex during casual encounters. According to a survey of twenty thousand college students, only 42 percent of the women, compared with 78 percent of the men, had experienced an orgasm in their last hookup. When that was broken down further, the results were even more notable. In relationship sex, 76 percent of the women reported having had an orgasm. During a hookup with someone they'd fooled around with four or more times, 34 percent of the women had an orgasm. However, during a sexual encounter with someone they had never been with before, only 11 percent of women had an orgasm.[41]

This disparity of pleasure may partly explain the difference between men and women's feelings about casual sex. But what about research demonstrating that women, unlike men, can't handle casual sex due to their chemistry? One of the most frequently made claims is that during sex, cisgender women release more of the "love" hormone, oxytocin, than do cisgender men. Since a primary role of oxytocin is to promote bonding, the logic goes that women are programmed to become emotionally adrift if sex doesn't lead to a relationship.

However, such thinking fails to take into account that it is much more likely that the effects of oxytocin aren't that specific and do not affect all women equally. As one 2013 review found, oxytocin alone is unlikely to affect "complex, high-order mental processes that are specific to social cognition."[42] Nor does this reasoning address the fact that even if one of oxytocin's roles is to promote bonding, humans have shown time and time again that we are not bound by our physical destiny. (If we were, an awful lot of medical professionals, from transplant surgeons to fertility specialists, would be out of work.)

Such logic also fails to explain the fact that people of all genders can have negative experiences with casual sex that have nothing to do with biology. A 2015 study published in the *Archives of Sexual Behavior* looked at how different motivations for sex impacted someone's response to it. They called these "autonomous" and "nonautonomous" casual sexual behaviors. In this case, "autonomous" reasons for casual sex fulfilled someone's own personal desires. These included things like being highly attracted to the other person, wanting to experiment and explore one's sexuality, and feeling like the encounter would be a valuable learning experience.

"Nonautonomous" reasons referred to reasons that were not fully free or independent, or that had an underlying goal separate from a person's sincere desire to have sex. Among these were things like being drunk or high, hoping the hookup would lead to a relationship, and seeking revenge on an ex. This study further found that, regardless of gender, those who had casual sex for autonomous reasons did not feel bad afterward. On the other hand, those who had casual sex for nonautonomous reasons typically experienced negative emotions.[43]

Really, like so much else, what many of these studies remind us is that it's not the casual nature of sex that is inherently a problem. But rather, it's the circumstances under which someone has sex and the social reactions to their sexual activity that most affect their experience. Sexism, a lack of attention to female pleasure, and poor treatment by people we have been intimate with are the things that contribute to a general hostile sexual climate. These are also the things that can mean that, particularly for women, casual sex becomes a negative experience.

Where We're at Now

Among all types of sex, from casual to committed, a range of studies have demonstrated that, far from having rampant sex and anonymous hookups, people of all ages are actually having less sex than in the past.[44] [45] There are myriad reasons suggested for this. Some of these, like a culture of overwork, a fear of becoming emotionally involved, online dating that rewards physical appearance and an uptick in the use of internet-enabled devices, are pretty concerning.

Others, like living in a post-AIDS world, an increase in antidepressant prescriptions, living at home longer, and coming of age in tough economic times, might be thought provoking but are understandable. Still other reasons may be more encouraging. Some of this sex decline could be due to factors like an increasing realization by young women that they do not owe their partners sex and that opting out is actually an option. Or that claiming an asexual identity is possible.

Ultimately, our biggest concern shouldn't be whether or not people are having sex with a committed or casual partner, or even if they are having sex at all. Really, what we should be thinking about are the motivations behind people's choices, how the actual experiences of sex play out, and then the ways in which people treat their partners and are treated by them, both during the act and following it.

WHEN IT COMES TO SEX, MEN AND WOMEN ARE ON TOTALLY DIFFERENT PLANETS: WHAT YOU MAY HAVE HEARD AND WHY THAT'S BS

WHAT YOU MAY HAVE HEARD:
When a woman says she isn't interested, it just means a man needs to work a little harder to convince her.

WHY THAT'S BS:
Since we live in a world that feeds people pretty clear dating scripts, it's true that plenty of women don't feel comfortable saying yes to sex and dating immediately when asked. But that doesn't mean that most women who say no secretly want a guy to work harder at convincing them. What it means is that we all have

to start taking what people say at face value and working to change the cultural norms that can make it seem like men and women are on different planets and need to go through archaic dating rituals before coming together.

• • •

WHAT YOU MAY HAVE HEARD:
Men just have higher sex drives than women.

WHY THAT'S BS:
Any time you talk about biology, you are getting into some complicated gender-essentialist stuff, which holds than women are inherently wired to seek romance and men are inherently wired to seek sex. But even if you are looking at cisgender folks, a lot of the science fails to account for the role of socialization, which tells boys that they are controlled by their sex drives while telling girls they not only have lower sex drives, but that they have to keep the ones they have under control. In fact, what the research actually shows is less straightforward. For one thing, when you include other factors in your study beyond how often someone desires sex, there is often a much smaller difference between men and women than we are led to believe.

• • •

WHAT YOU MAY HAVE HEARD:
Women use sex to get love. Men use love to get sex.

WHY THAT'S BS:
You know the old idea that a woman won't have sex until a man tells her he loves her, and that he gives her the old "Yeah, yeah, baby, I love you" just to get in her pants? All that does is ignore men's emotions and women's sexual desire, and reinforce the idea that men and women can never find common ground, or that the bedroom is a battleground. The truth is, women have sex for many reasons, including love, desire, connection, stress relief, and so on. Similarly, men love for many reasons, and their love should not be diminished or dismissed as simply a ploy for sex.

• • •

WHAT YOU MAY HAVE HEARD:
In queer relationships, one person takes on the male role and one person takes on the female role during sex.

WHY THAT'S BS:
This is just a plain old reductive notion based on the (incorrect) idea that there even is such a thing as a "male" or a "female" role in sex. It also ignores the fact that plenty of LGBTQ+ folks have no interest in recreating cishet sex norms. The thing, is binary stereotypes almost never reflect the wide range of real-life experiences.

WHAT IT ALL COMES DOWN TO

If you accept the idea that sexual expression is a fundamental human right, then it becomes a lot easier to shed the lifetime of sexual shame and guilt that so many people carry.

Acknowledging that there is nothing inherently wrong with expressing one's own sexuality, and letting others do the same, will go a long way toward challenging some pretty negative forces—like those that promote the idea that it's the right of cishet men to feel pleasure via the bodies of cishet women, or that pretend the primary goal of sex is procreation. These views deny the fact that everyone has an equal right to pleasure, or that opting out of sex altogether should be a legitimate option. And they result in attempts to either hide the existence of sex, commodify it, or exert control through tactics that draw on shame, fear, or outright aggression.

It's easy to default to commonly held wisdom about sex. But a lot of what we think we *know* isn't based on a universal truth, but rather on beliefs and traditions. That's why it's so important to question our underlying assumptions about sex and challenge the shaky rationale upon which so many of these have been built. Doing that will help make space for healthier expressions of sexuality, and will allow people from all walks of life to do their walking with far more positive results.

PURSUING PLEASURE: A PERSONAL CHECKLIST

Place a check beside the statements that you believe to be true and fill in the blanks where appropriate.

1. ❏ It is important for me to be able to orgasm alone.
2. ❏ I can achieve orgasm through masturbating.
3. ❏ It is important for me to be able to orgasm with a partner.
4. ❏ I can achieve orgasm with a partner.
5. ❏ I am able to achieve orgasm as often as I want.
6. ❏ I believe that a sexual experience can be satisfying, even if I do not have an orgasm.
7. ❏ I know how it is easiest for me to reach orgasm. This is by:

....
....
....
....
....
....
....
....

8. ❏ People should not expect to climax from sex every time.
9. ❏ I am comfortable with the amount of time it takes me to reach orgasm.
10. ❏ I can tell my partner how best to help me reach orgasm.

11. ❏ I can identify three things that turn me on. They are:

....

....

....

....

....

....

....

12. ❏ If I have a partner, they know what these three things are.

13. ❏ It is normal for healthy men to occasionally experience early ejaculation or to have difficulties achieving an erection.

14. ❏ Most women reach orgasm through clitoral rather than vaginal stimulation.

15. ❏ I am comfortable with the fact that I may not always be able to perform sexually.

16. ❏ Even if I am not getting turned on, I will still try to have sex so as not to disappoint my partner.

17. ❏ If sex hurts or is uncomfortable, I can tell my partner to stop what they are doing.

18. ❏ I am open to working on improving my sexual arousal response.

If you answered yes to number 18, complete the following section.

In order to work on my sexual arousal I would:

▸ Tell my partner that I am not having orgasms.

▸ Discuss turn-ons and sexual fantasies with a partner.

▸ Masturbate.

▸ Show a partner how I masturbate to orgasm.

▸ Devote time to practicing achieving or delaying orgasm.

▸ Use a sex toy.

▸ Use an artificial lubricant.

▸ Consult my health-care provider.

▸ See a sex therapist.

▸ Strategize to come up with additional solutions like:

....

....

....

Once you have completed the checklist, ask yourself the following questions:

1. Which of my responses surprised me?
2. What about this list would I most like to change?
3. What questions were most difficult to answer and why?
4. Am I willing to take steps in order to help improve my sexual experience?
5. How significant a role do I think my communication style plays in my experience?

CHAPTER 3

CONSENT— (I PROMISE) IT'S NOT THAT COMPLICATED

Not too long ago, I was having coffee with an old friend, and the question of when something was rape versus when it was just bad sex came up. "Of course there's a gray area," she said. "I've been in a few situations where I didn't really say yes, and I didn't really say no. Especially when I was younger. I wouldn't call those times rape, though. They just kind of sucked, or were weird."

Shortly after that conversation, I read the 2018 Roxane Gay anthology *Not That Bad*, which is a collection of personal essays detailing sexual assaults that didn't quite rise to the level of the commonly imagined rape narrative of violent, forced intercourse.[1] After I read it, I thought about my friend's dismissal of her experiences, and then I thought about the fact that we have been trying to name these types of violations for an awfully long time. I mean, thirty years ago, *Ms.* magazine published *I Never Called It Rape*, one of the first books to address date rape, a concept that, at the time, had only recently entered the public consciousness.

It was pretty overwhelming to think we might still be

stuck in the same place we were thirty years ago. So I reminded myself that that culture has evolved in a lot of ways since then. For one thing, many more people are, in fact, calling such experiences rape than they were in the past. For another, there is more and more discussion about what it means to actually have someone's consent for sex in the first place, and of all the forms nonconsensual sex can take.

Consent is something that we now understand as the idea that someone has agreed to have sex with another person of their own free will, without pressure or coercion, and without the influence of drugs or alcohol. That might seem straightforward, yet a lot of folks find it tough to always be guided by these principles.

It's true that many nonconsensual encounters are the result of a real disregard for others, or of deliberate abuse. However, others are the byproduct of cultural messages telling women to stay silent about their desires and telling men to take any sex they can get. Or they are the result of a society in which a lot of people find it hard to talk about sex, let alone about consent, at all.

These days, it can actually be hard to remember just how new it is to discuss consent at all. Between feminist advocacy, Title IX activism that calls for colleges to take sexual violence seriously, and the fight for affirmative "yes means yes" consent on the one side, and the inevitable men's rights activism pushback and enduring #MeToo critiques of "What about due process for innocent men?" on the other, it can seem like the consent conversation is everywhere. It sure wasn't always this way. In 1991, when Antioch College created an "Ask First" consent policy, which defined consent "as the act of willingly and verbally agreeing to engage in specific sexual conduct," it was widely derided.[2] The school and the policy were mocked by everyone from *Saturday Night Live* to radio shock jocks for attempting to formalize what was seen as normal college behavior at the behest of uptight, antisex, man-hating feminists.

Looking back now, some have pointed out that Antioch was at the vanguard, opening the door to something campuses across the country have now been scrambling to put in place. As three of the innovators of the policy, Chrystelle Evans, Juliet Brown, and Bethany Saltman, said in a 2018 interview with the *Daily* podcast, the pushback they got at the time was humiliating and unexpected. In part that was because the campus they entered in the 1990s felt sex affirming and exciting, and they saw the consent policy they crafted as a cutting-edge way to address something most people at the time still didn't even recognize as a problem.

Reflecting on the past few decades, Saltman mused, "It's very upsetting to me to think we were doing this twenty-five years ago and [only] now are many colleges thinking about talking about this."[3]

Yet while more and more institutions have adopted rules that once seemed outrageous, that doesn't mean that the matter is closed. Consent advocates may not be the outliers they once were. But they are still the target of ire, and the topic continues to be mocked and dissected endlessly. There are plenty of reasons for that. One is that we are all the products of a complicated American history regarding sexual violence, and untangling our modern views from this ugly inheritance turns out to be tortuous.

This is a history that saw only women as rape victims

and then placed on them the responsibility for either preventing rape or proving it occurred. It is one where a woman's body was considered the property of her father or husband, and so any crimes against her were viewed in relation to how they impacted these men. It is a history where Black women actually were property and so couldn't legally be raped. Then even after Black women were not legally considered property, they were still often not actually viewed in the same way as white women, which allowed their experiences of rape to be discounted. And it is a history where a woman's consent for sex was unnecessary, since the only place she was supposed to be having it was in a marriage to a husband who was never expected to ask.

This legacy is the cornerstone of our modern society, which explains why the simple idea that all sex should be wanted by all people has become something fraught and complex. It shouldn't be. But getting to the heart of why this simple concept seems so cumbersome can take a little digging. So this chapter will dive into the history of sexual assault, to help us consider where we started, how far we have come, and how a deliberately invented mythology defining rape in very limited terms has to be undone in order to actually dismantle the hostile sexual culture so many of us traverse.

SURE, THINGS HAVE CHANGED, BUT . . .

Sometime a few years after it came out, I watched the 1988 movie *The Accused* at a sleepover, and it has stayed with me ever since. In it, Jodie Foster plays the fictionalized version of a Massachusetts woman who had been gang-raped at a bar five years earlier and then had to endure courtroom and public scrutiny of her prior actions. That movie helped open the doors to mainstream conversations about sexual violence and victim blaming. It also premiered at a time when the legal system—responding to advocacy by women's rights activists—was finally beginning to change as well.

Advocates had long been fighting to change antiquated rape laws, and starting in the late 1970s and early 1980s, this fight was focusing on many of the issues highlighted in *The Accused*. One of their goals was the passage of rape shield statutes, which prohibited a standard tactic long used by prosecutors hoping to discredit victims: namely the introduction of any evidence relating to the past sexual behavior of the victim during a rape trial. Another was eliminating some long-standing requirements for rape survivors to win convictions, including corroboration of the assault (often in the form of a witness) and proof of active resistance (often in the form of defensive injuries).

At the same time, there was a parallel fight to criminalize marital rape. This had not been illegal anywhere until the 1970s, and was only outlawed in all fifty states in 1993, when laws in Oklahoma and North Carolina caught up to those in the rest of the country. Then in 1994, the federal Violence Against Women Act passed. This was indeed a triumph, but after the House passed an amended version in 2012, which eliminated some basic protections for immigrants, indigenous Americans, and LBGTQ+ victims of domestic violence, we were reminded that laws are only as strong as the elected officials charged with upholding them.

A decade into the 2000s, college activism around campus sexual assault became a key issue. Student activists, fed up with their colleges' internal mishandling of sexual assault cases, began to make noise, and in 2011, the Obama administration wrote something called the Dear Colleague letter. Authored by the Department of Education's Office for Civil Rights, the letter declared, "The sexual harassment of students, including sexual violence, interferes with students' right to receive an education free from discrimination and, in the case of sexual violence, is a crime."[4] Students were then able to file complaints under Title IX when their sexual assault cases were not handled properly by their colleges or universities.

Driving home the severity of this issue was California's 2014 passage of the first affirmative consent law. This required college students to obtain "affirmative, conscious, and voluntary agreement [that is] ongoing throughout a sexual activity."[5] A number of other states subsequently passed similar laws.

However, despite these laws, sexual assault is still a huge problem. One out of every six American women has been the victim of an attempted or completed rape in her lifetime. That's a number that climbs to one in three for indigenous women. For men this number is one in thirty. LGBTQ+ folks experience even higher rates than most of the rest of the population, and in this group trans women, particularly trans women of color, face incredibly high incidence of assault.[6]

As much as we try to dismantle the culture that permits these crimes to continue, we also know that this culture is a deeply entrenched one. So, what can we do? For a lot of people, the answer is to support things like these new affirmative consent laws.

To be sure, I was among those who initially applauded

such bills when they first began to emerge, but legislation is not without its issues. I love the fact that these bills now tend to mandate consent education. But I also worry. In a country where Black and minority men are far more likely to see jail time than white men, it's very possible that the punitive aspect of these laws will not create the cultural sea change that many hope for, but rather will be used primarily to punish people who are already disenfranchised. While we can take heart that in 2018 a prison-reform bill passed, the racial disparity of our criminal justice system remains.

It's not that there isn't a need for legislation. But making new laws without looking at the environment of sexual hostility that makes them necessary is a mistake. Now, it goes without saying that changing culture is one of the hardest battles around, but if our past is any indication, it is also something that can indeed be done. Luckily, much of the groundwork is already underway.

So those of us who are fired up just need to take the baton and keep running. We need to keep debunking rape myths (see below for some examples), and we need to keep focusing on holistic consent education that starts in preschool and goes all the way through college. We need to continue critiquing a narrative that supports male hostility, and we need to keep fighting the inevitable backlash against these efforts. We also need to keep pushing for equitable legislative actions, with our eyes open to the problems that can accompany the passage of new laws.

REPORTING A SEXUAL ASSAULT TO THE POLICE: WHAT YOU MAY HAVE HEARD AND WHY THAT'S BS

WHAT YOU MAY HAVE HEARD:
If it was really rape, the victim would have reported it to the police.

WHY THAT'S BS:
According to the United States Justice Department's National Crime Victimization Survey, 60 percent of sexual assaults are *not* reported to the police.[7] And an even greater rate was found by a British government study, which put their number at 83 percent.[8] Reporting can be hard for anyone, but it can be particularly complicated for certain people, including men who might fear hostile or dismissive responses from authorities; for LGBTQ+ victims, for whom trans- and homophobia are real barriers; for undocumented immigrants, for whom any encounter with authorities can bring the fear of deportation; and for people of color, who face racism in the system as an added barrier.

• • •

WHAT YOU MAY HAVE HEARD:
If a rape really happened, then our legal system will ensure that justice is served.

WHY THAT'S BS:
Not only is it notoriously hard to gain convictions in rape trials, but many victims know that despite

rape shield laws, they will often be put on trial themselves. Additionally, many communities—*particularly those made up of marginalized groups*—have fraught relationships with the police. This can make the decision to report a sexual assault a particularly complicated one.

• • •

WHAT YOU MAY HAVE HEARD:
If you know who did it, there's no reason not to report.

WHY THAT'S BS:
According to the National Institute of Justice, seven in ten rape victims were assaulted by an intimate partner, relative, friend, or acquaintance, and among college women that number rises to nine out of ten. Reporting a sexual assault when the assailant is a friend, a partner, a relative, or even a casual acquaintance can be that much harder, due to fears about the impact on one's family, employment, or housing, or the possibility of retaliation.

SETTING THE RECORD STRAIGHT

When it comes to sexual assault prevention, there is a lot of lingering misinformation that hampers prevention efforts. See if you can answer these questions:

1) About _____ percent of rape claims prove to be false accusations.

2) On US campuses, about _____ percent of rapes occur while the perpetrator or the victim is under the influence of alcohol or other drugs.

3) About _____ percent of rapes involve a male victim.

4) _____ is the most common "date rape" drug.
True or False:

5) Most of the men accused after #MeToo ended up with criminal convictions.

6) If someone starts having sex but indicates they want to stop midway through, it isn't really rape if the other person keeps going.

7) If someone is raped while drunk, they are at least somewhat responsible for letting things get out of control.

8) Women need to take some responsibility for preventing sexual assault and should just use common sense, like not wearing revealing clothes or going home with men they don't know.

9) When a man is very sexually aroused, he may not even realize that a woman is resisting.

10) There is sometimes a gray area when it comes to sex, where it isn't really rape and it isn't really consensual.

The answers are: 2 to 8 percent of charges turn out to be unfounded, about 90 percent of campus sexual assaults involve situations where the perpetrators or victims are drinking, about 10 percent of rapes are of males, alcohol is the most common "rape drug," and just a handful of post-#MeToo accusations even resulted in charges, let alone convictions.

And as for the other true or false questions? Well, if you ask me, none of them are actually based on fact. Think about number 6. Just like anything else in life, from walking out of a movie you already bought tickets to, to sending back a meal you didn't like, people should have the right to change their minds about sex. There's much confusion around number 7, and I go into that in detail in the sidebar on "Sex Under the Influence." But the short answer is, it's up to the person instigating sex to make sure that their partner is capable of consent. Just because you decided to drink alcohol, it doesn't give another person the right to your body in any way, shape, or form. Number 8 is just plain old victim blaming, number 9 is trading on some off-base notions about male desire and biology, and number 10? Yes, sometimes people aren't sure if someone is consenting. But instead of going for it, that just means they need to hold off on sex until they are totally certain. Of course, real life can make this a little more complicated, and I'll cover this issue more later in the chapter.

Don't worry if you didn't get all the answers right. It's also okay if you have a different take on some of them than I do. But the fact that a lot of people probably miss the mark on at least a few of these questions is also a reminder that when it comes to this topic, our information isn't always totally accurate. And that's something that can make sexual violence a whole lot harder to combat.

SEX UNDER THE INFLUENCE

Though people who are incapacitated by substances cannot consent to sex, plenty of people have consensual sex after using drugs or alcohol. But the introduction of substances into sex can definitely make situations riskier and can make it a lot harder to determine whether there is, in fact, consent.

Here are a few things to keep in mind in order to keep yourself and others safe:

1) It is safer to have sex under the influence with an established partner than with a new hookup. It's also safer to have sex after drinking with someone with whom you have previously had sober sex, and whose likes and dislikes and boundaries you have a clear sense of.

2) Assuming you've been with this person before, drunk or high sex is not the time to introduce a new sex act that you've not previously tried.

3) Check in even more than you would regularly. Touch base periodically with the person you are having sex with and ask if they are still enjoying themselves, need a break, or want to do something differently. Then listen to their response.

4) Remember that people can get drunker and more high even after they have stopped consuming substances. So a person who might have seemed rela-

tively sober when you started hooking up might be getting more inebriated while you are making out and may no longer be able to consent. Additionally, you never really know how drunk or high someone is. Just because someone seems to be communicating coherently, that doesn't mean they aren't too drunk to actually consent.

5) If you are too drunk to use a condom properly, then you are too drunk to have sex.

ENHANCING EMPATHY

So how do we combat sexual violence? First we must untangle some of the most entrenched attitudes about it. I think about my very first semester in college: I had a professor who lectured that rape was a natural act, expected in primates and humans alike. That notion appalled me then, and I reject it now. Rape isn't natural. It's a reality, sure. But just like we reject violence, rape is by no means a reality that any of us ever has to accept on any level, in any form, or with any justification.

At the time, I simply wrote this guy off as a relic. And he was that. And maybe he would have been unreachable had I tried to discuss this with him. But to effectively fight rape and the culture that allows it, we also need to reach out to people like this, ideally long before they have a pulpit. We may be required to exercise a little patience in helping people really *get* it, even with people whose views we find abhorrent. That might not be your initial instinct. It isn't always mine. But this is why it's so helpful to include the concept of empathy in our conversations about consent. Doing so can clearly help support victims. It can also help us understand and tackle the climates that create perpetrators.

Empathy is the ability to understand and to share the feelings of another, to put ourselves in someone else's shoes, and to connect to the emotional state of a different person. Like love, empathy is not finite, and it can grow from a place where little or none existed before. I often tell my own kids that I grew new love with each of their three births. Empathy is not all that different. It can be grown and, in many cases, it can be learned.

I regularly work on developing empathy with my students. Starting in middle school, we do exercises where I ask them to imagine how another person would respond in any given situation. "How would you feel if you found out you won a trip to Hawaii? How would you feel if you lost your new phone, had your dog go missing, weren't invited to a party, got cast as the lead in the school play? Now imagine you are another kid in the class, even one you aren't particularly fond of: How do you think they would feel in those situations? Would they feel the same as you do, or differently?"

I do a similar exercise with my high school and college students. We look at a range of scenarios involving interpersonal conflict, and I ask, "Whom do you relate to? The perpetrator? The victim? The bystander? Now imagine how the person in another role feels. Does that line up with the feelings of the role you first imagined yourself in? If not, is there a way to bridge that gap?"

Nevertheless, empathy is more than just envisioning how someone else feels. Empathy also means that we recognize others as fully formed humans. There will always be those who use someone else's very humanity to degrade and harm them. But for many more of us, it is the act of seeing others more as an object than as a person that allows us to debase them. So, when we see the humanity of others, when we see their thoughts and feelings as equal to our own, it's just harder to commit violence of any type against them. This can explain why researchers have determined that increasing empathy helps decrease sexual violence.[9]

But true empathy can be a gut punch, so many people avoid it. To really feel what someone else feels can be devastating and heartbreaking. When it comes to sexual assault, many of us have shielded ourselves from a reality that just seems too distressing to contemplate by hardening our hearts or by accepting rape myths of the *she was asking for it, was playing hard to get, got what she deserved* variety.

The idea that you, or people you know, could commit rape is so upsetting that we have to tell ourselves that the victim was lying, or at least that they misinterpreted or misunderstood the situation. Conversely, the idea that you could be a victim yourself is even more terrifying, and rape myths also have the power to inure us to the fact that we could ourselves be prey. They let us think that as long as we follow the rules, we will be safe. Still, what happens if we *are* sexually assaulted? Even then, some victims take comfort in the myths and, in the words of the *Ms.* report, "never call it rape." *I wasn't "really" raped*, they can tell themselves. Or, *next time, I'll do something different to avoid danger.*

This notion, that following the rules can offer protection, is further supported by individuals who subscribe to something called the just world belief. This view holds that people get what they deserve and that there are no "innocent victims." Adopting this view can make someone's environments feel stable and ordered, and it offers them the comfort of believing that they have control over their fate.

For many people, the rape myth/just world belief combination is a necessary security blanket, without which it could just seem too scary to leave the house every morning. But while such views might feel comforting, they offer no real-world protection. Even worse, they actually perpetuate harm by shifting blame from perpetrators to victims, and they actively shut down people's ability to empathize.

Of course, acceptance of rape myths isn't all about the comforting narrative. It's also about misogyny. A study published in the *Journal of Interpersonal Violence* found that rape myth acceptance (RMA) in men was "strongly associated with hostile attitudes and behaviors toward women, thus supporting the feminist premise that sexism perpetuates RMA. RMA was also found to be correlated with other 'isms,' such as racism, heterosexism, classism, and ageism."[10]

Luckily, there is hope for change. Researchers writing in the journal *Sex Roles* found that having more frequent and "higher-quality" contact with counterstereotypical, high-status women decreased rape myth acceptance across all genders. It also decreased men's intentions to rape, and it decreased women's interpretations of rape as an expression of sex, making them more likely to see rape as an act of violence.

"High-quality" contact with women meant that participants were doing more than just exchanging a passing greeting, and to be considered "nonstereotyp-ical," a woman either had to have a nontraditional job or they had to be in a position of power or authority. The researchers found that when participants had more involved interactions with women in these categories, they had their expectations challenged, were able to see the world through someone else's eyes, and were exposed to views different from their own.[11] In other words, this type of contact was an almost perfect method of helping develop empathy.

Needless to say, empathy alone won't eliminate rape, but it is most certainly an important piece of the rape-prevention puzzle.

IS THERE A GRAY AREA WHEN IT COMES TO CONSENT?

When I ask my students if they think there is a gray area when it comes to consent, a lot of them waver. *Maybe?* they offer. *I mean, there probably shouldn't be, but there is . . .* they say.

I get that.

Here's my take. There is no "gray" about consent. Either someone has agreed to what is happening or they haven't.

But there are situations where one person deeply believes that they have consent and another truly believes that they were violated. (sometimes called consent "accidents".)

In large part, this book is designed to help people get to a place where this confusion is eliminated, and where the gendered pressures that tell boys from an early age to never take no for an answer and that tell girls to play hard to get are no more. Often it is these gendered pressures, or it is power imbalances between people of any gender, working alongside misinterpreted communications (both willfully misinterpreted or not) that result in people claiming the gray space exists.

So no—I don't believe in gray rape or gray consent. But I do believe the society that we live in creates conditions in which some people can feel entitled to make assumptions about consent and in which others don't always feel empowered to voice their needs. These conditions allow problematic social norms and narratives to take over, and they mean that folks default to their own rules of thumb about when they have consent, something that is just risky and ill advised.

FOCUSING ON INTIMATE JUSTICE

Another feature of rape prevention is the role of "intimate justice." Intimate justice is an interdisciplinary concept that was developed by Sara McClelland, a psychologist at the University of Michigan. It is designed to address intimate partner violence by broadening the definition of what that actually looks like.

Intimate justice tries to stop the normalization of sex that is unsatisfying, painful, or abusive and clearly labels it as harmful. This normalization happens in a lot of ways, many of which we discussed in previous chapters. One area that McClelland has specifically looked at is how people's perceptions of their own sexual experiences have traditionally been measured in research.

Often researchers use questions asking if a person finds their sex life "satisfying." McClelland determined that this kind of question is problematic, since everyone defines "satisfaction" differently. People's individual identifiers (like their gender, sexual orientation, class, race, religion, and ability), as well as their larger cultural and political spheres, the privileges they enjoy, or the stigmas they face, all color their understanding of pain and pleasure in sex. They also impact one's understanding of acceptable sexual behaviors.

So for women and gender and sexual minorities, reports of what is satisfactory or "good enough" in their sexual encounters often sound like anything but. Though for some folks in these groups, satisfactory sex refers to encounters that they physically and emotionally enjoyed, for far too many others, satisfactory sex can refer to sex that isn't accompanied by immediate threat. Or that wasn't physically painful. Or that simply ended quickly. Or that was with someone who wasn't abusive.

Conversely, when a cishet man reports that he finds his sex life satisfying or acceptable, he is more likely to be thinking about his physical experience.

Given this understanding, McClelland suggests that a better question than "Is your sex life satisfying?" is instead "How much do you expect from sex, and did you get it?" This second question allows people from varying backgrounds and circumstances to contextualize their experiences, and it can help researchers understand that those who expect little may report being satisfied with little.[12]

For example, since plenty of women with male partners expect sex to be painful, it would stand to reason that if someone had this expectation, when sex simply wasn't uncomfortable, even if it didn't actually feel all that plea-surable, it might still be considered satisfying. This could also be the case for women who expect male partners to orgasm but who don't have this expectation of themselves. Sex in those cases might be considered perfectly fine, even if it didn't feel particularly good.

Another example would be the impact on LGBTQ+ youth and partner choices. We know that teens in this group are less likely to expect to find a life partner than are cishet youth.[13] One troubling outcome of this lower expectation is that the fear of not meeting someone, or of being alone, can result in a higher risk of accepting an abusive partner.

Similarly, many people, particularly women and sexual and gender minorities, assume that unwanted sex is just a fact of life. This worldview interprets forced sex that doesn't follow the "real rape" narrative (more on that below) as simply part of the expected order of things (kind of like my old professor claimed), and not as the violation that it really is. As a result, this mind-set means that unwanted sex is more likely to be tolerated and less likely to be identified as coercive.

Since many of us adopt these patterns on some level, it is helpful to ask yourself:

> ▸ What do I consider satisfactory or acceptable sex?
> ▸ What is "good enough" for me?
> ▸ Do I expect to experience physical pleasure? If so, what does this look like?
> ▸ Do I expect my partner to experience physical pleasure? If so, what does this look like?

▸ Do I think that it's inevitable that I sometimes find sex painful? That my partner does?

▸ Do I think it's normal for a person to expect sex regardless of what their partner wants?

▸ Do I expect my partner to ask me if I want to have sex every time they initiate it?

▸ Do I ask my partner if they want to have sex every time I initiate it?

▸ Is it acceptable for a partner to use my body in the way that they most enjoy, even if I don't like what they're doing?

▸ Is it acceptable to use my partner's body in the way I most enjoy, even if they don't like what I'm doing?

▸ Is it my partner's duty to sexually please me?

Do any of your answers make you wonder if the sex you're having is equally enjoyed by both partners? Do any of your answers make you think that some of the sex you're having is not wholly consensual?

If so, consider a few more possibilities.

If you are initiating sex without the complete buy-in of a partner, why might you be doing this? Do you feel entitled to sex? How do you feel about your partner? Do you respect their feelings and opinions? If not, why not? Is it because you think they are in some way inferior or have a duty to accommodate your desires? Do you think your desires are more important than those of your partner? Can your partner decide not to have sex? What happens when they are not interested? Are they free to express this? If they never express a lack of interest in sex, do you think it's likely that they always want to have sex, and in the same way that you do, every time? If not, why might they not be sharing this? Could their reluctance to share be due to their cultural beliefs, the way they were raised, past sexual trauma, or the result of a power imbalance in your relationship?

If any of your answers gave you pause, are you willing to examine those issues further? To change your behaviors? If not, what is stopping you from doing so?

Now, if you are the partner who feels that you might not have an equal say in your sex life, consider those questions from your perspective. Do you think your partner understands their role in your sex life? Do you feel respected by your partner? Can you share your feelings on sex? Can you determine when you do or do not have sex? Is this a relationship that you would consider ending? If not, why not? Is there anything about the relationship that is salvageable? What? Is that worth sticking around for?

We know many relationships are rife with nonconsensual sex (in fact, almost 30 percent of rapes are committed by intimate partners[14]). We also know that many relationships endure despite this, and that a lot of people don't think about the forced or unwanted sex in their relationships as a deal-breaker. As Lux Alptraum writes in *Faking It: The Lies Women Tell About Sex— and the Truths They Reveal*, "A woman who opts to have sex because it's preferable to being physically abused may be exercising some form of agency, but it's a limited sort that highlights her lack of power far more than it highlights her freedom of choice."[15]

While it would be easy to just advise everyone in unequal sexual situations to walk out, the reality for many people is that this isn't possible or desired. Or, it isn't possible or desired at the present moment. Maybe someone feels responsible for their partner. Maybe they've had their self- esteem destroyed by them. Maybe they have a life together that includes children or shared finances. Maybe it feels too dangerous to leave. So if someone does stay, for as long as they stay, working on how to heal and reorient the sexual relationship is crucial to survival on a range of levels, both mental and physical. People can consider therapy for themselves and their partner, work against becoming isolated from family and friends, and if it is safe to do so, even broach the issue with a partner. Help is also available from places like the National Domestic Violence hotline, which you can find online or at 800-799-7233.

Ultimately, whether in the context of a relationship or not, there are multiple contributing factors to nonconsensual sex, and understanding what they are is a good way to help dismantle them.

THE IDEA OF "REAL" RAPE

In 2011, the FBI proudly released a report showing that violent crime, including the crime of rape, was on the decline. Sadly, while this sounded good, when it came to rape, the numbers weren't telling the whole story. Why not? In part, that was because the FBI had only been tracking rape in very limited terms, as the "carnal knowledge of a female, forcibly and against her will."

This meant that many forms of sexual assault, including rapes of males and nonbinary folks, drug- and alcohol-facilitated rapes, rapes where there wasn't penetration, rapes where there wasn't physical force, and statutory rapes were left out. These categories simply hadn't been on the radar of those who originally wrote the laws. The impact of this omission was that an estimated 40 percent of rapes were excluded from official FBI statistics.[16]

Far from calming an anxious public, the FBI's announcement resulted in notable outcry, and only six months later, in January 2012, the agency revised the definition of rape. It was about time, since it had been using the same criteria since 1929! The new definition covered victims and attackers of any gender, and it included instances in which the victim was incapable of giving consent because of the influence of drugs or alcohol or because of age. Additionally, physical resistance was no longer a required element for classifying a rape.

Even though legal definitions have gotten some updates in recent years, it is still common to distinguish between "real rape" and anything else. This understanding positions *real rape* as a crime committed by a male stranger who is violently propelled by uncontrollable deviant sexual urges against a female victim.

Even to this day, many Americans also have a very racialized notion of rape, imagining the "average" rape as one where a Black man attacks a white woman. This is a false notion with insidious roots in America's history of slavery and racial prejudice. It goes without saying, not everyone is impacted by the same sexual stereotypes. While Black and Latino men are often seen as hypersexual, Asian men are often seen as nonsexual.

We also have a lot of unfounded notions about the types of people who *are* and *aren't* "real" victims. According to research on police stereotypes, those excluded from the "real victim" narrative include people of color, LGBTQ+ folks, survivors of prior rapes, people with mental health conditions or other disabilities, sex workers, poor and working-class individuals, homeless people, and any man.[17] Of course, plenty of people with intersecting identities fall into many of these categories. This can mean they are multiply discounted, since in this view, the only legitimate victim is a cishet white woman who is morally pure and fought back valiantly against her attacker.

Really, it wasn't so long ago (in 2011) that the *New York Times* covered the horrific gang rape of an eleven-year-old child by a pack of boys and men. The article reported that the girl "dressed older than her age, wearing makeup and fashions more appropriate to a woman in her 20s." And that "She would hang out with teenage boys at a playground."[18] It is worth noting that this idea of looking "older" is one that is particularly dangerous for children of color, and particularly for Black kids, who are often taken to be much older than their real age. This is something that was confirmed by a study out of Georgetown Law Center that found "adults view Black girls as less innocent and more adult-like than their white peers."[19] The result is that for girls, "looking older" can mean increased risk of sexualization and a decreased sense that they need to be protected. For kids of all genders, it can mean increased risk of violence at the hands of authorities like the police, or awful encounters with adults in positions of power across the board.

The *New York Times* article also played the sympathy card for the rapists by citing the concerns of community members. "'It's just destroyed our community,' said . . . a hospital worker who says she knows several of the defendants. 'These boys have to live with this the rest of their lives.'"

Similar notions also emerged in sentencing during

the notorious Brock Turner case. The father of the Stanford University student who was found guilty of raping a drunk and unconscious woman pleaded for leniency during the rape trial on the basis that his son's future would be compromised. In a letter to the judge, the senior Turner wrote of his son, "These verdicts have broken and shattered him and our family in so many ways. His life will never be the one that he dreamed about and worked so hard to achieve. That is a steep price to pay for 20 minutes of action out of 20 plus years of his life."[20]

Turner was convicted of sexual assault. However, citing this letter and others, the judge sentenced him to only six months in jail. He was released after three. This caused outrage in some circles over the perceived lenience of the sentence and the sense that Turner got off easy, being a wealthy, white college athlete. That perception of biased lenience was not just alarmism. As CNN reported at the time, it is common for white college athletes who are convicted of first-time sexual offenses to receive little or no jail time, if they are even charged in the first place.[21]

This case was a reminder that while there have been advances in how the legal system deals with sexual assault, we are still often stuck in a really regressive place. Prosecutors may remain reluctant to pursue cases they don't think they can win. So, even though it is no longer a legal requirement, victims without eyewitnesses or evidence (like videos or photos), or those who don't fit the perfect victim model are far less likely to see their cases tried than those who can live up to a "real victim" standard.

Americans have inherited a long and dangerous history of men determining when rape occurred, and what, if any, the punishments for this crime should be. Rape laws were almost exclusively written by white men, and since these men also served as law enforcement, judges, and jurors, they could then help determine who was arrested and criminally charged. Unsurprisingly, the authors of rape laws had a self-serving interest to promote myths about rape and rapists that would protect their own status.

In her book *Redefining Rape: Sexual Violence in the Era of Suffrage and Segregation*, Stanford University historian Estelle Freedman explains that rape laws enshrined these men's sexual privilege into law and "contributed to the immunities enjoyed by white men who seduced, harassed, or assaulted women of any race."[22] Needless to say, white men accused of rape would often get their charges reduced.

These laws did little for the female victims of rape. They offered minimal protection to white women who were raped by upper-status white men. They also provided almost no protection at all for women of color, and they perpetuated the idea of the supposed Black rapist attacking virtuous white women. This myth has long been used to excuse racist violence perpetrated in the name of white women, and as modern studies tell us, it is one that is still incredibly powerful.[23] [24] Of course, we don't really need studies to tell us that. Just consider the horrific 2015 massacre of nine Black churchgoers in Charleston, South Carolina, by a white male shooter who declared, "You rape our women and you're taking over our country. And you have to go."[25]

I shouldn't even have to turn to statistics to demonstrate how off base the myth of the lurking Black male rapist is, but considering how much power it still holds, it pays to be clear: according to the Rape, Abuse & Incest

National Network, the overwhelming majority of rapists are white males. That doesn't mean that Black men cannot be assailants. But what the *myth* of the lurking Black male rapist does is shift blame as way to continue the tradition of protecting white men, and in doing so, it obscures the fact that almost 90 percent of all rape cases involve people of the same race.[26]

At the same time, that myth emphasizes white female victims and erases the experiences of Black women who are survivors of sexual assault. And it is crucial to realize how deeply Black women victims can suffer. As maya finoh and jasmine Sankofa write at the ACLU, "Studies have shown that Black girls, women, and nonbinary people are hypervulnerable to abuse [and] when abuse occurs, they are less likely to be believed and supported."[27]

Another issue in the "real rape" narrative is the idea that a victim must physically resist and is often injured in the process. This belief is also deeply flawed, since the last thing most people do when being sexually assaulted is fight off their attacker.

As Marissa Korbel writes in *Harper's Bazaar*, "I, too, have had sex I didn't want because sex was the least bad option. Sex was a known variable. Think of it as a harm reduction tactic. Fighting and screaming and kicking and yelling at a man? Unknown outcomes. Would he hit me back? Would he let me go? Would I fight and lose? If I lost, would he have sex with me anyway, only more violently?"[28] Korbel's experience is a common one. Sure, some people's fight-or-flight responses kick in during an assault. But many others freeze. Or, if it seems like a better tactic, they appease.

Of course, if even an eleven-year-old girl can have her

legitimacy as a *real* rape victim questioned, and if the potential harm to a promising young man can lessen his jail time, it's little wonder that people are so skeptical of this crime. But since the vast majority of assaults don't look like the mythological telling of them, it is imperative that the record is set straight and that the idea of the "real rape" narrative be laid to rest once and for all. Because when you combine the "real rape" narrative with a "perfect victim" narrative that holds that victims need to be "virtuous" women, maybe even virgins, who physically try to fend off a violent stranger, it becomes clear just how hard it is to check off all the right boxes to make a rape "count."

RAPE TRAUMA: WHAT YOU MAY HAVE HEARD AND WHY THAT'S BS

WHAT YOU MAY HAVE HEARD:
Rape is the worst thing that can ever happen to someone.

WHY THAT'S BS:
The "real rape" and "perfect victim" narratives make a lot of assumptions about survivors. One of these is the idea that rape is the absolute worst thing that can happen to a person, and that absent of years of therapy or personal growth work, it is impossible to fully heal. The fact is, for many survivors, the trauma of rape is not easily shed. But others walk a different path, and for many people, what prolongs trauma is the way they are treated as a rape survivor. The shame, disbelief, and blame so many people

experience after a rape can actually be harder to overcome than the violation of the attack itself.

• • •

WHAT YOU MAY HAVE HEARD:
After rape, survivors view their lives through the lens of the assault.

WHY THAT'S BS:
We love to tell people how they should feel about their rapes, but doing so simply disempowers people who have already had their agency stripped from them through an act of violence. Telling survivors how they should respond is just another way we reinforce the idea that there is only one way to be a "rape victim."

As Maria Marcello, a rape survivor, wrote on *Medium*, "The violation of my body doesn't define me. People assume I'm traumatized, I suppose because society sees rape as the most traumatic thing that can happen to a woman, simultaneously life-shattering and life-defining. For some, that violation of a woman's body is a fate worse than death. For me it wasn't."[29]

• • •

WHAT YOU MAY HAVE HEARD:
We should never shy away from calling rape what it is.

WHY THAT'S BS:
Survivors of rape may not want to be associated with this label. They might have experienced what others

would call rape, but that doesn't mean that they want to identify with this word. Not everyone who has endured rape will understand sexual violence as distinct from other forms of violence, and those people may not want to be put in a separate category. Even as we endeavor to name this crime as a way to shine a light on its ubiquity, we also need to provide space for those for whom this name does not fit.

SEXUALITY SPOTLIGHT: FALSE RAPE CLAIMS

Do you know the best way to derail any progress on sexual assault? Hype the possibility of the false rape accusation.

This is a possibility that a lot of people seem to think is staggeringly common. For example, one study found that 40 percent of those surveyed felt rape accusations were often false.[30] Another survey done with college students put that percent at fifty![31]

But these estimates are wildly off base. According to reports based on multiple academic and police studies, the actual number of "false" rape claims is between 2 and 8 percent.[32] [33]

And even that high end of 8 percent is probably inflated. That's because this number reflects an amalgamation of different situations, including cases where an accuser recants their testimony. This commonly happens when a victim feels that going through the legal system would be too painful, expensive, or ineffectual—even if their accusation wasn't false. This statistic also includes accusations that are considered "unfounded." Again, this does not mean an assault didn't happen, but rather it means that there is not enough evidence for authorities to classify it.

This is not uncommon when the crime is one that rarely has witnesses. And this statistic also includes situations where someone is actually determined to have lied.

The combination of those three situations all contribute to a false-accusation percentage range that is just a whole lot lower than what many people think. Combine that with the fact that the vast majority of rapes simply go unreported, and it becomes clear that while the *idea* of the false rape claim looms large, the instances when this actually happens are really quite uncommon.

We also tend to be totally off base in our assumptions about why those cases that do turn out to be false actually occur. As Dara Lind writes at *Vox*, contrary to popular belief, the motivations we assume to propel false rape accusations, namely revenge and guilt over regretted sex, simply don't factor into most of the situations where a claim turns out to be untrue.[34] Rather, studies from police departments within the United States and other countries have found that the two most common reasons for a false claim are that a person needed an alibi or an excuse, or that someone had a history of making false claims across a whole range of issues![35]

That second category can reflect significant mental health issues. And the first one? Often these are teens who might fear very real punishments, or even abuse, following the discovery of sexual activity by an angry parent.

Ultimately, understanding where these false claims typically come from is an important thing to take into consideration for all of us. But it's particularly crucial for those worried that any act of consensual sex could land them in jail if the person they slept with suddenly had a change of heart about the experience.

What's the Background?

The idea of the false rape claim has been around an awfully long time. The topic comes up in the Bible, in Greek mythology, and in contemporary novels and movies galore (think *Gone Girl*).

Sometimes people accused of rape simply claim that sex just never occurred at all. But more often, the claim is not that sex didn't happen at all, but rather that it did happen, and it was consensual.

There have been plenty of cases where celebrities and high-profile athletes have been accused of rape or sexual assault, and after the accusation became public, the accusers had their photos and phone numbers plastered across the internet, received death threats, and saw their sex lives dragged through court as proof that what happened was actually consensual.

Armed with this information, attorneys and media outlets have painted those accusers of not being worthy of belief. When, after months of this grilling, the accusers decline to testify, prosecutors drop the cases. That's usually widely taken to mean that the accuser must have lied about the encounter. Eventually, the celebrity or athlete might half-heartedly apologize for "misreading the situation," but rarely do they pay any professional price.

We as a society often jump to conclusions about the motivations of accusers. The public discourse during these cases rarely considers other reasons why the accuser may have dropped their case. If such an incident is remembered at all, it is usually recalled as a derailed false rape claim by a money- (or fame-) hungry person against a celebrity, and not as a case where rape charges were potentially dropped after a harassed victim decided they simply couldn't take it anymore.

Why It's a Problem

The difficulty in reporting a sexual assault is well documented. According to RAINN, approximately three out of four rapes go unreported, only forty-six out of a thousand rapists are arrested, only nine out of a thousand prosecuted, and only 4.6 out of a thousand will ever go to jail.[36]

Those numbers are a lot lower than the reporting and conviction rate for crimes like robbery or battery,[37] and in a country that has a long history of lengthy jail sentences for just about every other offense, it is a glaring reminder to victims that speaking up is no guarantee of justice. Survivors of sexual assault also know that their story is likely to be picked apart and that they risk being branded liars if their experience doesn't follow the expected narrative, or if it reveals even the most minuscule change in story, something that is known to occur regularly with crime victims of all types.

In some cases, that branding can even get them charged with offenses themselves! As Ken Armstrong and T. Christian Miller, the authors of *A False Report: A True Story of Rape in America* explain, time and time again, rape victims who don't fit the model are accused of fabricating their stories and then find themselves being treated as criminals. They share the experience of an eighteen-year-old woman they refer to as Marie who reported being raped by a man who broke into her apartment. "Police detectives treated small inconsistencies in her account—common among trauma victims—as major discrepancies. Instead of interviewing her as a victim, they interrogated her as a suspect. Under pressure, Marie eventually recanted—and was charged with false reporting, punishable by up to a year in jail."[38]

Ultimately, the police arrested a serial rapist and determined that he had raped Marie and that her story was anything but false. But there are plenty of cases where arrests are not made, and victims of rape become victims of the criminal justice system as well.

So not only do victims have to worry about being disbelieved, they also have to contend with the possibility that the judicial system, which they had turned to for help, can just as easily turn on them.

Where We're at Now

The combined forces of the #MeToo movement and Title IX activism on college campuses have opened the door to a whole new round of fear mongering around false rape claims. Some seem to be motivated by legitimate panic that innocent men will be hurt by overblown or altogether made-up accusations. Others seem to be propelled by those wanting to continue getting away with the same things they always have.

Take Candice E. Jackson, then the top civil rights official at the Department of Education. During an interview with the *New York Times* she asserted that "90 percent of [college campus rape accusations] fall into the category of *we were both drunk, we broke up, and six months later I found myself under a Title IX investigation because she just decided that our last sleeping together was not quite right.*"[39] Such logic was then reflected by that department's rollbacks of protections for victims of sexual assault on college campuses.

Or just think about all the post-#MeToo pushback, which included laments like, *now men who are falsely accused won't be believed*, and *what about due process and innocent until proven guilty?*

Yes, we live in a time of the social media soapbox, where people who would have never had a platform in the past can now find a massive stage and a large audience. This can most certainly be both influential and abusive. However, as the general public, it is not our duty to hold ourselves to the same standards as a judge and jury. We can believe victims and support due process all at the same time.

When it was first established, the legal system was designed to protect the interests of many of the kinds of men who have been accused of late. That system still puts the burden of proof on victims to demonstrate that they have been harmed. #MeToo didn't change these legal requirements. And, given the fact that so many of these crimes happen without witnesses and behind closed doors, proving sexual assaults occurred is a uniquely burdensome ask.

Plus, most of the men who had a public charge of harassment levied at them did not face any criminal proceedings. There have been plenty of denials and some mea culpas. But there hasn't been a barrage of falsified charges hurled at people who had done no wrong with the sole intention of destroying their careers. There hasn't been a flood of arrests. And even in this new climate, detractors are just using new ammunition—saying that #MeToo is a "witch hunt"—to lob old fears, including the idea that men will be falsely accused of rape.

When we compare how few people are actually victims

of a false accusation, as opposed to how many people are actually victims of rape—and, maybe even more tellingly, when we consider the fact that a man is far more likely to be a victim of sexual assault himself than he is to be the victim of a false rape claim—it becomes easier to remember that the true fight is still one for sexual safety, and not one to make men immune from accusation.

CONSENT: WHAT YOU MAY HAVE HEARD AND WHY THAT'S BS

WHAT YOU MAY HAVE HEARD:
Consent just means doing a lot of guesswork.

WHY THAT'S BS:
When it comes to consent, people might feel confused or unsure. But it's not like jumping off a diving board despite your reservations. In a sexual scenario, if you aren't sure, then you don't have consent. If you try to talk yourself into thinking that the person is consenting, then you don't have consent. If you make assumptions about what another person wants to do because they weren't explicit, then you don't have consent. That being said, if two consenting adults have sex one night and the next morning one of them regrets it, that is not rape.

• • •

WHAT YOU MAY HAVE HEARD:
If someone really wants to have sex, they will enthusiastically say yes.

WHY THAT'S BS:

The idea that someone can easily say yes to sex that they *do* want to have doesn't take into account the role of gender or culture. Since many women feel shame for being interested in sex, it can be hard for them to enthusiastically agree to sex, or to say what they want, for fear of being seen as easy, even if they do want to have sex. Plus, in many cultures it's considered rude to be direct. That is often especially true when it comes to sex.

While it would be great if everyone was at a place where they could verbalize their desires, until that happens, people with partners who don't feel comfortable using words to convey what they want to do sexually are going to have to work to develop communication strategies, potentially through agreed-upon, clear body language, to determine whether there is consent. But these strategies are usually a lot easier to employ with a partner you know well on other levels, rather than with a person you aren't as intimately acquainted with. Still, if you're with a partner you aren't intimately acquainted with, do not assume that your partner just has a difficult time saying yes. Wait until you have clear consent before engaging in sexual activity.

• • •

WHAT YOU MAY HAVE HEARD:

Consent means different things to different people.

WHY THAT'S BS:

Consent is consent. That being said, how we convey

consent will be different in different circumstances. People who are with new partners will have to establish how they communicate consent, while people in longer-standing relationships may have already determined the boundaries of their sexual comfort levels. But translating your understanding of how to communicate consent from a past partner to a current one is a risky move, and you need to make sure that all parties are on the same page all the time.

• • •

WHAT YOU MAY HAVE HEARD:
A lot of sexual assaults occur due to misunderstandings about whether someone gave consent.

WHY THAT'S BS:
There are times when someone really isn't sure if another person wants to have sex. But this uncertainty is not an excuse for committing an assault. People are capable of understanding that they can't always tell if they have consent. And if they can't tell, then they are capable of simply not having sex until they are sure. Your potential lost opportunity will cause a lot less harm than a potentially stolen one.

WHAT IT ALL COMES DOWN TO
Our culture of sexual violence is often sustained by myriad tangled and often contradictory justifications that simultaneously blame victims for assaults and then deny that those very assaults even happened.

In this climate, many people are reluctant to label

what they experience as sexual violence, let alone as rape. It's common to fear the ramifications of naming, and to doubt the truth of our own experiences. That isn't surprising given the strength of the *real rape* narrative and the complaints about how complicated it is nowadays to obtain authentic consent (a notion built more on willful disregard than on real befuddlement).

Ultimately, though, when we dismantle many of the hostile forces supporting sexual violence, there will no longer be room to pretend that ensuring consent is too demanding, to deny the scope of the problem, or to hold victims of sexual violence responsible for their assaults. Instead we will be able to envision the creation of a world where every single person can feel sexually safe regardless of how they choose to move through it.

DISMANTLING SEXUAL VIOLENCE

Sexual violence is often justified by turning the tables on the victims and holding them responsible for assaults. That's a problem, so think about how you could respond to the following situations in a way that actually supports the victim/survivor.

1) Your friend tells you that sometimes her live-in boyfriend has sex with her even when she doesn't want to. "I mean, he pays more of the rent since I'm in school, and he takes really good care of me. So I know I owe him," she says.

....

....

....

....

....

2) Your teenage daughter calls you crying. She is drunk and at a party you told her not to go to. When you arrive to pick her up, she tells you that an older boy did "stuff" to her and she thinks some kids took pictures.

....

....

....

....

....

....

....

3) You meet your sister for drinks one night. She turns up seeming really rattled. After a few minutes, she tells you some guy on the subway pushed his penis into her butt and when she screamed, he called her a slut. A few other guys on the train laughed, and the rest of the people just pretended not to notice.

....

....

....

....

....

....

4) Your friend tells you about a mutual acquaintance who performed oral sex on a passed-out guy at a party. When you express dismay, your friend says, "What are you so upset about? I bet he was psyched to get a blow job!"

....
....
....
....
....
....
....

5) Your coworker asks to talk to you one day. They say that your mutual colleague has been sexually harassing them, and that they are planning on filing a formal complaint. When you ask for details, your coworker says the colleague started by asking about their dating life and talking about their own. On a few occasions, the colleague gave your coworker a spontaneous shoulder rub, which caused your coworker to physically squirm away. Then last week, the colleague commented on your coworker's butt, saying that tighter jeans would better show it off. You have never had any interactions like this with the colleague in question.

....
....
....
....
....
....

Now, for each of your responses, ask yourself:

- ▸ Did my response support the victim/survivor?
- ▸ Did my response come with any lesson for the victim/survivor about what they should have done differently? If so, could I reword it to avoid that component?
- ▸ Did it offer any advice for the victim/survivor for now or in the future?
- ▸ Is there a way to offer support without admonishment or advice?
- ▸ Does a response absent advice make me uncomfortable? If so, why is that?
- ▸ Did my response ask what the victim/survivor wanted to do?

For a lot of people, the natural instinct is to hold a victim/survivor somewhat accountable for their situation. There are a lot of reasons for that. People who identify with the victim/survivor may want to feel that the victim/survivor has more control over the situation. Many people personalize the situation and would like to think that they would never make those mistakes, or that they could protect themselves.

Others identify with the perpetrator and worry that they could find themselves in that position unwittingly. Or they think about their past actions in a new light and try to rationalize what they suspect is unacceptable behavior.

The problem is, these are self-protective measures

that don't do anything to help challenge hostile climates or support victims.

So how might we respond in a supportive way to situations like the ones presented above? Start practicing saying things like:

▶ That sounds really hard.
▶ I'm so sorry you had that experience.
▶ No one deserves to have that happen, no matter what they did first.
▶ Actually, that is against the law.
▶ Thank you for confiding in me.
▶ Do you want to get more help?

These phrases are great even if you feel like you don't know what to say, since they are supportive, correct misinformation, offer the victim choices, and hold people accountable for their actions, all without forcing you to be an expert in a field you may know little about.

CHAPTER 4

LITTLE KIDS,
BIG QUESTIONS

THINK OF THE CHILDREN!

Not too long ago, a social media friend who generally posts kid pics with a little mainstream liberal fare
sprinkled throughout her feed raised the alarm about a
subway ad regarding treatment for polycystic ovarian
syndrome, which included "painful sex" and "heavy
periods" among the condition's symptoms. "Is it necessary for my kids to have to read about sex on our morning
commute?" she wrote.

Save for one remark from a woman who herself had
the condition, all of the comments on the post were from
parents of the six- to twelve-year-old set and were along
the lines of, "My kids don't even know about sex yet,"
and, "That's awful, you should complain." One jokester
took the "You can tell kids sex is always painful if you're
not married" approach.

I didn't weigh in. But I was reminded just how many
folks simply assume that learning about the fact of sex is
damaging to kids. In fact, a study commissioned by the
Classification and Rating Administration found that while

80 percent of parents surveyed reported concern over their kids seeing graphic sex scenes, only 64 percent were upset about their kids seeing graphic violence. Furthermore, only 56 percent of those parents were worried about the depiction of realistic violence, while a comparatively high 70 percent were distressed by full-frontal nudity.[1]

If that isn't a clear statement on our anxieties, I don't know what is.

Most of those anxieties are motivated by concern over children. Who would want to expose kids to ideas that might be scary or keep them up at night? But sometimes the way we safeguard kids can be misguided and cause more harm than it prevents. If the goal of this book is to help dismantle hostile sexual climates, it's important to understand that parts of this process have to begin early, and that working with kids now is the best way to set them up for success later.

Some of this work, like tackling gender stereotypes, the impact of sexism and homophobia, and the *boys will be boys* message, can even be started with toddlers and then continue as kids get older. Whether we like it or not, children are impacted by the same sexual climate as everyone else, and it is the job of caring adults to intervene and push back against its harmful aspects. Sometimes that can make us feel caught between two impulses: the desire to protect children from knowledge they are too young for and the need to give them skills to address complicated issues they may encounter, even if those are issues we wish we could shield them from for as long as possible.

This chapter strives to help you strike that balance so that young people can feel safe in the world themselves, and then can be part of making it safer for others as well.

ABOUT AGE APPROPRIATENESS

Though some adults think children will be damaged by a conversation about sex, and so decide not to cover this topic at all, and others hold off on conversations because they imagine school will cover the basics in sex ed, many parents default to the idea that they will get to the sex discussion with their kids when the question comes up. This is a comforting fallback, borne of the idea that parents are best able to gauge if their children are ready for information. But waiting for a child to bring up an issue means a lot of kids, and a lot of questions, will fall through the cracks.

Just think: if adults find it hard to talk about sex, imagine how much harder doing so might seem to a child who has undoubtedly gotten the message that this topic is taboo. Even if they aren't asking, that doesn't mean that children aren't curious or don't need information.

This can be true for all kids, but it is particularly the case for LGBTQ+ children, as issues of sexual identity and orientation are often left out of conversations altogether. Failing to talk about things like gender or sexual orientation can make a child feel utterly alone and isolated.

So don't wait for a kid to ask about sex, or gender, or sexual orientations. Just start talking about the subject often and early. That means talking to toddlers and preschoolers about all the parts of their bodies, including the genitals, equally. It means talking about LGBTQ+ people and different types of family structures. It means explaining the basics of reproduction to elementary school–aged kids (or younger), without glossing over the fact that most people have sex because it feels good and not just to make a baby. It means telling kids that their bodies are theirs and theirs alone, that no one should touch them in a way that makes them feel scared or uncomfortable, and that if they are ever told to keep touching a secret, this is a sign that they need to do just the opposite.

When you have these conversations, use clear language, make sure you are understood and that the kid is following what you are saying, and if you don't know an answer, let kids know that, too. Cory Silverberg's books, *What Makes a Baby* and *Sex Is a Funny Word*, are great to give to or read with kids. And if you need help talking about gender identity and sexual orientation, there are also really solid books about LGBTQ+ families for kids of all ages that a simple Amazon search can help you find. For young kids, I like Maya Gonzalez's work and her book *They She He Me: Free to Be!*

Another excellent book that came out recently is *Beyond Birds and Bees: Bringing Home a New Message to Our Kids About Sex, Love, and Equality* by Bonnie J. Rough. Using books as a guide can be a really easy way to normalize conversations without making you worry that you may be saying the wrong thing.

Rest assured that despite your worries, you will not scar a kid by giving them accurate information about sexuality. What they are much more likely to be upset by are the things they see online or hear from their misinformed peers. One of the best things we can do for kids is to help them become responsible consumers of the messages and media around them. Pointing out the problematic nature of a song or a movie is going to go a lot further than is censoring things you disapprove of. Having such conversations falls under the category of educating kids about sex, as opposed to just letting them absorb what the world is telling them about the topic.

I still think about how confused I was when a second-grade classmate explained to me that there was this thing called humping, which involved a man putting his penis inside a woman's bum and making her poop before she ended up pregnant.

And I recall the year I spent convinced, at age ten, that I had AIDS because, despite my mother's many warnings about hygiene, I had used a bathroom in the park without putting toilet paper down on the seat and had emerged from the stall to see graffiti declaring: "This bathroom is infested with AIDS!"

Conversely, when my parents gave me a copy of some 1980s *Where did I come from?*–type book, I might have been a little surprised, and maybe even embarrassed, but I sure wasn't disturbed or damaged, and I got a lot of my misinformation cleared up in the process.

BODY PARTS AND BODY SAFETY

All children need to know all body parts. That means you don't ignore the penis parts, the vagina, clitoris, and vulva parts, or the anus and buttocks parts. Kids need to know that it's okay to talk about these parts, and it's okay to touch these parts themselves. But they also need to know that if it isn't in a helping way, it's not okay for older kids, or for teens or adults, to touch them on their genitals, to kiss them with their mouths open, or to make the kid touch those parts on anyone else. Kids of all ages need to know that they can tell grown-ups they trust if this happens.

A lot of people call these the *private parts* when talking to children. In general, I'm not a huge fan of this term, since it can make it seem like there are parts of the body that should not be discussed in polite company. However, when talking about abuse, it can be helpful to use this term because kids tend to be more comfortable with it. When I teach about personal body safety with younger kids, I explain that in this context, *the private parts* are parts of the body like nipples and breasts, buttocks and the anus, the penis and testicles, and the vagina and vulva. Kids can also think of these parts as those that are often covered by a bathing suit.

But when I use that term, I tell kids that just because I am calling these parts *private*, that doesn't mean that they are off-limits to talk about. If someone touches these parts, then the child needs to tell a person they trust as soon as they can. Or, if it happened a little while back, or a long time ago, they should tell an adult they trust as soon as they can.

I also try to avoid classifying touch as good or bad, since a lot of "bad" touch feels physically good. I never want a child to internalize the idea that an abusive touch from one person means that the touching of private parts in general is bad, since in the future, they may desire such touch from another person. Plus, sometimes things that feel bad, say, getting a cavity filled, are actually medically necessary, and so are actually *good* for you. Because of that, I prefer to talk about *safe* and *unsafe* touch.

Safe touch feels okay, acceptable, and positive, and it is touch that makes kids feel loved or taken care of. Or it is touch that is related to a medical need or to hygiene. On the other hand, unsafe touch feels uncomfortable, embarrassing, painful, or scary. It happens when someone touches a kid's body parts for reasons that don't have to do with taking care of that kid.

I also talk about *confusing* touch. Confusing touch may start out feeling good or normal, but it may end up feeling bad or scary. If a child (or another adult) is dismissing the seriousness of an incident, you might want to say, "A lot of unsafe touch crosses the line and is a form of sexual abuse." It can also be helpful to use that term when explaining why some kinds of touch aren't okay. But you might not want to label a child's experiences in the moment, if they're telling you about something that's going on. Sometimes in those moments, it works to just call unsafe touch "really not okay."

Another term that can help explain sexual abuse to kids is *secret touching*. This is something that Cory Silverberg describes in his excellent book for kids *Sex Is a Funny Word*. He calls it *secret touching* because, as he says, "No matter where someone touches you or where you touch them, they make you keep it a secret. They want you to keep it a secret because they know what they are doing is wrong, and they don't want other people to find out. They might try to scare you so you won't tell. They might be nice to you so you won't tell."[2] Framing touching in this way makes this kind of secret a red flag for kids and a sign they need to tell a trusted grown-up what is going on.

BEYOND BOYS WILL BE . . .

In recent years, you may have noticed more than a few little boys walking around with a T-shirt sporting a play on the phrase *boys will be boys*. I've seen kids in shirts that declare "Boys will be . . . decent human beings," "Boys will be . . . held accountable for their actions," and more. And while there is a good argument to be made against the commodification of these messages, their prevalence is also a reminder that more and more people are, at the very least, questioning traditional ideas about how to raise boys.

The *boys will be boys* message excuses boys' bad behavior as something built in to their gender. But as psychologist Cordelia Fine demonstrates in *Testosterone Rex*, there are simply no biological absolutes when it comes to behavior.[3] Defaulting to a chemical explanation distracts us from the real causes of gender differences and allows us to avoid the harder work of examining what may really be causing some boys to be aggressive.

Elizabeth J. Meyer, a professor at the University of Colorado and the author of books on ending bullying and sexism in schools, explains in an article for *Psychology Today* that a *boys will be boys* default links "aggressive behaviors with a child's sex assigned at birth and ignores all the other environmental (family, media influences, messages at school, etc.) and individual factors (personality, nutrition, body chemistry, etc.) that might be influencing behavior. It creates an easy excuse to fall back on so adults don't have to examine other reasons for such aggressive behaviors."[4]

So how do we dismantle a message that can feel fundamental to our understanding of normal childhood behavior? One way is to revisit the idea of how sexism hurts boys. We know that while studies have found that girls tend to learn that there is a range of emotions they are permitted to express, many boys grow up learning that they need to hide all emotions except anger.[5] Boys as young as two may learn that feelings of sadness, rejection, isolation, and fear should only be funneled into expressions of rage. This message starts the first time they hear, "Boys don't cry," and then is reinforced throughout their lives.

We also know that parents, and especially fathers, don't show as much physical love to sons as they do to daughters. Plus, there are also plenty of parents who believe that they need to "toughen" sons up, often by encouraging aggression in sports. Boys are also physically punished more than girls, which can create a cycle of violence. Then there is the fact that games and activities for boys often simulate war or fighting.

The impact on boys can be pretty awful. According to the American Psychological Association, boys who are socialized toward "traditional masculinity ideology" (which the organization describes as being antifemininity, avoiding the appearance of weakness, and stressing achievement, adventure, risk, and violence) experience many negative effects.[6] Boys and men make up 77 percent of all deaths by suicide.[7] We also know that men are most likely to perpetrate intimate partner violence,[8] and that boys and men have been responsible for all but a handful of the over 160 mass shootings that have occurred since the 1960s.[9]

The situation sounds dire, but it isn't hopeless. There are concrete things adults can do to push back against the cultural forces that grow these men. For example, adults can reinforce positive behaviors over negative ones, and challenge places where we hold boys to different expectations than girls. One way to do this is by letting boys own their more vulnerable feelings, by allowing them to cry and show fear, and by teaching them to handle rejection and failure. We also need to respect boys' bodily autonomy and not push them into unsafe spaces just because they are male. Boys should learn that they don't need to wrestle, climb high trees, or jump off diving boards to prove anything.

Adults can also set an expectation that boys express empathy. Many people assume that girls will be considerate and tender and that boys will be thoughtless. There is no reason not to expect a boy to be caring toward others who are sad, scared, or upset, and there is no reason not to expect them to understand when playful teasing crosses the line to harmful bullying. Boys also have to learn to stop when someone says no. In my house we all use the word *donuts* (like *do not*, but clearly out of context) during teasing or play that has gone too far to show that we are serious about wanting someone to stop what they're doing. My children claim to think it is silly, but they all pull that word out, and it works.

Adults also simply shouldn't overlook bad behavior just because we assume that boys are naturally badly behaved. We need to stop chalking up violence to some inherently male quality, and instead we need to challenge a larger culture of violence.

When we start to take these steps, we send the message

to boys that their gender isn't an excuse for crossing boundaries, that they can be held accountable for their actions, and that we expect them to grow up with respect and concern for people of all genders.

KIDS AND CLOTHES

A few years ago, a friend texted me, "How do you explain to an eleven-year-old that short shorts are not age appropriate, and what they represent, and the whole sex appeal thing? She does not get it. She sees it as stylish, and I see it as *no way*."

Here's the thing: it's always important to remind ourselves that kids shouldn't be asked to shoulder the responsibility of how other people respond to them. Nevertheless, they should know that certain responses are possible based on how they present themselves in the world.

If you feel like you need to talk to a kid about revealing clothes, you can say something like, "That's a great outfit and you look amazing in everything you wear, but not everyone is comfortable seeing so much skin on a kid, and people might make comments about your clothes or your body that could make you feel weird."

If the kid is okay with that, I say let them wear what they want to wear.

We often put our adult fears onto children who probably just like what they're wearing, want to be trendy, or feel good in their clothes. And, yes, maybe they also want attention, but guaranteed they don't want it from grown-ups who are actually sexualizing that kid. It's much more likely that if a kid wants *that* kind of attention, it's wanted from other kids, which, big picture, isn't such a bad thing.

Typically, we worry about girls' outfits the most. But any time we talk to girls about their clothes, we then need to also talk to boys about making girls feel safe. We need to tell them not to stare at girls rudely and to respect girls regardless of what they wear.

And if a girl gets some nasty comments about her clothes or her body and comes back to report to us, the last thing we need to do is make her feel like it's her fault and like she invited those comments based on her outfit. Support that kid, tell them it stinks that the world thinks it's okay to comment when they see skin on a kid or that it's acceptable to talk about a girl's body. Reassure them they didn't do anything wrong. Ask them if they still feel comfortable in what they were wearing, or if they'd rather wear something else.

Of course, it isn't only girls in short shorts who have to navigate how the world responds to what they look like. A boy who wears something deemed too "feminine" may have just as difficult a time—even more so in some cases, since their choice of expression may not fit within cishet norms and expectations of how they identify. This is ever more complicated, as families and schools may increasingly support boys wearing whatever they want, but if the larger society hasn't caught up, boys can still be mercilessly bullied for such presentation.

So while I utterly welcome this kind of support and

try to offer it to my own kids, I also think it's okay to acknowledge how hard it can be for a boy to move through the world when he is pushing gender boundaries in his presentation even a little. Just consider the relative freedom afforded to girls who want to wear jeans and sweatshirts, compared to boys who even just want to paint their nails or wear a bright color.

And what about LGBTQ+ kids who present as visibly queer and who often encounter particularly intense hostility? Here, too, I think a similar approach is warranted. Support children in their queer presentation, but also have honest conversations with kids about possible reactions to how they look. They should know that some of these reactions will be positive and welcoming and can make them feel like part of a community. Others might be hostile. Many adults worry about kids becoming a visible target, and it is okay to share that concern.

As with so many issues, there is the world we want to live in and the world we actually live in, and since those two realities are seldom in perfect harmony, neither will our responses always be.

MAKING SPACE FOR A RANGE OF IDENTITIES

Another great way to help children grow up to respect other people is to help them understand that all identities are valid and to normalize what it means to be LGBTQ+. Little kids should know about the range of identities that are out there. Sometimes adults gloss over this topic because they lump conversations about sexual orientation and gender identity together with conversations about sex, and then they default to the reasoning "kids are too young to know about this." Though it's obvious that sexual orientation and gender identity can affect someone's sexual expression, for younger kids, the LGBTQ+ part of who someone is will often be much more about identity and love and families than it is about sex.

Since children tend to live in families, family is often the most important thing in their lives. So when kids are toddlers and preschoolers, talking about identity in the family context can seem completely ordinary. Make it natural to mention that this family has one dad, that family has two dads, this kid is being raised by grandparents, that one has stepsiblings, two moms, foster kids, etc.

Some cishet people might feel like it's rude to point out that Uncle Bill is gay, and that doing so might reduce Bill to his sexual orientation. But pretending that everyone is exactly the same erases the beautiful variety of identities in the world and sets a limited expectation for what kids should think is normal. Really, rather than othering, open discussions about LGBTQ+ identities emphasize the humanity of all people.

Of course, discussing identities is different from outing someone against their will. Don't do that. Ever. But people who are open about their identities should not have those identities ignored or hidden when children are around. That teaches kids there is something shameful, bad, or weird about this key part of who people are. So make an effort to weave in the stories of LGBTQ+ friends, classmates, teachers, family, neighbors, and public figures as an easy way to let kids see that there are a million ways to be in the world. You can also work to present same-gender romantic experiences in the same way you do cross-gender experiences. For example, even though my primary relationships have been with men, my kids know that before I was with their fathers, I had dated a few women, in the same way they know I had other boyfriends at earlier points in my life. Obviously, if you identify as LGBTQ+, then these conversations will be different than if you don't, but nobody embodies every identity out there, so there is generally space to reference a range of experiences.

A lot of us would like to think we are open-minded and treat everyone identically regardless of their identities. But just like a lot of white folks are really uncomfortable with the idea that they might be racist or even benefit from a racist system, a lot of cishet folks find it really tough to confront their own biases about gender and sexual orientation. Nevertheless, it's important to examine your own biases before talking with kids.

Homophobia, both the kind you are aware of (say, knowing you are uncomfortable with the idea of two men kissing) and the kind that is harder to admit to (say, a discomfort with the idea that your own child could be gay) can color the way you talk about sexual orientation and gender identities. It can make these conversations less about love, childrearing, and community and more about stereotypes and fears. For instance, you might unwittingly pass along your own prejudiced belief that gay men are pedophiles, or that trans people have a mental illness or are secretly trying to trick people, or that lesbians just haven't met the right man yet. Try really hard not to put your potentially problematic adult associations onto kids and then assume that a conversation is too mature for them.

Whether you are a parent or someone who works with children, consider these questions to help you think about where you might be coming from and how that could affect the way you talk about the issue with kids:

▸ Do you view sexual orientation and gender identity as a choice (and as a bad one if a person is LGBTQ+)?

▸ Do you belong to a religious group that is hostile to LGBTQ+ issues? If so, do you agree with those teachings? Do you want to leave your place of worship? If you can't or don't want to leave, can you find out what your religion *actually* says about sexual orientation? Most homophobic religious beliefs are based on how leaders understand specific texts, not on the fundamental tenets of a religion. Do you wish to change the culture of hostility toward LGBTQ+ people within your religious group?

▸ Is there something about being LGBTQ+ that makes you uncomfortable? What is it? Are these feelings based on hostile assumptions and stereotypes? Do some reading, and you will often be surprised by how misinformed many pervasive views are. The websites mykidisgay .com, PFLAG.org (which stands for Parents and Friends of Lesbians and Gays, and was the first support and ally group for families of LGBTQ+ folks), and genderspectrum.org (which works to create gender-inclusive environments and offers support groups) have a lot of great resources.

It's also super important to be sensitive to the possibility that the child you are talking to may be LGBTQ+ or questioning themselves. A lot of LGBTQ+ adults recall knowing they were queer as early as kindergarten or even before but not having the language to describe their identity until later. These days a lot more kids do have the language, and that fact, combined with more open atmospheres, means we are seeing kids coming out as young as elementary school. This would have been unthinkable in the not-too-distant past. Coming out that young can be really freeing for kids who can live authentically from an early age. It can also be scary and can open them up to hostility and bullying at home and at school.

So the more we teach children that difference is not something to fear, but rather something to celebrate, the stronger and safer our communities will be for children of all identities. LGBTQ+ kids will be less likely to be persecuted, hetero boys will be less likely to express their masculinity in hostile ways, and girls will not have to endure the dangers that so often accompany them now.

LGBTQ+ IDENTITIES: WHAT YOU MIGHT HAVE HEARD AND WHY THAT'S BS

WHAT YOU MAY HAVE HEARD:
Kids will have a way harder life if they are LGBTQ+.

WHY THAT'S BS:
Despite the fears of a lot of well-meaning adults, being LGBTQ+ is not something that inherently causes hardship. What's hard for queer kids is living

in a hostile and trans- and homophobic world. While adults can't shield kids from all the world's cruelties, supportive, loving parents, teachers, and religious leaders offer the best protection against everything from depression to anxiety, and the best role models for navigating the larger world.

Plus, while it's true that LGBTQ+ youth have higher rates of suicide than cishet kids, it doesn't have to be that way. Brian Mustanski, the director of the Northwestern University Institute for Sexual and Gender Minority Health and Wellbeing, conducted a decade-long study on self-harm and suicidal thoughts among queer youth and found that social support from family and friends helps protect LGBTQ+ children from thoughts of suicide.[10]

• • •

WHAT YOU MAY HAVE HEARD:
Children are too young to know that they are LGBTQ+.

WHY THAT'S BS:
Some kids will know their sexual orientation or gender identity from a really young age—think preschool—whether or not they have the language for it. Others will identify this aspect of themselves far later in life. But the last thing any child needs is for an adult to dismiss such a core aspect of their identity with a tossed-off "You're too young to know" or "You're probably going through a phase." Even if a questioning kid ends up determining that they aren't

queer, what harm does it do to support them through the process of figuring it out?

• • •

WHAT YOU MAY HAVE HEARD:
If you don't stick to traditional gender roles, kids will get confused and grow up gay.

WHY THAT'S BS:
What *is* confused is a lot of people's understanding of sex (biology), gender (identity), and sexual orientation (broadly, whom you find attractive). But the fact is, enforcing rigid gender norms will do nothing to change whom someone is attracted to. What it might do, however, is make them feel pretty bad about themselves.

Despite the fact that various groups claim to be able to change sexual orientation and gender identity through therapy, this just isn't possible. Adults who think taking dolls away from boys or wrestling girls into dresses will help keep them on a heterosexual path should know that groups including the American Psychological Association have come out against sexual orientation change efforts (SOCE) as not only ineffective, but also deeply harmful,[11] and more and more states are banning "conversion therapy" for minors as a result.

SEVEN WAYS TO HELP KIDS BECOME GOOD SEXUAL CITIZENS

Plenty of adults want to help young people get on solid sexual footing. Here are the seven most important ways to help get them started.

One: Open the door to conversations about sexuality.

The American Academy of Pediatrics believes that preschoolers should be getting sex education that teaches body safety and the proper names for genitals as a protective strategy against abuse.[12] On the other hand, opponents of sex ed have labeled the efforts to teach children about sexuality as *pornographic* and *perverse*. Using slogans like "Too much too soon," these folks argue that children need to be protected from information about sex, lest it traumatize them or inspire them to act.

But this fear is misguided. A wise sex educator friend of mine uses the analogy that all kids see adults driving cars every day and most turn out just fine. Sure, a few will get behind the wheel and crash long before they get a license. But that doesn't mean we hide cars from kids or ban driver's ed. When it comes to driving, not only do we know that most kids won't be taking the car out for a spin before they're sixteen, but we also know that they will be better drivers after they learn the basics. Isn't it about time that we start treating sex in the same way?

Two: Establish the importance of consent.

When I was a kid, no one talked about the idea of consent. You kissed your relatives, sat on people's laps, held hands with a classmate, all without anyone ever asking how you felt about it.

These days, a lot of folks are realizing that this can be a problem, since when we act as if children don't need to give permission to be touched, they then feel as if they don't have the right to say no to unwanted touch now or in the future.

I know in my house it was heartbreaking to tell my eight-year-old that he couldn't hug his sisters when they didn't want him to (which for a few months was a good amount of the time). But I also thought that making this clear was an important life lesson. Of course, you don't want to go over the top with these messages and make people feel like they are walking on eggshells and that any misread signal is cause for alarm. In families, and in life, there are times when people simply have to touch each other. Still, the underlying message for kids needs to be one where they feel they have some control over their bodies and what they do with them.

Three: Check your gendered messages.

Kids are hit with gendered messages from day one. Girls learn that they will benefit from looking and acting feminine, which is typically interpreted to mean they are conventionally attractive, nonconfrontational, and compassionate. Boys learn that to be seen as an alpha male in society, they need to be physically strong and dominant over others.

These messages are confusing enough for adults, let alone for kids. That's why challenging these ideas and celebrating nonconventional gender behaviors can help young people escape some of the more harmful effects of living in a very gendered world.

Four: Prepare for rejection.

Everyone is going to get rejected at some point in life. But kids need to learn that if someone isn't interested, far from just continuing to pursue that person, they need to back off and accept the fact that there will always be times when you don't get what you want in this life. It's crucial to teach kids of all genders that, while painful, rejection is normal and not a statement on their worth as a person. This will teach kids resilience and prevent retaliatory behavior, which can emerge when people assume that anything they want should be theirs to get. As Elayne Savage writes in *Don't Take It Personally: The Art of Dealing With Rejection*, "Three important characteristics contribute to resiliency in children: development of a sense of self, self-determination, and the capacity to depersonalize . . . and distinguish which actions are directed toward them and which are not."[13]

Five: Address bad behavior when you see it.

A lot of adults have no problem correcting kids for their bad manners, klutziness, and irresponsibility. But some of us find it harder to comment on inappropriate sexual stuff. It just seems too personal or intimate, and as a result, we often don't want to go there. Or if we do, we give them a vague "That's not appropriate" without going into detail about why.

Now, I'm not talking about embarrassing girls for wearing revealing clothes. That has never helped anyone. But if you think your child is crossing someone's boundaries, pursuing a crush with too much intensity, making offensive jokes and comments that they may or may not understand, or slut shaming someone on social media, raise the issue. If your kid's behavior might be harmful to themselves or others, let them know how you feel. And all that stuff about the dangers of dismissing certain behaviors with a *boys will be boys* excuse? Yep, that applies here, too.

Six: Empower kids to speak up.

I sometimes wish the children in my life, be they my own kids or my students, would just listen to me, accept the wisdom of my years, and not question every little thing. But those questions and that pushback? Sure, it might get exhausting or even smack of entitlement or brattiness, but it is also such an amazing sign of a confident child.

Children are so disenfranchised in our society that anything we can do to equip them with skills that build their sense of self, and that help them stay safe, happy, well adjusted, resilient, and respectful, is crucial. But about that respect thing: even though a lot of cultures and families stress respect for adults, kids will be much better served if they are comfortable telling people no— especially older peers or adults. Respect should not mean acceptance of intolerable and unacceptable actions. What we want is kids who will be able to get out of scary or uncomfortable situations. They will be better able to do that if we teach them the importance of maintaining other people's boundaries as well as their own.

As an adult in a child's life, listen when they confide in you and try to avoid the temptation to blame young people for getting into bad situations (*didn't I tell you, warn you, explain that . . .*). Those kinds of admonishments will just teach young people that speaking up is pointless, which will continue a dangerous cycle.

Seven: Allow them to make mistakes.

Part of being a child in the world is making mistakes. And, yes, some mistakes are more egregious than others. But if we are given the chance, mistakes are how we learn and grow and evolve. The job of adults is to help lessen the impact and intensity of a child's failures, and to help them move forward on a better path when they stumble. Kids should not live in fear that one misstep will brand them forever. We are not the same people throughout our life spans. When we label children or remove them from their schools or communities for their failures, the message we send is a fearful one of banishment, not a message that acknowledges that people can grow and change.

In schools, traditional disciplinary actions are usually of the "punish, suspend, and expel" variety and, in recent years, have too often included the involvement of law enforcement, even in elementary school! Such tactics haven't been found to reduce problems, and they have been found to disproportionately punish students of color.[14] Yet so many education institutions still rely heavily on them.

SEXUALITY SPOTLIGHT: KIDS WHO BUY INTO GENDER STEREOTYPES

When my youngest was three, she confidently informed me, "Girls don't like LEGO."

Despite my best efforts to present her with an idea of the world where LEGO didn't have a gender, her statement didn't surprise me. At a similar age, my son had told me boys didn't have long hair. And, as a toddler, my older daughter had rejected the brown dump truck T-shirt and black dinosaur sneakers that her father had offered in favor of glittery princess garb.

Their comments made me cringe and question my role in perpetuating these messages. But I tried to remind myself that partly what my kids were demonstrating was how an understanding of gender often develops in children.

So what does that look like? By about two, children typically start to learn gender-role behavior, and by three they are increasingly aware of some of the social meanings associated with those roles. Many children also become what has been called "gender detectives," who are on the hunt for evidence that confirms their growing understanding that people are different depending on whether they are male or female.

Going through this phase is a perfectly normal response to living in a gendered world. But that doesn't let adults off the hook. Though it might seem to fall on deaf ears, it's still important to lay the groundwork that challenges a child's assumptions about which activities fall into the boys' category and which fall into the girls'.

And that is a challenge, since children, like the rest of us, are constantly bombarded with messages about gender at every turn. I mean, even in my own home, whom did my littlest see playing with LEGO? It wasn't me or her sister. Nope, it was her older brother and his mainly male pals.

The other thing that I've learned is that as much as I'd like to present my kids with a vision of a world that is less gendered, obscuring the existence of gender bias has its pitfalls. Take the fact that for years, I secretly hid shaving my legs from my kids because I didn't want them to think that shaving was expected of women. It seemed like a good idea until I realized that if I kept doing that, they'd grow up thinking that adult women didn't have leg hair. So I let them in on the secret. I did have leg hair. I just removed it in a time-consuming and occasionally painful social ritual. But I also told my daughters that in no way did they have to do the same thing, and I told my son that he *was* welcome to do so when he was older. If he wanted.

When I first made the decision, concealing this part of my grooming ritual seemed like a good way to avoid putting certain expectations on my children. But what I initially failed to consider was that doing so just set up an impossible standard, not unlike the ads for razors that show a woman shaving what appear to be already hair-free legs. It can be tempting to try to curate the world around us into one that reflects our values. But pretending the world is more egalitarian than it is sure isn't going to fool kids when they can see with their own eyes that this simply isn't the case.

One of the most pervasive issues is that of media messaging. As psychotherapist Katie Hurley, the author of the book *The Happy Kid Handbook: How to Raise Joyful Children in a Stressful World*, explains, while it might be tempting to hide things like magazines with sexist ads from kids, children will be bombarded with similar marketing strategies every time they leave the house. So talking about what such images mean, and asking things like, "What do you think of this? Tell me what might be wrong with this picture. Is this what women you know really look like?" is going to help kids understand the prevalence of gendered messaging, teach them to critique what they are being sold, and give them skills to resist the pressure to conform to unrealistic expectations.[15]

Parents, teachers, and other adults who work with kids can model positive behavior and do what they think is right for the children in their lives, while explaining that what they're doing may not be reflected by the wider culture. It is possible to help children see beyond the limited box of what it means to be a person in a gendered world, while simultaneously acknowledging the reality of the world they are going to have to navigate. That can take some work. Still, it's work that can be well worthwhile, since kids who are raised in heavily gendered environments are more likely to subscribe to traditional beliefs on gender, often to the detriment of themselves and others.

What's the Background?

Recent decades have seen significant changes on gender. Yet many notions about differences between men and women—particularly that men are strong, powerful, aggressive, breadwinning heads of the family, while women are maternal, nurturing, weak, and emotional—continue to be accepted as "natural" or as simply the way things are. As a result, these are the versions of masculinity and femininity that children most frequently encounter.

For example, a 2017 Common Sense Media report found that kids as young as two learn from screens which toys, skills, and activities are typically associated with each gender, and by the time they are eight, these interests are coupled with messages about men's and women's innately gendered qualities.[16]

But it's not only on screen that gendered norms are maintained. Plenty of parents and educators still adhere to gender bias, both conscious and not. Teachers often model gender stereotypical behavior or have different expectations for students based on gender (say, assuming boys will bounce off the walls while girls will be "better" behaved). Even the most casual of interactions can carry this weight. For one thing, plenty of teachers divide a class into groups of boys and girls, something that one study found reinforced the idea in children that they should not seek out cross-gender playmates.[17]

Language is also a tough thing to change. It wasn't so long ago that, having consciously stopped referring to a mixed-gender group of students as "guys," I found myself saying, "Hi, there, ladies," to a group of kids I took to be girls. Only this particular group of middle schoolers was made up of kids who identified both as girls and as nonbinary. The group was awfully nice about my blunder, but I knew I messed up the second the phrase left my mouth.

Everywhere they turn, children are reminded that the world around them is categorized into male and female. If they are lucky, they will be granted just a little freedom to explore what this means. But even so, it's the rare child who can grow up free of messaging about what it means to be a boy or a girl, or who is allowed to forget that they are being gendered at every turn.

Why It's a Problem

While it isn't a problem for kids to pursue interests that are typically associated with one gender or the other, adults still need to push back when their ideas about gender are off base. A lot of our everyday gendering behaviors might seem innocuous, but studies have found they leave significant negative effects.

Maria do Mar Pereira, the author of the book *Doing Gender in the Playground*, explains, "Trying to live up to these unreal ideas of masculinity and femininity leads to a range of problems: low self-esteem, bullying, physical and verbal violence, [and] health problems." Specifically:

girls who experience this pressure are more likely to have body-image issues, boys are more likely to be violent, and both boys and girls under gender pressure report higher levels of stress and anxiety.[18]

Adding even more credence to these concerns was a 2017 study published in the *Journal of Adolescent Health.* This compared young people's attitudes about gender in Ecuador, Bolivia, Belgium, Scotland, the United States, South Africa, Malawi, Kenya, the Democratic Republic of Congo, Burkina Faso, Nigeria, Egypt, Vietnam, China, and India. It found that by age ten, in societies that are both conservative and liberal, children believe harmful stereotypes about gender.

In each country surveyed, it was considered more acceptable for girls than boys to challenge gender conventions. Even so, girls were often much more limited in their opportunities outside the domestic realm, in large part as a result of anxiety over their sexuality. The authors write, "Around the world pubertal boys are viewed as predators and girls as potential targets and victims. Messages such as—do not sit like that, do not wear that, do not talk to him, boys will ruin your future—support the gender division of power while promo[ting] sex segregation . . . In some places, girls come to internalize these norms to an even a greater extent than boys."

Additionally, globally, children were found to believe that girls are vulnerable and in need of protection, and that their physical appearance was their most crucial asset, while boys were understood to be strong and independent. Yet what we know from the data is that in reality, boys were more likely to engage in physical violence and be the victims of it. They were more likely to die from unintentional injuries, and they were more prone to substance abuse and suicide than were girls. Notably, Edinburgh, Scotland, was the only city where boys and girls did not think the boy must always take the initiative in a relationship.[19]

As this study and others remind us, while adhering to and reinforcing gender stereotypes might seem like a simple matter of personal choice and expression, the consequences of doing so are anything but. Today's children may be exposed to a widening view of gender. But gender stereotypes and expectations are a very successful method for perpetuating a long-standing system of gender inequality that typically disadvantages women, stifles men, and excludes those who don't fit into binary gender boxes.

Where We're at Now

Traditional ideas about how boys and girls should move through the world often go unquestioned and result in a lot of children having gender bias. But regularly identifying this bias and allowing kids of all genders to express themselves in a variety of ways is an important first step to a sexually safer world.

Adults trying to dismantle gender stereotypes may wonder how many of a child's choices are a result of that child's natural and authentic personal interests, how many are a response to the gendered world they are forced to navigate, and whether it is even possible to separate the two. Needless to say, the answer isn't always obvious. Just like you can't make a transgender or gender-nonconforming kid become cisgender by forcing them to wear clothing that they find oppressive, we also can't make girls who prefer to spend hours primping in the bathroom happily throw on some overalls and lop off their hair, or make boys who just want to run around smashing things become interested in throwing a stuffed-animal tea party if that isn't their thing.

As much as we might hope for it, we cannot expect children to subvert gender roles just because we want them to. Even the best intentioned adult can find this a really tough thing to do! Many parents truly believe that girls and boys should be treated the same. But as in many areas of our daily lives, our desires and our actions are not always in sync.

A 2018 Australian survey of parents of children three and under found that the significant majority reported wanting to challenge gender stereotypes with their kids. However, the survey also found that the majority of these parents were replicating gender bias with their kids. For example, the parents of young girls were more comfortable with the idea of them engaging in masculine-typed play, such as playing with trucks, whereas parents of young boys had lower levels of comfort in regard to their sons' participation in feminine-typed play, such as playing with dolls. Furthermore, more mothers were comfortable with the idea of their child acting in opposition to gender stereotypes than were fathers, and more mothers than fathers were comfortable with the idea of their young sons crying when feeling sad.[20]

Humans are messy and contradictory, and we cannot be expected to single-handedly challenge a complicated system that thrives on maintaining the status quo. But that doesn't mean we can't try to make changes, and that doesn't mean that we aren't making any progress.

"THEYBIES": RAISING KIDS GENDER-FREE

What's the best way to escape the confines of gender stereotypes? For a growing number of parents, the answer is to raise their young children gender-free. These families use gender-neutral pronouns, don't reveal the child's biological sex to the outside world, and make a concerted effort to provide their children with a wide range of clothes, books, toys, and experiences that have no correlation to the child's biology.

There are a lot of reasons folks are exploring this option. We know that people begin to assign gendered attributes to a fetus the second they learn its genetic sex, and then continue to gender people from the second they are born (cooing at baby girls and noting their beauty, talking about how strong a baby boy's grip is) until the moment they die.

For some families, raising young kids gender-free, or gender creative, is a way to subvert these early messages as they wait for the child to come into their own gender identity authentically, on their own terms, and without many of the gendered social impacts we often don't even realize exist.

Consider: Why do so many people talk about wild boy energy? It that really baked in to a Y chromosome, or is it a product of how we treat boys? How is it that so many little girls seem to love baby dolls? A natural instinct for mothering? Or the fact that these girls are babied and given dolls since infancy?

As Kyl Myers writes of raising her toddler in what she calls a gender-creative style of parenting, "I have also seen enough scientific evidence to know that gender-creative socialization has beneficial outcomes. Children who grow up without strict gender roles feel free to explore their own identities and grow up to have more egalitarian romantic relationships and contribute equally to household income and parenting; gender equality leads to healthier and happier children and adults and more profitable businesses and more progressive public policies."[21]

Children raised by parents with a flexible approach to gender don't have gender hidden from them. They certainly see the world around them, and most will identify as a gender pretty young. But an early challenge to traditional gender roles is intended to help children start off from a place where they are not hindered or limited by what so many of us understand about what it means to be a boy or a girl, a woman or a man, in this world.

WHAT IT ALL COMES DOWN TO

For too long we have defaulted to the idea that protecting children from exploitation means protecting them from the fact of sex, a word that can be interpreted so broadly as to allow for censorship of everything from conversations about sexual orientation to lessons on puberty. When we combine this with our continued reliance on old gender stereotypes, the results can be concerning.

As adults, it can be hard to pinpoint all the places where we need to intervene or all the ways in which we are contributing to problems. We all want to grow healthy and safe kids who can be trusted to one day navigate the world on their own. But in order to make this a reality for the most children possible, we are going to have to clearly address where we have stumbled up to this point. And we'll need to understand that excusing or ignoring potentially problematic behaviors not only harms children today, but will also hurt them and their communities in the future.

HOW COULD YOU REACT?

Think about the following situations and consider how you could respond.

1) Your sister's six-year-old son turns up at your house in a princess dress for a family party.

....
....
....
....

2) A nine-year-old student in your fourth-grade class has clearly violated your school's dress code by wearing a tank top that shows her bra strap.

....
....
....
....
....
....

3) While driving your eleven-year-old child and their friend to the movies, you overhear them having what

they think is a private conversation about how *slutty* a girl in their class is.

....

....

....

....

....

....

....

4) You find your preschooler playing a naked doctor game with a similar-aged child.

....

....

....

....

....

....

....

Now, imagine your goal in responding is not to punish, but rather to help a child feel supported. Is there anything you would change about your response? If you imagine being angry in this situation, ask yourself if your anger is directed at the right person. If not, how can you channel this anger to help a child feel safe and to develop a positive view of sexuality?

Here are a few suggestions on how to do that:

▶ In the first question, include a comment about how great your nephew looks and a word of support for your sister about what a great job she is doing with her kid.

▸ In the second one, you could talk to the administration about the problems with the policy, rather than addressing a young child already dealing with early puberty in a way that might upset her.

▸ In the third, you could either decide to talk to both kids right then, or choose to talk to your own child after the fact about the harm of slut shaming.

▸ For the forth, instead of flying into a panic, a better tactic could be to calmly explain that while it is normal to be curious about friends' bodies, you also have rules about keeping your clothes on when playing.

▸ If you are able to start a discussion from a place of education and support rather than from anger or shame, you are likely to see far more encouraging results.

CHAPTER 5

THE TEEN
SEX SITUATION

THIS MODERN WORLD . . .

Worrying about the impact of sex on teens is nothing new. Today, there's a focus on easy access to porn, hookup culture, and sexting. A few years back, it was bicuriosity, rainbow parties (where boys would allegedly compete to see how many girls they could convince to leave a blow-job lipstick ring on their penises), and girls who were supposedly using anal sex to preserve their virginity.

Twenty years ago, it was teen pregnancy. Prior to that it was drug-addicted runaway high school prostitutes. Before that came panic over hippies and free love. Even earlier there was fretting about everything from "going steady" to flappers, and even girls who wanted to ride bicycles and cut their hair short, things that, at various points, made adults worry about the potential lead-in to sex.

Clearly, some of these concerns warranted more attention than others. But living in a constant state of sex panic means it can be hard to differentiate between those issues that really are a problem and those that are the product of overblown alarmism. This chapter looks at which issues we really need to worry about (say, depriving teens of comprehensive sex education), where we can relax (say, around healthy teen relationships that might involve consensual sex), and why focusing our energies on the wrong things harms young people now and sets them up to perpetuate hostile sexual climates later.

WHERE ARE KIDS AT TODAY?

There's a common belief that today's young people are more sexually active and more sexually savvy than at any other time in history. We know the first part sure isn't true. According to the Centers for Disease Control's Youth Risk Behavior Survey, the number of teens who reported ever having had sex dropped from 54 percent in 1991 to 40 percent in 2017.[1]

But what about the second part—the idea that teens are just that much more sexually precocious or knowledgeable than in the past? Even with all the unfettered access to the internet and to porn that is now only a click away, I still don't buy it.

Partly that's because I keep on seeing the same issues come up again and again. For years I answered questions from teens online, first for Planned Parenthood's teen website, then for an LGBTQ+ youth site, then on the website gURL.com, and most recently for an app called Okayso. What I find heartbreaking is to realize that the anonymous questions I got back in the early 2000s aren't all that different from those I'm still getting today. Questions like: *My boyfriend just went in me for a second, can I get pregnant? Every time I try to put on a condom I lose my erection. I can only have an orgasm from masturbating, not from sex. I hate my man boobs. If you*

*have sex with another guy, does that mean you're gay?
There's this white stuff in my underwear. Is it normal?
Why does it hurt every time I do it?* And *How do I know
I'm ready for sex?*

Some questions fall into a category I like to call "highly
improbable teenage paranoia." An example of this is a
boy who wrote that he was terrified that he had given
his baby cousin an STI because he'd changed her diaper
after masturbating, the girl who thought she was pregnant after using soap she suspected the previous user had
ejaculated on, and the teen who was convinced that he
had contracted HIV by sitting naked in some standing
water next to his sink. Mind you, this kid wasn't HIV
positive, but he just thought getting anything in his anus
would make him so.

Then there are those teens who are in complete and utter
denial, girls who say things like, *I only let my boyfriend
come in me when it's two weeks before my period, so I
know I'm not pregnant. But why do you think I haven't
gotten my period in six months and am getting a fat
stomach?* And boys who complain that they are leaking
green discharge and experiencing extreme pain when
they pee and want to know if lactose intolerance might be
causing their discomfort. (Actual questions!)

Plenty of the questions are a sad reminder of the
impact of abstinence-only education and a culture so
deeply uncomfortable with adolescent sexuality that
it tries to hide sexual information online with clunky
internet filters, passes draconian abortion laws, and finds
it acceptable to have kids take virginity pledges in school.
To be sure, some things have changed. For example, the
average teen has a far greater understanding of gender

identities, sexual orientations, consent, and sexual abuse than ever before. And plenty of kids do get solid information from the internet.

But in an era when porn accounts for an awful lot of sex education (the current generation of teens is often stunned to find out that adult women do indeed have pubic hair and don't have multiple orgasms seconds after a penis is roughly shoved into their vagina), and when abstinence education makes up the difference, it is little wonder that even if answers are theoretically just a Google search away, so many kids are still in the dark.

That's why any adult who can muster the courage needs to counter these forces with accurate information that challenges our culture of sexual shame.

TEEN SEX: WHAT YOU MAY HAVE HEARD AND WHY THAT'S BS

WHAT YOU MAY HAVE HEARD:
Today's teens are having sex younger and with more partners than ever in the past.

WHY THAT'S BS:
Actually, the opposite is true. According to the Centers for Disease Control's Youth Risk Behavior Survey, in 1991, 54 percent of teens had ever had sex. In 2017 that number was 40 percent. Similarly, in 1991, 19 percent of high school students reported having sex with four or more people, while in 2017 that number had dropped to 9.7 percent, and back in 1991, over 10 percent of teens reported having

had sex before age thirteen, while in 2017, less than 3.4 percent had.[2]

• • •

WHAT YOU MAY HAVE HEARD:
No one dates on college campuses anymore—they just hook up.

WHY THAT'S BS:
After studying data from the Online College Social Life Survey, of over twenty-four thousand students at over twenty institutions, Lisa Wade, the author of the book *American Hookup*, determined that college students today have hooked up on average just eight times in four years, and a third of students haven't hooked up at all. She writes, "Contemporary students boast no more sexual partners than their parents did at their age, and many have fewer."[3]

• • •

WHAT YOU MAY HAVE HEARD:
The rise of social media and dating apps has led to a massive uptick in casual sex.

WHY THAT'S BS:
With the numbers of people reporting less sex than in previous generations, it has been posited that technology could be leading to more casual sext than casual sex. Some researchers, like psychologist Jean Twenge, have suggested that with the rise of smartphones, people are literally choosing tech over sex.

THE TRUTH ABOUT TEEN SEX

Ask the average adult if they think it's a good idea for teens to become sexually active, and most will give you an unequivocal no before citing the physical and emotional risks associated with this decision. But a lot of those nos are the product of off-base assumptions, which themselves are a result of the fact that all we normally hear about teen sex are the negatives. There are a number of reasons for that. One is that it's just really hard to challenge collective knowledge that falls into the *everybody knows* category (in this case *everybody knows it's dangerous for teens to have sex*).

Another is related to the type of research that gets highlighted. As sociologist Mike Males points out in his book, *Teenage Sex and Pregnancy*, many of the statistics used to prove that teen sex is inherently risky simply are not based on good science. He writes, "The bulk of surveys today are not designed to pinpoint teen behaviors, but to produce the most alarming numbers possible. You do not get funding or grants in today's highly competitive fiscal climate by finding that teens do not really have burgeoning problems in the areas you are asking for money to address."[4]

But even in this climate there have been some positive findings. For example, studies have determined that being in a respectful sexual relationship with a caring partner can actually help teens develop better social relationships in early adulthood[5] and can help boost self-esteem.[6] Having a healthy relationship while still in the teen years can be good practice for dealing with relationships later in life, when people are on their own without the same kind of safety net that parents and schools typically provide.

Plus, teens can be taught by their parents and schools to spot relationship red flags, which will help them avoid unhealthy situations later on.

Additionally, despite what adults may fear, teens who are sexually active are not automatically on a dangerous path. In some cases, they may even be less likely to get in trouble! Clinical psychologist Paige Harden has determined, for example, that for older adolescents, sexual activity that occurs in romantic relationships is actually associated with less delinquent behavior than is found in other teens.[7] That might seem counterintuitive, but think about it: a teen couple is a lot more likely to sit around watching movies on a Friday night than they are to be rampaging in the streets. Similarly, having someone in their corner, like a supportive boyfriend or girlfriend, can help teens deal with the stresses of adolescence in more positive ways. That's true for all teens, but for LGBTQ+ teens, supportive boyfriends and girlfriends have even been found to help protect against suicidal thoughts.[8] [9]

Our sense of what motivates teens to have sex can also be off base. A study conducted by researchers at the Indiana University School of Medicine found that, contrary to popular belief, teen girls aren't always driven to have sex out of depression, rebellion, or by a need for social acceptance. The authors noted that there are a number of studies that have found a link between depressed moods and taking sexual risks, which have reinforced the idea that sexually active teens are acting out. But they go on to explain that their research revealed something different. Among the girls they studied (specifically, a group who chose to start having sex again after periods of abstinence), the unifying factor behind their decisions to have sex again was that the teens were happy in secure relationships. They write, "Our data present a more nuanced picture, in which sexual intercourse is associated with important relationship attributes, such as partner support and perceptions of relationship quality."[10]

There are also a lot of assumptions about the emotional impact of sex on teens. Many people expect that sex will unleash a flood of feelings and that teens will be devastated and destroyed by the experience. So when a teen is upset following sex, we tend to attribute their negative reactions to the fact of sex itself. But a distraught teen could be responding to things like bad treatment by peers, the end of a relationship, or the fact that a romantic fantasy didn't live up to expectations. Obviously, a lot of teens have emotional reactions to sex, but when we chalk that all up simply to sex itself, we then have an excuse to ignore the potentially more complicated underlying issues.

Americans might also do well to consider the research of Amy Schalet, a sociologist at the University of Massachusetts and the author of *Not Under My Roof: Parents, Teens, and the Culture of Sex*. Schalet has looked at the difference in attitudes about teen sexuality between Dutch and American parents. She found that while the American parents were typically opposed to teens having sex at all, the Dutch parents believed that teens were able to have healthy sexual experiences in the context of a loving relationship. To encourage their teens to sustain these relationships, parents of teen couples got to know each other, invited their children's partners over for meals and on family outings, took their teens for health care when needed, and—probably most surprising for a lot of Americans—allowed teen couples to have sleepovers.[11]

This tactic seems to be paying off. The Dutch rate of teen pregnancy is four times lower than is ours, and their abortion rate is half.[12] They have much lower rates of sexually transmitted infections, and their rate of condom use in 2017 was 70 percent,[13] while America's dropped to 54 percent that same year. That's actually 10 percent lower than it was in 2003![14]

It can be really hard for American teens to have healthy sexual experiences. Some get a fear-driven and shame-based message about sex from their families and schools. Some live in a place where it's actually illegal for anyone under the age of consent to even have sex with another teen the same age (check your state's laws about that!). The result is that those teens who become sexually active often feel guilty about their actions and live in fear of being found out. This makes them more likely to numb the experience with drugs or alcohol and less likely to use protection, since doing so requires acknowledging that sex isn't something that "just happened."

And it makes it unlikely that teens will turn to parents, teachers, or health-care providers when they're in trouble, or even when they just want to talk through an experience. Sex in this climate worries me a lot. But I don't chalk up my concerns to the simple fact of teen sex. Rather, I think it's the decidedly punitive way in which we force sexually active teens to have sex that makes so much teen sex unwanted, unpleasurable, and unsafe. So for all those reasons, when my students ask what I think about teens having sex, I tell them this: for the vast majority of adolescents in the United States today, through no fault of their own, and maybe for reasons that differ from those of other adults, I honestly think it can be a pretty bad idea.

QUESTIONS FOR TEENS WHO ARE THINKING ABOUT BECOMING SEXUALLY ACTIVE

One of the most common teen questions about sex is: *How do I know if I'm ready?* One way to help determine this is to think about whether a teen is "sexually competent." This is a term developed by British researchers that refers to the ability to ensure that sex that is consensual, protected, mutually enjoyed, and not the result of external influences. With this definition in mind, and following protocol I learned working on Planned Parenthood's teen website many years ago, here are some questions I think it is wise to ask teens who are considering having sex:[15]

1. Do you want to be in a relationship before you have sex?
2. Do you think you might feel differently about your partner after having sex? Are you comfortable with that? What if they feel differently about you?
3. Are you having sex to make someone your boyfriend or girlfriend?
4. Are you having sex because you're worried that your partner will break up with you if you don't?
5. What if you break up after having sex?
6. Do you know how to practice safer sex?
7. Do you have access to condoms? Are you comfortable using them with your partner?

8. If you have sex with someone where pregnancy is a possibility, do you know how to use contraception? Do you know how to get emergency contraception if you need it?

9. Do you know how you would feel about an unplanned pregnancy, and what you would want to do about it? Do you know your options around parenting, adoption, and abortion?

10. Do you know how your partner feels about dealing with an unplanned pregnancy? What would you do if you didn't see eye to eye on that?

11. Do you feel comfortable seeing a healthcare provider and getting tested or treated for STIs?

12. Are you comfortable telling your partner what you do and don't like sexually?

13. Would you feel comfortable telling your partner if something didn't feel good? Would you feel comfortable telling your partner to stop if you weren't enjoying the experience?

14. If something goes wrong or you have an emergency, do you have an adult you can talk to?

15. Are you comfortable stopping what you're doing if your partner changes their mind?

16. Do you know what the laws about teen sex are in your state or country?

WHAT ARE WE UP AGAINST?

Whether or not a teen decides to become sexually active, they will all be subject to a range of messages about sex. These come from parents—some of whom may talk about sex and bodies casually over breakfast, and others of whom may blush when they hear that a sextet will be playing a concert this weekend. They come from the media, where the hot mom/schlubby dad couple is just an expected trope, and where rape and sexual harassment are presented as passionate or romantic. They come from schools, which may teach nothing at all, embrace abstinence-only education, or turn to a more comprehensive model. They also come from religious leaders, from cultural backgrounds, from their communities, and, of course, from their friends and peers. This can fuel conflict when these messages, as often happens, are in opposition.

Increasingly, they also come from porn, which is often a substitute for real sex education. In porn, fantasy is sold as reality. Actors typically have unbelievable bodies, which are portrayed as the height of sex appeal. In this genre, one rarely sees communication about likes and dislikes or about safer sex, and people's identities are sold as fetish to a presumed cishet male audience.

Teens should know that it is actually illegal for them to see porn before they are eighteen but that there is absolutely nothing psychologically wrong with getting turned on by porn. That being said, they should also know that what they're seeing is a fantasy that shouldn't determine how they expect their own sex lives to look. As Al Vernacchio, a sexuality educator and the author of the book *For Goodness Sex*, says, no kid thinks that they can learn how to drive by watching *The Fast and the Furious*, but far too many assume porn to be a decent teacher when it comes to sex.[16]

Though most adults agree that porn is the last place teens should learn about sex, there is little other agreement on how to address this issue. For some folks, the answer is doubling down on abstinence-only education, promoting strict gender roles, and advocating for ever more punitive legislation. For others, it's hoping that schools will cover the important stuff or ordering a *how to talk to your kids about sex* book.

Then there are folks who are fighting for comprehensive sex education and against legislation that would restrict access to sexual health services and information for minors. But this latter path is a tough one that requires pushing back against a culture in which a lot of young Americans grow up learning about sex from the internet, if they learn about it at all, where we are quick to crack down on any perceived misstep, and where people are then expected to be knowledgeable and capable sex partners as adults. And while some kids grow into this role just fine, a whole lot of others simply don't.

Fortunately, it doesn't have to be that way, and there are things that anyone who cares about teens can do to help. For example, one goal is for teens to develop *sexual competency* (which I mention in the sidebar on helping teens determine if they are ready for sex). This is a concept developed by a group of London-based researchers who determined that in order for teens to avoid negative experiences with early sex, they should develop concrete skills prior to becoming sexually active. These skills include:

▸ The ability to use contraception and practice safer sex.

▸ The understanding that sex should be consensual and desired by all partners.

▸ The ability to avoid having sex as a result of external factors, such as pressure or substance use.[17]

Of course, the basic fact of being underage means that teens can't always advocate for themselves. So it is up to adults to help teens develop these skills and others. Whether someone has kids now or plans to in the future, whether someone works with teens or simply cares about young people, they can still benefit from having a clearer understanding of what's really going on with teens so they can help teach them how to become sexually healthy and competent adults.

TEEN PREGNANCY AND POVERTY

Despite the numbers having dropped in recent years, the United States still has the highest teen pregnancy rate in the fully industrialized world. Our rate is twice that of neighboring Canada, twice that of the United Kingdom, four times that of the Netherlands, and seventeen times as high as the rate reported by Japan. There are an awful lot of reasons for this. Some commonly cited ones are a lack of access to birth control and abortion, a lack of sex education, and shame over sex.

There's another significant factor: poverty. Various

studies have found that high poverty levels and low educational attainment among women directly correlate to the likelihood of having a baby during high school.[18] But so often we get it wrong, warning kids that having a baby will make them poor, rather than the other way round.

Now, this shouldn't be surprising, since it continues a trend of blaming individuals for systemic problems rather than trying to tackle those problems at their root. Still, it bears mentioning that while no one will pretend that being a teen mom is an easy path, plenty of teen moms and their kids turn out just fine, and reminding teen parents of this is a good way to give them hope for a positive future. My favorite example is Stanley Ann Dunham, a teen mom who completed her PhD in anthropology, embarked on a successful career that took her around the world, and, as a single mom, raised two children, including a son who would go on to do some pretty great things, most notably becoming America's forty-fourth president, Barack Obama.

THE SITUATION WITH SEX EDUCATION

One of the best ways to help set teens on a positive path is to fight for *comprehensive* sexuality education. American sex education has actually been around an awfully long time. In 1892, the National Education Association (NEA) passed a resolution calling for "moral education in the schools." A few schools around the country then began teaching versions of sex education (often with push-back from institutions like the Catholic Church). Then by 1912, the NEA sought teacher training programs in sexuality education, and after the First World War—and the resulting rise of STIs among soldiers—Congress passed the Chamberlain-Kahn Act, which provided funds to educate soldiers about syphilis and gonorrhea.

By the 1920s, between 20 and 40 percent of US school systems had programs in social hygiene, a fair number of which addressed sexuality. Then in the 1930s, the US Office of Education got involved in creating curricula and in training teachers in this area. In the 1940s, groups like the US Public Health Service began calling for sex education, and by the 1950s, national sex-education programs had been created by the American School Health Association, the American Medical Association, and the National Education Association.

Of course, what passed as sex ed was often problematic. It tended to focus on hygiene, warned girls about falling prey to bad boys, and warned boys to stay out of public bathrooms where pedophiles lurked (see the troubling sex ed film of the 1960s *Boys Beware* for an example of that!). But the discipline was gaining speed. Encouraged by people like Alfred Kinsey, in the 1940s and '50s, courses in human sexuality began to appear on college campuses. In 1964, the medical director at Planned Parenthood, a doctor named Mary Calderone, founded the Sexuality Information and Education Council of the United States (SIECUS), a forward-thinking organization that still exists today.[19]

The next two decades saw a range of responses to sex education. Somewhat paradoxically, sex education both had a heyday in the 1960s and '70s and also was met with a lot of pushback. Starting in the 1960s, groups—often related to conservative Christian organizations—began to actively oppose sex education in the schools. But at the same time, sex education was also evolving. Many schools were teaching "life skills" and "family life" education classes that wove in sex education.

When HIV and AIDS emerged in the early '80s, debates over sex ed were nothing new. But around the country, as one set of parents was fighting for comprehensive sex ed that included a discussion of condoms and sexual orientation, others were protesting any program that acknowledged the existence of sex for anything other than procreation.

By the mid-1990s, deep in the AIDS crisis, every state had passed mandates for AIDS education. This meant a far greater number of students across the country were finally getting sex education that actually included a conversation about safer sex and sexual orientation. That education was going to shift once again after Bill Clinton signed the Personal Responsibility and Work Opportunity Reconciliation Act of 1996 (often referred to as the welfare-reform act) into law. This act included provisions for school programs designed to prevent sex outside of marriage, called abstinence-only education.[20] This pairing was legitimized by hyping the myth of the welfare-draining teen mom driving around in her Rolls-Royce, and by pointing to data showing that the 1990s had seen a rise in teen births.

Of course, what was not highlighted was the fact that this decade had also seen a decline in access to reproductive health services for teens and a new wave of laws restricting abortion access for minors. And those large-living teen moms on welfare? Just another way of demonizing kids in an already desperate situation.

When George W. Bush came into office a few years later, he dramatically increased the funding for these abstinence-only programs. In the first few years of this newly conceived abstinence education, only California rejected the funding. However, by 2005, two other states had also decided to turn it down, and by 2008, fewer than half the states were still accepting it. This was largely the result of more and more studies demonstrating how catastrophically abstinence education was failing. For instance, teens who got abstinence-only education weren't having any less sex than those who didn't. However, those who went through the programs were more likely to become pregnant or contract an STI, since they never learned about safer sex or contraception. Plus, they were also receiving very troubling messages about gender, sexual orientation, and sexual assault.

So when the Obama administration arrived, much of the federal funding for these programs was cut. As a result, abstinence only began to decline even more notably during this time. Of course, that was all set to change when the Trump administration took over in January of 2017 and almost immediately pledged $300 million to abstinence-only funding.[21] Trump then named a longtime abstinence-education advocate, Valerie Huber, to oversee programs that, in a move intended to deflect attention from the criticisms of the programs, were now being rebranded as "sexual risk avoidance."[22]

So just what is abstinence-only education? Basically, it's a program that replaces sex education in many American schools and that teaches that the only appropriate time to have sex is in the context of a heterosexual marriage. Classes either don't include information about contraception or condoms or they discuss these devices exclusively in terms of failure rates. Any mention of sexual expression is limited to reproduction, and the only time non-cishet orientations are mentioned is in relation to risks like suicide and disease.

Numerous studies have found that abstinence-only education doesn't even succeed at its troubling goal of limiting sex to a procreative act between husband and wife.[23] Additionally, countless studies, including one published in late 2017 in the *Journal of Adolescence*, confirmed that students who receive this form of education not only still have sex, but they are less likely than their better-educated peers to use condoms or contraception when they do.[24] Another study published in February of 2019 in the *Journal of Adolescent Health* also found that in some states, receiving abstinence education actually increased teen pregnancies.[25] As a result, groups like the American Academy of Pediatrics and the Society of Adolescent Health and Medicine have come out against these approaches.[26] [27]

Federally funded abstinence programs require schools to follow a very rigid curriculum. Here are the government's stated requirements:

- has as its exclusive purpose teaching the social, psychological, and health gains to be realized by abstaining from sexual activity;
- teaches abstinence from sexual activity outside marriage as the expected standard for all school-age children;
- teaches that abstinence from sexual activity is the only certain way to avoid out-of-wedlock

pregnancy, sexually transmitted diseases, and other associated health problems;

▸ teaches that a mutually faithful monogamous relationship in the context of marriage is the expected standard for human sexual activity;

▸ teaches that sexual activity outside the context of marriage is likely to have harmful psychological and physical effects;

▸ teaches that bearing children out of wedlock is likely to have harmful consequences for the child, the child's parents, and society.[28]

There are just so many problems with these points. Despite the claims, these are simply not universal values, and they are not based on facts. As a health teacher who does a lot of (comprehensive) sex education, the idea that I would tell students that sex outside of marriage was likely to have harmful effects that marriage would somehow miraculously shield them from is beyond offensive. The simple institution of marriage does not offer automatic protection from emotional distress, unplanned pregnancy, STIs, or sexual assault, and to pretend that it does is just plain dangerous.

Marriage is also not a universal value, and in a country where we're seeing rising rates of single adults[29] and significant numbers of unmarried parents,[30] the innate superiority of marriage sure isn't a message that is appropriate for all children. Plus, from my own perspective, as a mom who has had kids both within and outside of a legal marriage, I can assure you that a legal document declaring a couple married does not automatically make a child healthier. And this "expected standard" stuff?

These are not universal expected standards by any means. Again, from my own experience being Jewish, these aren't my standards, and they sure aren't the expectation for a whole lot of other folks from a whole lot of different backgrounds.

Additionally, abstinence programs have been found to perpetuate negative stereotypes about LGBTQ+ folks, about sexually active girls, and about any positive expressions of sexuality in general. That's not surprising when we remember that in many programs, teachers are simply not allowed to discuss LGBTQ+ issues or sexual orientation at all, and much of what passes for consent and sexual assault education is of the *boys have no self-control so don't lead them on* variety. Plus, many programs are expressly barred from mentioning that there is a legal medical procedure called an abortion, and a significant number prevent teachers from answering even the most basic question about what a condom is.

Programs across the country compare girls who have had sex to a cup of spit, to dirty tape, or to a smelly sneaker, and they use all manner of disgusting visual representations to get their points across. This message is jarring for any sexually active teen (not to mention survivors of sexual assault!) and can be very damaging to their self-esteem and sexual expression.

There is hope, however. While many states will take federal funding for abstinence programs, a few, like California and Colorado, have passed laws ensuring comprehensive sex education. A handful of states now also require that schools specifically teach LGBTQ+-inclusive sex education.

WHEN TEACHING CAN GET YOU
IN TROUBLE

As a health educator, it is pretty unnerving to encounter stories of teachers who've gotten into trouble for discussing sex or sexual orientation, since for many folks in my field, this is often the intended subject of a lesson.

But educators get in trouble more often than you might think.

For example, a few years ago, Wisconsin mandated a sex-education curriculum that required schools to teach about condoms and other forms of birth control. Sounds pretty straightforward, right? It would have been, until a DA announced that teachers who followed this law could end up in jail for breaking another: namely, contributing to the delinquency of minors. Ultimately, the DA lost his bid for reelection, and then the law mandating sex education was repealed, so no one was charged.[31] But this was far from an isolated case. Something similar happened in Utah, when a Salt Lake City teacher with over thirty years' experience was put on paid administrative leave and threatened with criminal charges after she answered students' questions about oral sex, masturbation, and what it meant to be gay.

That incident prompted Utah representative Carl Wimmer (a guy who also wanted to criminalize miscarriages[32]) to suggest introducing a law that would make it illegal for teachers to answer students' sex questions, and that would also set up a teacher registry listing the names of those educators who dared to do so! That law didn't pass.[33]

However, a number of states do have what are nicknamed "no promo homo" laws. These are local or state education laws that forbid teachers of health and sexuality education from discussing LGBTQ+ people or topics in a positive light—if at all.

Some laws—for example, in Alabama and South Carolina—even require that teachers actively portray LGBTQ+ people in a negative or inaccurate way.[34] This is a clear method of discrimination against LGBTQ+ folks, similar to bathroom bills that force people to use bathrooms associated with their sex assignment at birth.

Yes, there are teachers out there who have engaged in criminal sexual behavior involving students. But the average teacher talking about sex ed sure isn't one of them. Like supporters of abstinence-only education, supporters of muzzling teachers are working under the premise that kids who don't know about sex won't have it, and that kids who don't hear about being gay won't stray from a cishet path.

Of course, these laws also have detractors, and those who want to fight against them will find allies in groups like the Gay Lesbian Straight Education Network (GLSEN) and the ACLU. Attending local school board meetings and voicing your opinion, actively supporting comprehensive sex education, and voting against these harmful measures when they emerge in municipal elections are also crucial tactics to help prevent their spread.

PRIORITIZING PLEASURE IS PROTECTIVE

Though there are a lot of great comprehensive sex-education programs out there, even some of the most solid ones tend to gloss over a key part of sexuality: namely, pleasure. For a lot of people, the idea of talking about the pleasure part of sex with teens makes them feel like they're giving the go-ahead to something they disapprove of, even in the context of a larger conversation.

But in reality, teens aren't going to start having sex simply because we mention that everyone should enjoy the sex they're having, any more than they're going to wait to have sex until marriage because they pledged abstinence. (One study found abstinence pledges put girls at a higher risk of contracting HPV and becoming pregnant than those who did not take such a pledge[35]). In fact, the vast majority of Americans (over 90 percent, according to a range of surveys) do not wait until marriage to have sex.[36] That's not surprising when we realize that the average age of marriage in the United States for women is currently 27.6 and for men 29.5. For interest's sake, back in 1968, those numbers were twenty-one and twenty-three, respectively. The fact is, the majority of those who are sexually active, married or not, aren't high school students, since only about 40 percent of teens in the United States have sex by the time they graduate.[37]

Multiple studies have also found that increasing a teen's knowledge about sex increases the likelihood that they will both delay sex and be safer if they do decide to become sexually active.[38] So letting them know that pleasure should be part of the equation is really just another tool we can draw on to help keep them safe. Teaching teens to expect pleasure out of their sexual experiences empowers them to take more control of their sexual safety, to say no to unwanted sex, and to take better care of their sexual health. It also helps them set limits.

Nevertheless, bringing up this issue can be complicated. So here are a few things to remember:

1. Talking about pleasure is an important part of any conversation you have with teens about sex, and doing so can help keep them safe.
2. LGBTQ+ issues should a part of the discussion. Sexism and cishet expectations of sex can harm LGBTQ+ teens when they don't receive crucial information and they feel erased from conversations.
3. Talk to kids before they become sexually active, so that if they do choose to have sex at some point, they aren't doing their learning on the fly.
4. Sex is not only about reproduction. While conversations about contraception are crucial, for the average teen, the pregnancy part is not the most relevant aspect of their sexuality.
5. On that note, don't pretend most people have sex to get pregnant. They don't.
6. Don't assume all kids are interested in having sex with someone else. Sex with a partner, or even dating, isn't something all teens are into. Teens should be assured that it's perfectly normal— and more common—to not be sexually active.

About that last point: some kids might have no interest in sex at all. For others, masturbation is a key component of their sexuality. Masturbation is perfectly healthy for people of any gender, but it can still get a bad rap, and the history of how it has been viewed can make people leery of the implications of mentioning self-pleasure.

As all sex educators know, twenty-five years ago, Bill Clinton's surgeon general, Joycelyn Elders, was fired for even hinting that masturbation was acceptable. When asked at an international AIDS conference if she believed that teaching children about masturbation could encourage safer sex practices, Elders answered, "I think that is something that is a part of human sexuality, and it's a part of something that perhaps should be taught. But we've not even taught our children the very basics."[39] Shortly thereafter she was out of a job.

I'd like to think we've progressed since then, but a lot of people still shy away from this part of the sex conversation. But just like talking about pleasure with teens can be protective, the same is true of masturbation, since it is the safest sex around. You won't get pregnant by masturbating. You won't get an STI. You won't have to navigate the complications of a sexual relationship with another person. What you will get is a better understanding of your body and the knowledge that you don't need another person to fulfill your sexual needs.

ADVOCATING FOR EMERGENCY CONTRACEPTION

Emergency contraception (EC) is a form of hormonal birth control (also called the morning-after pill) that you take after sex, not before. It has been around in various forms since at least the 1970s worldwide.

Contrary to what some folks think, EC is not an abortion pill, and it won't end a pregnancy once one is already in place. The main way EC works is by preventing a person from ovulating, just like the regular birth control pill. With no egg released, there can be no fertilization. If someone happened to ovulate before having sex, EC still works to inhibit the joining of sperm and egg and thickens cervical mucus.

According to family planning expert and health educator Dawn Stacey at Verywell Health, EC also won't work after fertilization of an egg. She writes, "The majority of the research finds that Plan B does not cause any changes in the lining of the uterus [. . . and so] researchers have concluded that this emergency contraceptive cannot prevent implantation of a fertilized egg."[40]

Though EC has been available in many countries, including Canada, for close to forty years, access to EC in the US has been incremental. Between the advent of the birth control pill in 1960 and the 1990s, some American providers would give women a pack of pills with the instruction to take five a day for five days as emergency contraception. But EC in its current form did not have FDA approval in the United States until 1999. After this, EC was available with a prescription.

In 2006, the FDA approved EC for women seventeen and older without a prescription, and for those under seventeen with a prescription. A few years later, in 2013, girls fifteen and over could get EC without a prescription from their local pharmacy, and the following year, progestin-only EC (like Plan B One-Step and its generic forms) were approved for unrestricted sale on store shelves. So today anyone can legally buy EC without needing to show proof of age.

However, pharmacies across the country fail to consistently stock EC, and multiple states have laws allowing pharmacies and/or pharmacists to refuse to dispense EC pills on the basis of moral or ethical objections, often in the form of conscience clauses.

Now, years after EC pills were first approved by the FDA, access to this form of birth control is still debated heavily by policy makers at both the state and federal levels, and it will likely continue to be a focus of policy discussions in the years to come.

THE ROLE OF REPRODUCTIVE HEALTH CARE

In addition to what they are learning or not learning in school about how sexuality can be expressed, another challenge for American teens is their ability to access reproductive health care. This is something that, for most of my youth, didn't really seem like a big deal. I was born in 1975, and arguments over abortion and contraception seemed like ancient history. By the time I had sex with my high school boyfriend, my biggest concern about protecting myself from pregnancy was not my fundamental right to use birth control, or even if the method I chose would be effective, but rather it was about keeping the fact that I was on the pill a secret from my parents (something they turned out to be a lot cooler with than my teenage self could have imagined).

For me, growing up after the legalization of birth control and abortion meant that the messages I got on reproductive health were fundamentally different from those of previous generations. I also grew up in Canada, so my understanding of health care was a little different. For example, the year that I was thirteen, a nurse from the local teen clinic came to my school to tell us about the services that they offered. These included some pretty standard stuff like throat swabs and flu shots, but also STI testing, emergency contraception, abortions, gynecological care, and rape crisis services. Everything was not only free, but also confidential.

Yet, as we are now seeing, the messages I got were also really different from what today's young people are hearing.

Younger generations have seen the rollback of the federal requirement that employers cover birth control, with the excuse that contraception could lead to risky sex.[41] They have witnessed the man who would become president say on the campaign trail that women who receive abortions should be punished if the medical procedure is banned in the US, and they have seen the appointment of judges to the Supreme Court that could make just such a ban far more likely to occur. They are living in a time when support for abortion rights has never been higher (a 2018 poll from NBC News and the *Wall Street Journal* found that 71 percent of American voters believe that *Roe* should stand[42]), yet over 90 percent of American counties don't have even one abortion provider.[43] It's a time when women who miscarry can see jail time,[44] and when what should be the simple act of obtaining reliable contraception can be anything but, since access to health care is so limited for so many.

Today in the United States, politics, geography, and finances play a huge role in determining access to services that people in many other countries can count on as basic human rights. A huge number of American minors continue to be uninsured or underinsured. Many simply can't obtain even the most basic health care, let alone that of a reproductive nature.

This issue seemed to be turning around with the Affordable Care Act (Obamacare), which was passed in 2010 with the goal of helping uninsured and under-insured individuals get access to more affordable health care. However, the constant political attacks and under-mining of this program mean the services it covers are not assured.

Still, it's not as if teens with private insurance are in the clear, either.

Suburban and rural teens are often unable to travel to the doctor without their parents. This might not seem like such a big deal for a routine physical, but it can be a huge issue when the matter is a sensitive one, say, about an issue involving mental health, or substance use, or, of course, sexual health. Indeed, teens who fear that doctors won't respect their privacy may avoid needed visits altogether.

One of the biggest issues is, of course, abortion. Even before states started passing laws that closed down clinics and restricted abortion access, getting an abortion was often financially and geographically out of reach, espe-cially for teens living in one of the majority of states with parental involvement laws. These laws require either getting parental permission for the procedure or literally getting a court date and convincing a judge that you as a teen are mature enough to forgo parental permission.

But even beyond abortion, young Americans live in a country where only 43 percent of teens between the ages of thirteen and seventeen are immunized with the recommended HPV vaccine doses,[45] and where a significant number of drugstores refuse to sell condoms and emergency contraception to minors, despite the fact that teens are legally able to obtain both. Additionally, federal laws, states laws, and even whether a clinic is publicly or privately funded can affect the type of care someone is entitled to.

For example, since 1970 there has been a program called Title X that has provided low-cost family planning services. In 1978, Congress amended Title X to place "a special emphasis on preventing unwanted pregnancies among sexually active adolescents," and it added services specifically for teenagers, since Congress recognized that teen pregnancies "are often unwanted, and are likely to have adverse health, social, and economic consequences for the individuals involved." Title X requires participating health-care providers to maintain patient-physician confidentiality, even if the patients are teens, and it does not require notification or consent of parents or guardians.

In 1981, something called the Adolescent Family Life Act passed. This bill included language encouraging "family participation" in adolescent reproductive health choices. That language opened the doors for the Department of Health and Human Services to claim that parental notification was needed when adolescents received family-planning services in states that had other laws requiring parental involvement in health care. However, two federal courts dismissed this claim, and as a result, clinics that get federal funding under Title X must still maintain minors' confidentiality. Those that don't get federal funding, however, are not bound by this rule.

This means that if a teen goes to a clinic that gets Title X money, they may have privacy from their parents. However, if that same teen goes to a clinic across the street that doesn't get Title X money, in one of the twenty-four states that do not allow minors to obtain contraceptives without parents' permission, their parents will be notified. (And it's worth noting that in Texas and Utah, even teen mothers must obtain their own parent's permission for contraception![46]

Unfortunately, even when minors legally have the right to privacy, confidentiality can be breached in all sorts of ways. Medical staff may be unaware of the laws, may fail to inquire about confidential conditions, or may accidentally inform parents. Minors can also receive what appears to be confidential care, yet the second an insurance statement arrives, or an office calls home to confirm an appointment, or a parent looks at a patient portal, that confidentiality means nothing.

Additionally, since abortion was only legalized nationwide in 1973, it was never a protected procedure under Title X. So even if a teen goes to a Title X clinic, they will need to follow their state's laws about abortion, which in most cases means that some form of parental involvement in the procedure is required. Of course, even finding a Title X clinic is not a given, since funding is constantly in jeopardy (see the ceaseless calls to "defund" Planned Parenthood).

Limiting access to reproductive health care is a huge

problem for anyone who needs services. However, for teens, the barriers that are so often put in place can be even more dangerous. A lack of preventive care means teens are less likely to protect themselves from unwanted pregnancy and STIs. Many don't even get basic medical conditions checked out. Plus, pregnant teens who are unable or afraid to talk to parents may put themselves in danger by seeking out unsafe illegal abortions. Notably, researchers from the Guttmacher Institute looked at two hundred thousand searches for "self-abortion" that were done in a one-month period in 2017. They determined that the majority were by conducted by adolescents and young adults facing an unintended pregnancy.[47] On top of this, if they do continue their pregnancies, teens may not seek prenatal care.

In recent years there have been significant gains in teen sexual health, like the decreasing levels of teen pregnancy and the FDA approval for the "morning-after pill" to be sold over the counter to minors without a prescription. But if the current trends continue, these gains may be lost. One place that we are already seeing this happen? The drop in the number of teens using birth control and condoms, and the huge rise in cases of STIs as reported by the Centers for Disease Control.

Ultimately, it would be great if teens involved their parents in their health care, and many do. But the reality is that there will always be young people who are simply unable to do this. Plus, studies have found that parental involvement laws do not cause teens to delay sexual activity, but rather they result in fewer teens seeking out reproductive health care.[48] This is why multiple medical and public health organizations, including the American Academy of Family Physicians, the American Academy of Pediatrics, the American College of Obstetricians and Gynecologists, the American Medical Women's Association, and the Society of Adolescent Medicines, oppose such laws.[49]

There are a few ways to address this. At the most basic level, we need to tackle the effects of abstinence-only education, since the result of this program is that even before they may discover that their access to reproductive health services is limited, students lack the basic knowledge about care they might need. Once they have accurate information, young people then need to be able to put what they have learned into practice.

We also need to oppose the ever-increasing legislation limiting access to abortion and contraception. We need to force retailers to respect laws mandating that they sell condoms regardless of age, and we need to challenge those who claim they don't sell to minors. Similarly, pharmacists should not be allowed to pick and choose which medications they sell and to whom based on their own views, and we should fight any *conscience* laws that allow this.

Conscience laws permit people like pharmacists, physicians, or other medical providers to withhold certain medical services for reasons of religion or personal belief, and they are a huge problem. For one thing, providers have a professional duty to meet a patient's legal medical needs, whatever their own views. For another, individual interpretation of certain medical procedures and medications is incredibly dangerous. Though Catholic hospitals have long declined to perform any services related to abortion, increasingly we're seeing pharmacists, emboldened by these laws, taking matters into their own hands. Some have denied pregnant women with nonviable (no longer living) fetuses medication to help them expel the fetus, on the grounds that they are opposed to abortion. Others have refused to dispense emergency contraception and other forms of birth control as a matter of, yes, conscience.[50]

So much of the debate over these issues comes down to matters of individual values, with people on both sides who claim they want what's best for teens. That's really tricky ground to tread. But if the ultimate goal is truly to grow healthy teens, my personal belief is that we have to give them the tools to take care of themselves. Depriving young people of any autonomy around their reproductive health care has resulted in a real crisis of teen sexual health that the current climate may only make worse.

THE PORN TALK: WHAT YOU MIGHT HAVE HEARD AND WHY THAT'S BS

WHAT YOU MAY HAVE HEARD:
If you talk to high school boys about porn, you've done your job.

WHY THAT'S BS:
Studies have found that a significant number of kids have seen some type of sexually explicit imagery by the time they're in middle school, whether intentionally or not, and plenty more have encountered it even younger. Adults can be a little clueless about this. Data from a 2016 Indiana University survey of more than six hundred pairs of children and their parents reveals a parental naïveté gap: half as many parents thought their children had seen porn as actually had.[51] Plus, leaving girls out of the conversation is a big mistake

since, like boys, they are likely to encounter porn in some form, and they need to know how to deal with it.

• • •

WHAT YOU MAY HAVE HEARD:

As long as I tell them porn is bad (or nasty, or inappropriate, or illegal, or sexist), I've done my job.

WHY THAT'S BS:

The issue of porn is important to discuss, but I'd never advise anyone to write off porn as simply "bad." Teens should understand that being interested in sex and naked bodies is perfectly normal. However, it's also understandable that adults are worried. They are worried about everything from the impact of porn on developing brains, to what it says about a child's sexual interests, to the legal or moral aspects of porn. Plenty of these worries are legitimate (it's true a lot of mainstream porn presents an unrealistic idea of what sex looks like), but not all of them need as much attention. For example, even if a child has watched some pretty kinky stuff, that doesn't mean there's anything "wrong" with them.

Explaining that porn is a) not made for kids and b) not representative of typical adult sex will go a lot further than simply acting as if the desire to view it is shocking or immoral. Of course, it's also wise to mention that it is illegal for anyone under eighteen to look at porn.

• • •

WHAT YOU MAY HAVE HEARD:
I don't need to bring up porn because they'll learn about it in their sex-ed classes.

WHY THAT'S BS:
Sure, some comprehensive sexuality-education classes cover porn, but those aren't the majority, and that's even assuming kids are getting *any* sex ed, which often doesn't start until long after they have come across porn.

In fact, since sex education in the United States is so weak, plenty of kids actually turn to porn to fill the information gaps left by parents and schools. So even a middle schooler can benefit from learning that the sex they might see online is intended for adults, that it is fantasy, and that it isn't made with a child audience in mind.

Teens should understand that actors in porn don't usually look like average adults and that they're often given the job because of specific physical characteristics. In porn, a lot of men have huge penises, and women often have really big breasts, no body hair, and thin bodies. These actors just aren't representative of what is "typical" for bodies.

Plus, porn sex tends to look pretty different from sex off camera. For one thing, most of the mainstream porn the average teen comes across is made for a cishet male audience. Male pleasure tends to take center stage, actors often jump into sex acts with no discussion, and it's rare to see condom use.

PROTECTING YOUNG PEOPLE FROM SEXUALIZATION

In addition to debates over sex education and reproductive health care, there is often disagreement about how to protect teens from sexualization, which refers to having sexuality forced, physically or psychologically, on someone rather than it being self-initiated. So a woman wearing a tank top who is just trying to dress for summer may be sexualized when a man leers at her and projects sexual meaning into her choice of clothing, or sees her outfit as an invitation or excuse to make a sexual advance. A girl who displays physical signs of puberty at age ten may be sexualized when we tell her an outfit is inappropriate for showing some skin, if we wouldn't think twice about a physically smaller kid of the same age wearing the same thing.

To be sure, plenty of people welcome sexual attention and want to promote a sexy image. But it's a concern when attention isn't welcome, and particularly troubling when sexual attention is given to a teen who doesn't want it or cannot consent to it. While anyone can be a victim of sexualization, many studies have found that girls and women are far more likely to be sexualized than are boys and men.[52] This occurs in interpersonal interactions, and it can also be seen when advertisers use female bodies posed in suggestive clothes and settings to sell their products. Or onscreen, when female characters serve as little more than receptacles for male desire.

Additionally, some people are harmed by sexualization on multiple levels. For example, girls of color and LGBTQ+ youth can simultaneously face sexualization and eroticization. Eroticization means that certain nonsexual qualities someone possesses (like their age or race) are viewed as something sexual. Then there is the effect of sexualization on cishet boys. Though less likely to be sexualized themselves, these boys can't escape the impact of living amid this flurry of messages telling them that, first and foremost, girls are sex objects.

A task force report from the American Psychological Association found that the impact of sexualization on girls can impact everything from cognitive functioning to physical and mental health and sexual expression.[53] We also know that girls exposed to lots of sexualized imagery are more likely to self-objectify or to judge themselves by their appearance, and that preteen and teen girls who buy into the idea that their greatest worth comes from their sexual appeal are also more likely to justify sexism.[54]

And while it might seem as if this is some uptight antisex handwringing, if the experts are to be believed, the sexualization of children, particularly in the media, is on the rise. According to the findings of a study published in the journal *Sex Roles*, there has over time been an increase in the number of images of low-cut shirts and high-heeled shoes paired with childlike characteristics like polka-dot prints, Mary Jane–style shoes, pigtails, and lollipop slurping.[55]

Additionally, there is also the phenomenon of age compression. This is a marketing term that refers to the "adultification" of young girls and the "youthification" of adult women, and it is used to sell everything from toys to junk food, clothing, video games, and auto parts.

Figuring out how to respond to a teen's sexual expression is complicated, since the same young person who wants to dip their toe into their sexual side, say, through their choice of clothing, might also be experiencing the negative impact of the expectations of the world around them.

So here are some things to consider if you are concerned:

▸ Is the teen exploring their sexuality alone or with a similarly aged peer? For example, are they sending flirty texts to another kid in their class?
▸ Are they simply seeking knowledge?
▸ If you're uncomfortable with the teen's choice of clothing, is this discomfort related to how the rest of the world will interpret it or how you interpret it, rather than what you think the fashion motivations are?

Ultimately, if you suspect that a young person is being forced into sexual situations by someone else, or is trying to enact a vision of sexuality that mimics harmful media or porn representations of sex, then they might indeed be feeling the harmful effects of sexualization around them. But if a teen wants to look cute and fashionable, is seeking the attention of a peer, has a crush, or is just plain curious about sex, then don't discount the possibility that they are acting in a developmentally healthy way.

It is true that teens may think an outfit is "cute and fashionable" exactly because our fashion sense is affected by the advertising messages around us, and a teen's fashion sense might very well mimic the harmful media messages that sexualize kids without them knowing it. But one of the worst things we can do is shame young people for being vulnerable to these messages. Teens can be incredibly sensitive, and being told by an adult that what they're doing is naive or inappropriate can cause them to shut down or, conversely, to double down. So as you address these concerns with them, make sure to do so in an empathetic way.

Nowhere is the messiness of this issue clearer than when it comes to school dress codes. Dress codes are common across the United States. They tend to focus on girls' clothes and are often justified with arguments about the need to protect girls from leering eyes or about the "distracting" nature of showing too much skin.

But what do girls learn when we tell them that there's something so dangerous about their bodies that they have to be covered up, lest they excite or "distract" boys? I don't know about you, but to me that sounds an awful lot like we're saying that their bodies are sex objects. Dress codes in our schools do little to help students focus. Rather, they turn the focus to what a girl is wearing. And they teach kids of all genders that girls' bodies are dangerous and sexual, and that it's the responsibility of those girls to prevent others, including both their peers and adults, from noticing this fact.

Most adults want to prevent children from being sexualized. But some strategies simply work better than others. Teens are increasingly being asked to remain sexless in a world that is throwing sex on them at every turn, and from an incredibly early age (baby beauty pageants, anyone?). The last thing teens need is for the adults who care about them to treat them as degenerates when some of the sex being thrown their way actually sticks.

TAKING ACTION ON UNFAIR DRESS CODES

Dress codes are often imposed unfairly on girls and LGBTQ+ youth. Here are some steps to help fight against unfair dress codes:

1) Get the facts

▸ Look over your local school's dress-code policy. It could very well be that some aspects need to be modernized. That can be a good angle to take that won't make it seem like you're attacking the school.

▸ When challenged, courts have tended to uphold dress codes. But they are supposed to be applied fairly. So, for example, a school can't allow an NRA T-shirt while banning one that says "feminist."

▸ Research doesn't back the claims that dress codes reduce discipline problems and increase grades. What has been found is the real harm that dress codes can cause by making students miss class time, by shaming and embarrassing them, and by listing violations in a student's disciplinary record.

2. Bring it up with school administrators

▸ Raise the issue with the principal and discuss what you've learned. Can't get in to see the principal by yourself? Try to rally a group of supporters, since there is power in numbers.

▸ Work on identifying at least one teacher or administrator who you think would be sympathetic, and get that person on your side.

▸ If this is a district-wide issue, consider attending a school board meeting. Bring it to the attention of people who can actually make changes.

3. Move beyond your school

▸ Sometimes getting community support is more effective than working with any one school. If you're involved with a community group, religious organization, or parent association, try to enlist these organizations as allies.

▸ Write a letter to your local paper. The smaller the paper, the more likely you are to get published.

▸ Take to social media. Bringing up your concerns online can be effective at mobilizing large groups of people, but remember, anything you put out there can last forever, so make sure to be thoughtful and respectful.

▸ Document what is going on.

SEXUALITY SPOTLIGHT: THE CRIMINALIZATION OF TEEN SEX

Nothing sends chills down a parent's spine quite like the threat posed by a sex offender. We are all unnerved by well-known cases like that of the three women in Cleveland, Michelle Knight, Amanda Berry, and Gina DeJesus (who were kidnapped and sexually assaulted for a decade), Jaycee Lee Dugard (who at eleven was kidnapped, sexually assaulted, and kept captive for eighteen years by a known sex offender), Elizabeth Smart (who was abducted at fourteen and sexually assaulted by a religious fanatic over a period of almost a year), or Shawn Hornbeck (who was snatched from his bicycle at eleven, also by a sexual predator, and held for five years before escaping).

Then there are the stories that hit closer to home. Last year, in my own neighborhood, a guy crawled through the window of an apartment building and raped an eleven-year-old girl in her bed as her younger brother slept in the bunk below. As the mom to a then twelve-year-old daughter, I could think of nothing else for days. These stories are just so horrifying that many people want to be able to pass laws allowing us to lock up the perpetrators and throw away the keys.

But while these cases are gruesome, they really aren't common. That's hard to remember when the news media, politicians, and TV shows make it seem like there is danger lurking around every corner. Combine this with the fact that no criminals are more vilified than are sex offenders, and you can see how easy it has become to target anyone—no matter how young—who is involved in something called a sex crime. That's true even if the illegality of the crime in question is, well, questionable.

This panic has resulted in far-reaching sex-offender registries. These registries can continue even past the completion of a sentence, and they tend to include restrictions that can prevent individuals from living near schools, churches or day cares; having contact with children; or even using the internet. While registries are often sold as a needed measure to protect children from predators, a study conducted by the National Institute of Justice and Rutgers University found that the ever-increasing laws requiring sex-offender registration have not made a difference in preventing future sex crimes against children.[56] What is particularly troubling is the fact that in recent years, teens (and even preteens!) have gotten caught in the fray and have been forced to register as sex offenders in staggering numbers.

What's the Background?

Sex-offender registries are the byproduct of 2006's Adam Walsh Child Protection and Safety Act, which was named after the six-year-old son of John Walsh (the host of the TV show *America's Most Wanted*), who was murdered by a sex offender. In addition to all its other requirements, this law requires states to add juveniles to their sex-offender lists. Though not all states have implemented the bill yet, more and more enact its rulings every year, both out of principle and under the threat of losing much-needed grant money if they do not.

The result of this law is nothing short of shocking. A study from Human Rights Watch found that over two hundred thousand people from states across the country were on the registry for crimes committed as minors.[57] Some of the youngest people on the registry have committed gruesome crimes. But others had consensual sex with a slightly younger peer, got busted sexting, literally played a prank, or were acting out as a result of suffering from sexual abuse themselves. The impact on these individuals is grim. In addition to laws requiring detention in juvenile facilities, the registry can be lifelong and can impose unbelievable limitations for minors. Registry rules might ban contact with other kids, which can prevent them from attending school or even living at home if there are siblings in the house. And underage mothers may be barred from seeing their children's father if he has been convicted of statutory rape, even if the father is eighteen and the mother sixteen and she wants him involved in their child's life.

Some states require a sex-offender designation be stamped on a license, which makes getting a job or applying to college (let alone obtaining financial aid) impossible. Plus, most states allow public access to sex-offender registries via the internet. As a result, anyone (including, of course, other teens, teachers, and employers) who can get online can identify registered sex offenders in their communities.

Teens are actually particularly vulnerable to landing on the registry for the simple reason that most of the sex they're having is with their peers. While that might seem like the natural course of teen development, it is also something that's illegal in many places, which many people simply don't realize. As a result, rules created with hardened criminals in mind, and that purport to protect kids, have disproportionally harmed them.

Johns Hopkins public health professor Elizabeth Letourneau addressed the crisis in a 2016 TEDMED talk that looked at the folly of focusing on punishment over prevention. She explained, "We know that incarcerating or detaining children, even briefly, reduces the likelihood that they'll graduate from high school and increases the likelihood they will commit more crimes. My research shows that sex-offender registration and public notification do nothing—nothing—to prevent juvenile sexual offending or improve community safety in any way. Instead, these policies cause harm."[58] Some of that research was published in 2018 in the journal *Psychology, Public Policy, and Law.* It also highlighted additional dangers for children on the sex-offender registry, including being more likely to be solicited by an adult for sex, more likely to be victims of violence and harassment, and more likely to have suicidal thoughts.[59]

It's also important to remember that, while only a small number of children who have sexual behavior problems in childhood will grow into adult pedophiles, there are indeed kids who need professional help, particularly in cases where there is a significant age or cognitive difference between the children involved in the incident, or if there is additional violence involved. But getting help can be terrifying, with the registry looming large. As the then executive director of the Texas Association Against Sexual Assault, told the *Dallas Morning News* when the registries first began to emerge, "If I found my 10-year-old child with my 7-year-old child, I would be very tempted—even after 30 years in the field—not to report my child just to keep them off the [sex offender] registry."[60]

Though boys are more likely to find themselves on such registries, girls are not immune. But the most common reason girls find themselves facing sex-related charges is not because they were over the age of consent and had consensual sex with a younger teen. Rather, most female teen sex offenders shoulder this label after being arrested for sex work while still minors themselves. Despite the fact that it is against the law for an adult to have sex with someone who is under the age of consent, if there is an exchange of money—even if it is money that a girl never sees because it is turned over to a pimp who is forcing her into the business—that girl can actually be considered a criminal.

Recently, a few states have attempted to correct this flawed system by offering protections for child prostitutes. But this path hasn't been a straightforward one. And in a country where a sixteen-year-old African American girl named Cyntoia Brown, who had been repeatedly abused and raped and forced into prostitution by a pimp, can be given a life sentence for the murder of the client she believed was going to kill her, it is a stark reminder of just how harshly youth, and particularly minority youth, are often viewed by the system. Brown was ultimately granted clemency and had her sentence commuted in early 2019,[61] but there are plenty of other girls sitting in prison under similar circumstances today.

Why It's a Problem

These days, laws designed with adult criminals in mind also get applied to teens and in some cases, even to children, whose activities are significantly different. Think about the crime of statutory rape. This refers to sex between people where one is under the legal age of consent. It is usually understood that in cases of statutory rape, a teen has consented to having sex. However, this consent isn't considered valid, since juveniles are regarded as too young to ever make that decision. Statutory rape is different from child molestation, which typically describes an adult abusing a prepubescent child. It is also legally different from sexual assault or "forcible" rape. The reason the word *rape* is used in this situation is because it's assumed that there must be pressure or manipulation involved if minors and adults are having sex.

The idea that children need special protections around sex is actually fairly new. In fact, America saw legal safeguards for animals before there were any specifically in place for kids! These days, children are seen as society's most vulnerable population, and over the past century, we have witnessed the emergence of a number of important measures designed to protect them. For example, today, most states set the age of consent for sex between sixteen and eighteen. This is a lot higher than it was a hundred years ago, when ten or twelve was the norm— or, in the case of Delaware, seven! Moral reformers of the day, already fighting for temperance, suffrage, and social purity, successfully advocated to raise the age, and by the 1920s, the age of consent for heterosexual sex was increased in almost all fifty states.

However, prohibitions against statutory rape began to be enforced more frequently in the 1990s. Notably, this was due to the passage of the same 1996 welfare-reform act (a bill that we now see had many far-reaching effects). In 1993, President Clinton even championed the bill with the claim that reducing welfare benefits "would be some incentive for people not to have dependent children out of wedlock."[62]

Sexual activity isn't the only area where we've seen strict

age limits legislated. We all know that the United States also has anti–child pornography laws. But many people would be shocked to discover how new these actually are. In fact, it wasn't until the passage of 1977's Protection of Children Against Sexual Exploitation Act that there was specific legislation banning child pornography and criminalizing sexually explicit images of children.

This law came about due to outcry following a 1975 magazine spread of a completely nude, oil-covered, ten-year-old Brooke Shields. Though there has been debate about whether nude images of children can ever be considered art (think Sally Mann's photos of her own nude children), the Shields photos caused widespread outcry both for what was seen as the obviously sexual nature of the poses, as well as the fact that *Sugar and Spice*, the publication in which they appeared, was known specifically for its sexually explicit imagery, and this spread fell right in line with that.

Obviously there is a need for legislation to protect children from exploitation. But due to the way some laws were written, we now have a legal system that can lump together adult predators, pedophiles, and teenagers exploring sex, and that can treat kids who post naked pictures of themselves to their social media the same way it treats child pornographers. To complicate matters further, state sex-offender laws can trump juvenile-offender laws (which generally result in milder penalties, shorter sentences, and sealed records). Additionally, our constitutional guarantee of states' rights has resulted in numerous situations where a sexually active teen may be doing something legal in one part of the country, but criminal in another.

It is little wonder, then, that minors have found themselves sitting in jail, or saddled with lifetime sexual-offender status for behaviors they honestly didn't know were crimes.

Enforcement across the board is also uneven. As Amy Adele Hasinoff explains in *Sexting Panic: Rethinking Criminalization, Privacy, and Consent,* in many cases it's up to the parents to determine if charges will be laid, and laws are often enforced based on the anger of the parents of the younger teen.[63] That's something that can be exacerbated in same-gender or cross-racial situations, where the parents' prejudice against the "offender" may also play a role.

A report from the Office of the Juvenile Defender found that LGBTQ+ teens continue to be disproportionately represented in child welfare and juvenile justice facilities, often for sexual activity, since as the report notes, "LGBTQ youth are more likely to be charged with sex offenses when engaging in consensual sexual conduct than youth with opposite-sex partners."[64]

America has a legacy of unequal laws regarding sex between men. While lesbians were rarely considered by lawmakers, many states passed unique prohibitions against sex between men. Often these laws imposed far harsher penalties for same-sex statutory rape cases than they did in comparable situations between opposite-sex partners. Though such disparities were supposed to be addressed by a landmark 2003 Supreme Court case called *Lawrence v. Texas* (see more about that in the sidebar on page 65), the impact of such views remains.

Charges against teens can also come about as the result of state laws mandating that doctors, therapists, teachers, and even parents report teen sexual activity, even if the

teens are the same age and in a relationship. But whatever their offense, and however it came to the attention
of the authorities, a teen who is convicted of a sex crime
can then find themselves on a sex-offender registry. For a
teen convicted of something like statutory rape, sexting,
or prostitution, the consequences of this system can be
devastating.

Obviously, teens *can* be dangerous sexual predators.
But they can also be victims, make childish mistakes,
exhibit bad judgment, or just partake in normal sexual
exploration. None of this should brand them as lifetime
sex criminals, something that Human Rights Watch calls
"both unnecessary from a public safety perspective and
harmful to the child."[65] Yet the practice of branding them
is more than a trend. Often it is federal law.

Where We're at Now

Since statutory rape laws allow teens to be charged with a
crime for having sex with a boyfriend or girlfriend who is
only a year or two younger, about a quarter of the states
have enacted "close-in-age" or "Romeo and Juliet" exceptions. These ensure that if a couple is close in age—even
if one person is over the age of consent—then the case
is looked at differently than if a twenty-five-year-old
had sex with a fifteen-year-old. Though teens may still
face charges under Romeo and Juliet clauses, they rarely
require jail time, parole, or sex-offender registration.

But what has captured more headlines over the past
decade are the teens who have found themselves in legal
trouble when their use of new technology collides with
old child pornography laws. These laws were written long
before anyone could have ever imagined that teens would

be able to electronically transmit nude images of themselves to others. Yet child pornography laws have been applied when just such a thing happens. Certainly, new technology can be used for criminal acts, but is that what we should call a boy's possession of a naked picture of his girlfriend?

Though some states are moving to exempt same-age sexting, underage teens across the country have been charged with crimes for sending sexual images of themselves to other minors. Take the case of a fourteen-year-old Minnesota girl who in 2017 sent a revealing selfie to a boy she liked via Snapchat. A conviction, or even a guilty plea to a lesser charge, would have required her to spend ten years on the sex-offender registry. As the ACLU lawyer defending her wrote, "[She] created the sext of her own body. She was not an exploited child victim. She was exhibiting normal adolescent behavior in the digital age . . . It is nonsensical to suggest that [she] is both a victim and the perpetrator of her own abuse."[66] Ultimately, the courts agreed, and the charges were dismissed.[67] This was a positive sign that the tides might be changing. Shortly after this, legislation exempting teens from child pornography charges for consensual underage sexting began to be introduced in a number of states. But even so, plenty of minors remain caught up in the fray.

There are lots of good reasons I'd advise teens to avoid sexting or posting nude pictures of themselves online. Doing so can expose them in ways they might not imagine. Once a picture leaves their possession, they have no control over it. And a lot of this sending is done under pressure. But living in fear of jail and having to register as a sex offender shouldn't be the main deterrents.

Criminalizing teen sex is taking a terrible toll on American youth, on victims of sex crimes and trafficking, and on families. Teens inadvertently break the law when they text naked pictures of themselves to others. Real victims of sexual assault and of actual child offenders may not get the help they need if parents are fearful of what could happen if they involve the authorities.

Despite what many people believe, it's not the internet and permissive values around sex that we should fear for our children, but rather a legal system that treats sexually active teens in the same way it does rapists or pedophiles, and in doing so, turns normal kids into sex offenders, locks them up, and throws away the key.

Think about it this way: if we assume that kids are too immature too consent to have sex or to view pornography, then how can we possibly turn around and say those same kids have to be held to adult standards when they post a naked picture of themselves online or have sex with a slightly younger peer? But in many cases, that's exactly what our legal system does. Hypocrisy about teens and sex is nothing new. Legislating contradictions into law without batting an eye is something else, and if we want to raise sexually healthy teens who will ultimately become sexually healthy adults, this sure isn't the way to do it.

OLDER PARTNERS: WHEN TO WORRY

A lot of teens have older partners. Sometimes this is okay. Other times, it can be a real problem. For example, teen girls with older partners are more likely to become pregnant than girls who are dating kids closer to their own age.[68] For LGBTQ+ teens, who might have been forced to leave home, an older partner can offer things like a place to live and emotional and financial support. But this can come at a cost, as LGBTQ+ youth with older partners are at a disproportionate risk for dating and sexual violence and exposure to STIs including HIV.[69]

Here are some things to watch out for with older partners:

Equality: Does the younger partner really have an equal say in the relationship? Are their ideas and opinions valued? One person shouldn't get to make all the decisions in a relationship.

Previous relationships: Does the older partner have a history of dating teens? If so, you might want to think about why they never date people their own age.

Power and control: No one should have to ask a partner for permission to do things, or get their approval to spend time with friends and family. Trust your instincts. If it seems like a teen is being controlled by an older partner, they probably are.

Compatibility: Does the couple get along and have fun together? Are they integrated into each other's social lives, peer groups, and families, or is the relationship isolated and compartmentalized? If there doesn't seem to be any common ground, that can be a sign of trouble.

Legality: Is the relationship even legal? Depending on the difference in their ages and the state and local laws, if the older person is above the age of consent and the younger person is below it, they can be charged with a crime for having sex, even if the younger person says they wanted to.

Plenty of adults have large age gaps in their relationships and it's not a big deal. But things are different for teens, both emotionally and legally.

WHAT IT ALL COMES DOWN TO

According to a May 2018 Gallup poll, Americans currently hold more liberal views about sex than at any other time in history. The majority of people now find things like birth control, sex outside of marriage, and gay and lesbian relationships to be "morally acceptable." The poll even found a 10 percent increase in the number of people reporting teen sex to be morally acceptable in the five years since the previous survey.[70]

But despite these changes in attitude, a lot of the mainstream messaging on teen sex defaults to the most conservative views. These views just don't reflect modern life, and they aren't helping teens stay safe. We can help young people navigate the sexual aspects of their lives with more fluidity, but only if we begin the hard work of talking about the topic and challenging some long-held beliefs and misperceptions about young people and sex.

In recent years, minors have both gained and lost on the sexuality front. They have gained access to information via the internet, and lost opportunities for further learning with abstinence-only education programs. They have gained the ability to express their sexual orientations and gender identities, and lost rights with the passage of things like bathroom bills that force people to only use facilities associated with their sex assigned at birth. They have gained the right to access emergency contraception, and lost control over their sexual health with the countless hoops they've had to jump through in order to get birth control or an abortion. They have gained acceptance when we have made greater allowances for sex without marriage, and lost their freedom when we've turned normal teen sexual behavior into a crime.

And those losses? They really sting.

What we really need to do is challenge the idea that sex itself is inherently dangerous for teens and start improving the conditions under which teens learn about sexuality and the ways they choose to either express it or not. It's the job of adults to help put young people on a safe path, but on the sex front, we just seem to keep on dropping the ball.

TACKLING TOUGH TEEN TOPICS

A lot of adults worry about how they will respond to issues involving teens when they arise, whether those issues are brought up by teens or by other adults. So thinking about a few situations before they come up can make you feel a lot more confident when a situation presents itself.

For each scenario below, consider what your immediate gut-level response would be, then think about a revised response that actively strives to be nuanced, compassionate, and teen positive, taking into consideration everything you've learned from this chapter. Next consider how you could rationalize that second response if you were challenged on it.

1) Your sixteen-year-old asks if their boyfriend or girlfriend can sleep over.

    Gut response: ....
....
....

    Revised response: ....
....
....

    Reasons for the revision: ....
....

2) A parent comments on the skimpy outfits that some of the girls are wearing, saying they are "asking for trouble."

    Gut response: ....
....
....

    Revised response: ....
....
....

Reasons for the revision: ....
....

3) You overhear your nephews talking about how oral sex is nasty on a girl but normal on a guy.

Gut response: ....
....
....

Revised response: ....
....
....

Reasons for the revision: ....
....

4) Your teenage babysitter mentions that her church is opposed to gay marriage and that she had turned down a babysitting job from a family with two moms.

Gut response: ....
....
....

Revised response: ....
....
....

Reasons for the revision: ....
....

5) Your neighbor asks you to sign a petition calling for the local school board to ban the local health center from doing sex-ed presentations in the local schools.

Gut response:
....
....
....

Revised response:
....
....
....

Reasons for the revision:
....
....

6) A teenager you are close to says that they have something to tell you but makes you promise not to tell anyone else. The something is that a kid they know was raped on a school trip by one of the college-aged chaperones.

Gut response:
....
....
....

Revised response:
....
....
....

Reasons for the revision:
....
....

Hopefully, this chapter and earlier ones gave you some solid information that you can draw from to help address these situations. You might feel that some of the scenarios are straightforward (say, comments about oral sex that you could point out as sexist). And some of these scenarios might feel more complex than others—the sleepover issue, for example. If you see the benefits of a sleepover but the parents of your child's partner feel differently, this can be a thorny topic to navigate. Same for if you identify slut shaming in the way that someone is talking about a girl's outfit, but you also are uncomfortable with the outfit, just for different reasons, maybe because of how the world might respond to her presentation.

But what about when you are asked to keep a secret? Especially one about something like sexual assault? It can be helpful to preemptively make it clear to teens that there are simply some secrets you won't be able to keep. Sometimes this is actually a relief for them. But this is a really tough situation for any adult to be in.

Personally, though I fully support a victim's right to decide to come forward about an assault or not, this gets tough when it comes to children and teens. As an adult, you very well might decide that a sexual assault is not a secret you can keep and that it is worth breaching a confidence in order to get help. In many situations, adults are just legally required to report sexual assaults of teens. I would advise, though, that whatever the reason, if you need to break a teen's confidence, you let the teens involved know. They might be incredibly upset, but they do deserve to have advanced knowledge.

We sometimes get caught up in the idea that there should be a perfect response to every situation. I don't believe that there is. But I do think that considering what you might say in any given scenario before the issue arises is one of the best ways to prepare for what can otherwise be uncomfortable moments.

CHAPTER 6

GETTING TO GOOD SEXUAL CITIZENSHIP

According to the World Health Organization, in addition to being affected by genetics, our health is impacted by our physical and social environment and by things like our education and our interpersonal relationships.[1] Needless to say, these social determinants also affect our sexual health and the climate surrounding sexual behavior.

To be sure, people who grow up with rigid cultural messages about appropriate gender roles for men and women, those who do not receive comprehensive sex education that covers sexual violence and consent, those who cannot access sexual and reproductive health care, and those who live in hostile and dangerous sexual environments are more likely to experience negative sexual health impacts. For some, the result can be an increased risk of victimization. For others, such climates increase the likelihood that they will become a perpetrator.

But it can be awfully hard to see and talk about factors other than individual intent when it comes to people who perpetrate harmful behavior.

As longtime feminist writer and Pulitzer Prize winner

Susan Faludi wrote in an op-ed in the *New York Times*, "Fighting the patriarch and fighting the patriarchy are also distinct—and the former tends to be more popular than the latter. It's easier to mobilize against a demon, as every military propagandist—and populist demagogue— knows. It's harder, and less electrifying, to forge the terms of peace. Declaring war is thrilling. Nation-building isn't."[2]

None of this is to say we should give abusers a pass. But we are not doing anyone any favors when we lose sight of the larger picture. So here in the final chapter, I'll give you a lens to help view the way hostility grows into violence, as well as concrete skills and tools that you can employ as you work toward creating healthier communities made up of good sexual citizens.

PULLING UP THE ROOTS OF INTERPERSONAL VIOLENCE

Hostile climates don't emerge out of the blue. Most grow from questionable seeds, which are nurtured into something malignant and then sustained by an enduring mythology. Attacking the roots of such beliefs can be one of the most effective ways to unearth them.

Using a pyramid model, where seemingly less harmful actions support increasingly violent ones, can help demonstrate what this looks like. The original concept for this model came out of the Anti-Defamation League's Pyramid of Hate, which was designed to help explain how average citizens could carry out the Holocaust during the Second World War.

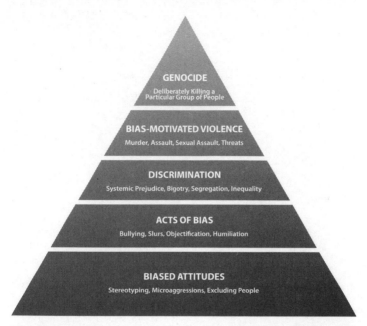

The concept of the Pyramid of Hate, developed by the Anti-Defamation League, demonstrates how the anger that drives genocide is built upon the tolerance of beliefs that originally appear innocuous, but which grow incrementally into something deadly.[3]

In recent years a range of organizations, notably a violence-prevention group out of Northeastern University called Mentors in Violence Prevention, began to adjust the pyramid model to focus on sexual violence.[4] I have continued to work with this model, and this is how I use the pyramid with my students:

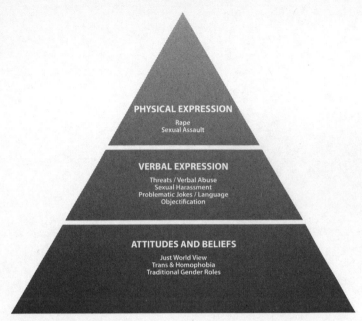

PHYSICAL EXPRESSION
Rape
Sexual Assault

VERBAL EXPRESSION
Threats / Verbal Abuse
Sexual Harassment
Problematic Jokes / Language
Objectification

ATTITUDES AND BELIEFS
Just World View
Trans & Homophobia
Traditional Gender Roles

Trivializing lower levels of the pyramid—attitudes and beliefs not necessarily tied to specific actions—has the effect of masking disturbing behavior behind accepted social conventions. Many attitudes and beliefs blame victims instead of perpetrators and in doing so bolster, sustain, and justify the expressions of sexual violence in the upper levels of the pyramid.

This version of the pyramid posits that, despite dismissals from the *can't you take a joke?* crowd, accepting sexist language, trans- and homophobia, and gender stereotypes is not harmless.

Rather, writing such things off as *no big deal* or *just the way things are* or *boys will be boys* desensitizes us to intensifying abuse. Likewise, justifications like *he doesn't mean anything by it* or *I was just flirting* condition us to dismiss increasingly dangerous and harmful behaviors as normal interpersonal interactions.

To think about it another way: How often do people randomly walk up to each other and begin throwing punches? It *can* happen, sure. But much more frequently, harsh words are exchanged before the first blow. Hostile language is often a warning sign of future violence.

Of course, it's also true that most people who use sexist terms don't violently attack others. So while language often plays a role, the progression from speech to physicality is typically gradual and nuanced, and it builds on other levels of the pyramid.

For example, consider the impact that the objectification of women plays in supporting violence. Objectifying someone means understanding them more as a *thing* than as a human. We see this when people (usually, but not exclusively, men) talk about *getting some*, or about *hitting that*, or about a *pair of tits*, as if they aren't attached to a person. We see it when porn calls trans women *chicks with dicks* and literally reduces them to a sex organ and a freak at the same time.

Objectifying another person is different from thinking they're sexy, which is a perfectly healthy response to someone you find attractive. When someone is objectified, the fact that there is a human person attached to the body of desire is utterly disregarded. How the person being objectified might feel is also disregarded. Objectification assumes their body is provided for another's enjoyment, and even if the sex is consensual, whether or not the person being objectified is having a positive, pleasurable experience is of little consequence. Sex in these circumstances is often just a one-sided event.

People who objectify women may rationalize their views through their support for a lower level of the pyramid: a belief in traditional gender roles. Among other things, these hold that a woman's primary place is in the domestic sphere, where she should meet her husband's sexual needs while simultaneously presenting herself as attractive but chaste to the rest of the world. Women who stray (even slightly) from this understanding of their role are then seen as fair game for objectification, or worse.

Such views can also serve as rationalization for higher-level violations like sexual harassment and assault. Many people who commit acts of verbal or physical sexual violence don't think of themselves as harassers or rapists and rely on common defenses such as *she was playing hard to get, what does she expect dressing like that?* and *she actually wanted it* to legitimize their behavior.

This line of thinking gives people a pass for degrading women whom they determine have stepped out of their *appropriate* female role. Harassment, and even violence, become a sort of vigilante justice used to maintain the social order or teach someone a lesson. Such thinking is particularly common in attacks against trans women.

While the pyramid model is useful for considering how attitudes and beliefs are connected to actions, it's important to acknowledge that it cannot explain all instances of sexual violence. Some people skip levels of the pyramid or don't fit into this exact model. To be sure, there are those who objectify women while outwardly fighting against gender stereotypes. Or those who sexually harass privately while simultaneously supporting feminist causes in the public sphere.

And far from dehumanizing those they denigrate through objectification, plenty of people instead use their victim's humanity as a way to humiliate and harm. As philosopher Kate Manne posits in her book, *Down Girl: The Logic of Misogyny*, "People may know full well that those they treat in brutally degrading and inhuman ways are fellow human beings, underneath a more or less thin veneer of false consciousness."[5] False consciousness is any belief that prevents a person from being able to understand the true nature of a situation. It came out of Marxist theory as a way to explain people's inability to see exploitation and oppression for what it is. By this, Manne is suggesting that many individuals who harm others—in the cases she refers to, men who rape or torture women—may very well know these women are as human as they themselves are. But in order to grant themselves permission to engage in horrific actions, they have to pretend that they are unaware of their victim's humanity.

Still, whether they act through objectification or humiliation, individuals who perpetuate this kind of harm tend to believe in many of the hostile and damaging narratives that so much sexual violence is built on. That's why work that targets the beliefs and attitudes at the base of the pyramid can help undercut the supports for the more violent actions. This work helps destabilize those who intend harm and prevent those who plead ignorance of the harm from making such claims. Addressing the impact of our word choices and our attitudes, and the effect of gender stereotypes, can also be a wake-up call for those who may think they are actively working against a hostile sexual culture, but who may stumble along the way.

ON BEING A BYSTANDER

Sometimes these stumbles come in the form of inaction. Historians and humanitarians have long tried to explain the phenomenon that allows people to step over a homeless person, ignore domestic violence, or vote to close borders to victims of global atrocities. In all of these cases, people who are not directly perpetuating harm tend to think of themselves as bystanders (sometimes innocent ones) with little power or responsibility.

But bystanders play a crucial role in determining community norms. Psychologist and Holocaust survivor Ervin Staub believes bystanders are far more important than people give them credit for. As he writes in his book *The Roots of Evil: The Origins of Genocide and Other Group Violence*, "Bystanders, people who witness but are not directly affected by the actions of perpetrators, help shape society by their reactions. Bystanders are often unaware of, or deny the significance of events or the consequences of their behavior. [But] bystanders can exert powerful influences. They can define the meaning of events and move others toward empathy or indifference. They can promote values and norms of caring, or by their passivity of participation in the system, they can affirm the perpetrators."[6]

Of course, there are different degrees of bystander behavior. For example, many people distinguish between collaborators, who actively help perpetuate harm, and passive bystanders, who don't work to prevent it.[7] However, the risk of this distinction is that if enough people agree by inaction that a behavior doesn't merit intervention, then society no longer questions the ethics of the behavior being addressed. This makes the harmful actions of perpetrators and collaborators more likely to be viewed as normal.

To complicate matters, humans are not consistent.

We may act in one situation and not in another. Think about a time you stood up for someone who needed you to have their back. Now think about a time when you saw someone being treated poorly but didn't say anything. Why do you think you responded to one situation but not another? Maybe the difference was the context. Do you imagine reacting similarly in a social situation, within your family, or out in public? With a friend, a teacher, an older relative, or a stranger? Or maybe you cared more about the first person, maybe the harm to them seemed greater, or maybe the risk to you personally seemed lower?

And there is risk from getting involved. We can be attacked ourselves. We can make things worse for the victim. Or we can be embarrassed if we misunderstood the situation, or if our help isn't wanted. But it's important to determine whether the risk we fear is related to real harm or whether it is related to our comfort level.

Discomfort can be awful. But it is generally something that can be overcome. And so many of us are so fearful about the social implications of our actions that we stand by when doing something could have dramatic results.

IDENTIFYING PROBLEMATIC BEHAVIORS

Intervening as a bystander can feel daunting. First, you need to determine that an event is problematic. Then you need to feel accountable. Finally, you need the skills and ability to act.

So how do you make that first determination and decide whether an incident even requires that an outsider become involved? This is particularly difficult in the sexual arena, where we are awash in so many confusing messages about what normal encounters look like. The result is a collective misunderstanding of sexual assault and what to do about it.

It's common to think the type of situation that would warrant intervention would be one where we see a man attacking a woman in a way that would mean he had to be physically pulled off her. But while most of us have witnessed problematic sexual interactions, it's pretty unlikely that we will ever be in a position where we would need to wrestle a sexual attacker off someone physically.

As Joan Tabachnick, an expert in the area of child sexual abuse prevention, explains in "Engaging Bystanders in Sexual Violence Prevention," it is the lead-up—the lower levels of the pyramid—that we come across on a much more regular basis. These, and not the imagined physical altercations, are the ones that present the real opportunities to interrupt violence.

Tabachnick writes, "If we limit our interventions to a culminating 'event,' we miss multiple opportunities to do something or say something before someone is harmed. Instead, [we should] think of the 'event' as being on a continuum of behaviors that demand specific interventions at each step. . . . Each situation is an opportunity to intervene by reinforcing positive behaviors BEFORE a behavior moves further toward sexual violence."[8]

For many people, those *before* behaviors are the ones that we have long written off as "no big deal" or "just the way people talk." Even if our gut is telling us something really different, it's common to assume that we are over-reacting or misinterpreting what we're seeing. Combine self-doubt with our fear of social embarrassment, or our sometimes legitimate fear of retaliation, and it's easy to see how we commonly miss valuable opportunities to de-escalate harm.

But what if you can't tell whether something is actually a problem? There are times when you might consider something to be harassment but the person you identify as a victim is totally unbothered or even welcomes the interaction.

That happened to me on the subway recently. While I was taking my kids home from school, I saw a group of teenage boys yell at another boy and push him against the subway door. I feared an uneven fight was going to break out, so I yelled, "Hey, you guys, knock it off!" Then I turned to the kid I thought was a victim and asked, "You okay?" He and all the other boys gave me their best collective teenage eye roll (matched only by the eye roll of my own children, who were trying to melt into the seat beside me), and he said, "We were just playing. Chill out." To demonstrate his point, he smacked one of the other kids with his backpack as they all laughed.

Okay, so they were playing and I was embarrassed. But that was one of those situations where embarrassment was the worst outcome of making a wrong call. I feared that the worst outcome if I'd done nothing was that a boy might have been injured or bullied. In far too many cases, the wrong call to stay silent can actually open the door to violence.

But we also know that making the wrong call can sometimes be deadly, particularly when it is a white person calling the cops on a person of color simply for living their life. In light of a number of well-publicized incidents, there has been an increased call for white people to think about their motivations and the impact of dialing 911.

That's why it's really helpful to try to develop the skills to assess a situation and determine if there is actually a threat—a hard thing to do, since everyone holds implicit biases and unconscious stereotypes. When implicit biases—those perceptions we have about people based on their identity or membership in group—go uninterrupted, they can result in dangerous misreadings of situations. So doing some work on recognizing your own biases long before you encounter a situation where they might come into play is a really wise idea. As a first step, you can start by even just taking an implicit bias test. There is a free one offered online by Harvard University. When it comes to interventions involving law enforcement, in particular, having a better understanding of your own biases can help you more accurately assess situations and can help you answer questions like: Is someone really in danger? Is someone actually hurt? And if I truly believe the answer is yes, is there anything I can do to help in a way that will make things better?

Many people have made the crucial point that so many calls to the police could be avoided by actually talking to someone before picking up the phone. There is a difference between intervening as a bystander to ask a question or have a conversation and intervening in a way that escalates the situation and potentially involves law enforcement.

So while I think intervening in situation that could be dangerous is crucial, and that we need to trust our instincts and question the social norms that prevent us from doing what we know in our hearts to be the right thing, it is just as important to really think about what our interpretation of a dangerous situation is based on. And we should always consider what an appropriate intervention should look like.

Taking social responsibly isn't an exact science, and people will undoubtedly make mistakes along the way. But while it is one thing to make the kind of mistake that ends in mild embarrassment, it is a whole different story when that mistake ends up with someone unjustly forced into a confrontation with police who never should have been called in the first place.

THE INTERVENTION PART

As I mentioned earlier, intervention doesn't always look like what we imagine, and there's a lot we can to do intervene in everyday situations so as to prevent increasing hostility. In their guide, Safe Passage, the Massachusetts-based anti–domestic violence group I mentioned in Chapter 1, offers a number of ideas. For example, was that news commentary unsettling? Were those song lyrics a little off? Did that joke make you uncomfortable? Did that guy really just say that to his girlfriend? To you? Instead of holding your tongue, their guide recommends that you try saying something like, "That's not funny," if something isn't. And if "that's not funny" doesn't fit the bill, they recommend other examples:

- ▸ "That's not okay."
- ▸ "Actually, a lot of guys wouldn't . . ."
- ▸ "I'm curious why you think that."
- ▸ "No one ever deserves to be sexually assaulted."
- ▸ "I don't think she's lying."
- ▸ "That wasn't your fault."
- ▸ "I'm worried about you. Do you need help?"

It is also a good idea to consider whether a set of guidelines for bystander intervention—often called "the Ds" of bystander intervention—are appropriate in your situation. This framework came out of the work of researchers like Victoria Banyard and Alan Berkowitz, and of groups like Mentors in Violence Prevention, Sex Signals, Hollaback!, Green Dot, Creative Interventions, and Showing Up for Racial Justice. Here is an overview of what the Ds of bystander intervention look like:

De-escalate: Ideally, we can prevent situations from escalating. There are also times when indirect intervention is the safest bet, such as when someone makes a hostile comment that you want to address, but you're in an unequal power dynamic. In such a case, you might want to redirect or minimize the statement. We don't always have the ability to help prevent interactions from becoming hostile, but in those situations that we do, working to reduce the intensity is key.

Direct: Confront a situation where someone else is being harmed or is at risk of being harmed. If you witness someone being sexually harassed, the direct approach might involve asking the person if everything is all right or if they need help. Or telling the harasser to back off. If you think a friend is being abused by a partner, a direct approach could be letting them know you're concerned and asking if you can help them find support.

Distract: You can try to distract aggressors. In a fight, this can allow people to cool off, and in cases of potential sexual violence, it can create an opportunity for the potential victim to get away. If you see someone who looks like they're being hit on in an uncomfortable way, you can approach the situation and ask either party an unrelated question, or try to entice the potential victim to come with you. "I think your car is getting a ticket" can be a good line to use. The goal of distraction is to interrupt the harmful behavior, not necessarily to confront it.

Delegate: Look for people to back you up when it is time to intervene. You can ask people around you if they feel as uncomfortable with what's going on as you do, maybe saying, "Does this look weird to you, too?" It could mean letting a train conductor know someone is harassing passengers. Or it could mean asking for help from fellow partygoers when you witness a fight or see sexual violence. You may also want to draw strength in numbers and get others on board to join you in confronting a situation. Delegating can create a shared sense of responsibility among community members.

Delay: If the first four Ds don't work for you or your situation, if you need to gather more information from an outside source, or if you feel like you missed an opportunity to intervene, you can also use a delayed response. This could mean following up and asking if someone is okay after the fact. A delayed response can still show victims that you care about what you witnessed and that you want to be there to support them.

The idea of de-escalation is a key component of antiviolence work and has increasingly been used in conjunction with bystander intervention training. One group that has been pairing these concepts is the Arab American Association of New York, which began offering trainings to teach people how to intervene in situations of potential violence, racism, and Islamophobia after an increase in anti-Muslim hate crimes. They suggest a number of de-escalation tactics to prevent situations from intensifying. These include:

> ▸ **Be a broken record.** Repeat the same thing over and over. Example: "Please step back. Please step back. Please step back."
> ▸ **Name the behavior.** Address the specific behavior as opposed to labeling the perpetrator. Example: "You are raising your voice."
> ▸ **Use I statements.** I statements can let the aggressor feel less threatened and put the onus on you. Example: "I feel scared when you say that."
> ▸ **Direct to "we."** Create an alliance with the perpetrator to help redirect their anger away from you. Example: "We don't talk about people like that."[9]

There is a range of situations that can call for intervention. Some may be physical, like a fight, sexual assault, or dating or domestic violence. Others might be verbal, like sexual harassment, purposeful misgendering of transgender and nonbinary folks, or violent, racist, sexist, or homophobic speech. Each situation will require different tactics, and not every situation will be one where it is safe to intervene. But when intervention is possible, doing so can make all the difference in the world.[¶]

For a long time, people who have spoken up about seemingly inconsequential misconduct have been called uptight, politically correct, and overly sensitive as a way to shut them up. Dismissing someone in such a way is an effective and powerful way to silence them. But claiming your voice is also powerful. And that's something a lot more people have the ability to do than they might realize.

Don't get me wrong—addressing interpersonal dynamics is no easy feat. I've been accused of being a humorless feminist since I was sixteen. There are still plenty of times when I find it hard to speak up, and many times I've kept silent when I wish I hadn't.

Intervening also doesn't come naturally for a lot of people. Maybe you grew up hearing messages like *it's none of your business*, *don't get involved*, or *you'll just make the situation worse*. Maybe you just hate conflict. Maybe you are afraid. Maybe you have been victimized yourself. Maybe intervening would reopen trauma. Maybe the danger to you is real.

Still, keeping your head down when you could safely speak up has the long-term effect of eroding everyone's safety, since we are all at greater risk when there isn't the common expectation that we have each other's backs. And it pays to remember that while intervening

---

¶ The suggestions offered in this book are intended to provide a general overview of the concepts associated with bystander intervention and de-escalation tactics. I urge readers to seek out real-life training and to further educate themselves on safety and preparedness in these areas.

can be hard, like anything else, it gets easier with practice.

ON SPEAKING UP: WHAT YOU MAY HAVE HEARD AND WHY THAT'S BS

WHAT YOU MAY HAVE HEARD:
Getting involved will only make it worse.

WHY THAT'S BS:
Ask yourself, what does "worse" look like? For a lot of folks, the answer is when a situation moves from potential violence to actual violence. It is rational to worry that speaking up could be the spark that sets off an explosion.

Now obviously, far too many white people look at a range of everyday situations involving people of color and do set off explosions. But in situations where there is hostility, threat, or sexual violence, speaking up could also be the water that douses the flame, since in most of these cases, intervention is not what causes violence to erupt. Rather, intervention can defuse a potentially dangerous situation and give people a second to calm down or get away.

• • •

WHAT YOU MAY HAVE HEARD:
She's probably into it.

WHY THAT'S BS:
If you witness an interaction that gives you a moment's

pause, but then try to tell yourself everything is cool, consider where that rationalization might be coming from.

Could it be that you are reverting to some old myths about rape? Maybe that people who look or act a certain way are inviting sex? Or that victims scream and yell, and that rapists are strangers who jump out of dark stairwells?

Temper these notions with the knowledge that most sexual assault occurs between people who know each other, and that most effective intervention is preventative and happens before a culminating event.

• • •

WHAT YOU MAY HAVE HEARD:
It's none of your business.

WHY THAT'S BS:
Sometimes things are none of your business, and there are plenty of cases (for example, if someone calls child protective services on kids who are simply walking to school alone along a route they know well) when outsiders can mess things up. So it is understandable to be nervous about intervening. I mean, who wants to ruin someone's life over a misinterpretation! But keep in mind, intervening doesn't necessarily mean calling the cops or reporting the behavior officially in any way. Often it just means asking a question to determine if someone feels safe, or addressing a concern with a neighbor via text message, or telling someone a joke isn't funny.

Holding back from addressing a situation for fear that you will be seen as a nosy busybody is risky. Many people don't want to seem judgmental, but there are plenty of things that warrant judgment, and thoughtfully raising an issue in a way that isn't going to harm the person in question can really help strengthen communities.

THE THING ABOUT FITTING IN

When I teach, I often talk about the difference between perception and reality. I like to point out that while the kid who got drunk, hooked up with four people, and went to the hospital with alcohol poisoning on Friday night might be all everyone is whispering about on Monday morning, there are a lot more kids who had dinner with their family, watched a movie at a friend's place, went to sleep, and got up early for soccer practice. The more frequent scenario isn't the most titillating one, so it doesn't get a lot of airtime. As a result, the perception of what is *normal* is often skewed by the attention we pay to one event over another.

Of course, this is not just a high school gossip phenomenon. We see this distortion in all areas of life, from news coverage of certain events (missing white girls garner more news coverage than missing girls of color, who may just be assumed by law enforcement to be "runaways"), to our assessments of risk (regularly driving down the highway is actually more fatal statistically than terrorist attacks), to the fictional stories we tell ourselves every day (as in, my partner didn't respond to my text because they're cheating, not because their battery died).

This gap between perception and reality has been

explained by something called the social norms theory. Developed in the 1980s by psychologist Alan Berkowitz (who was also involved in creating the four Ds of bystander intervention) and sociologist H. Wesley Perkins, social norms theory was originally intended to address college drinking patterns. More recently, Berkowitz has done a lot of work on the role of social norm perceptions in sexual assault.

His research shows that people often mistakenly believe that others are more engaged in, or more tolerant of, harmful actions than they themselves are. The impact of this is significant. As Berkowitz and colleagues write in the journal *Violence Against Women*, "Men misperceive other men's attitudes and also the frequency with which others engage in risky behaviors (such as sexually aggressive behaviors). This misperception then provides them with 'permission' to engage in such behavior."[10] These men misidentify the social "norm." Not only are they able to rationalize their own aggressive behaviors as normal, but they are then able to trivialize problematic behavior that isn't violent, since they believe that it's not that bad compared to other men's behavior. Such harmful or abusive behavior might very well contradict these men's own stated values and beliefs.

Berkowitz's research has also demonstrated that both men and women overestimate a lot of behaviors and beliefs, including other people's comfort with stereotypical masculinity, the level of sexual activity of their peers, men's willingness to use force for sex, and the amount of unwanted sexual activity that actually occurs. They also assume others believe a lot of misinformation about what causes rape.

On the other hand, he found that both men and women tend to *underestimate* their peers' discomfort with language and behavior that objectifies or degrades women, and they underestimate other people's willingness to intervene in hostile or aggressive situations.[11]

It makes a kind of twisted sense that people who themselves harass or assault would like to think others are doing the same, since if the behavior is common and socially accepted, then their own actions are normalized and justified. But what is more puzzling is why those who do not commit such acts would overestimate others doing so. One possibility is that this overestimation is the product of living in a culture that tolerates the conditions that allow sexual assault to occur.

That culture is ever evolving, and it is worth noting that this research was conducted before the #MeToo movement took off. Since the #MeToo movement was all about bringing sexual assault and harassment to light and showing how prevalent it really is, you might be surprised to learn that people were overestimating how much unwanted sexual activity occurs. But what this time frame highlights is the possibility that, even as society collectively disbelieved victims in a pre-#MeToo era, there was also always some part of our collective understanding that knew rape was happening a lot more than many people wanted to publicly acknowledge.

Just think about our earlier discussion of perceptions of victims' humanity. It's certainly possible that, as Kate Manne posits, people adopted a "thin veneer" of false consciousness in this arena in order to continue a tradition of rape denial while allowing rape to continue unfettered. In other words, at least on a gut level, people know that forced sex is rape, but if we don't call it that, then similar rapes can keep going on and anyone who dares name them will be branded as hysterical.

In a climate where it is both common to assume rape occurs regularly and to simultaneously deny the existence of widespread rape, and amid the flurry of information Americans have learned about masculinity, femininity, and sex, it's not surprising that people would assume those around them are actually acting on the messages that we all receive. Some of these messages parrot the same tired tropes we have long heard about sexual violence, including: *All men would rape if they got a chance. Guys just think with their dicks. No man wants to cockblock another guy.*

But research shows that most men don't harass, abuse, and assault, nor would they ever want to. Ironically, when we promote a culture where men are seen as sex-crazed dogs, those men who *are* abusers are more easily able to get away with things that are clearly unacceptable, like catcalling or badgering women for sex under the guise of giving them compliments. *Boys will be boys*, right? And *men will be men*.

In order to challenge the idea that men lack a moral compass when it comes to sex, we need to actively speak up about the fact that men can be sensitive, compassionate, attentive, respectful, and loving. And we need to encourage one another to support these qualities, rather than mocking them or doubting them when they appear. Just like bystanders need to be given the tools to intervene, men in our culture need to know that most other guys aren't actually living up to the harsh expectations we have of them.

Berkowitz explains that bystander intervention arises from a need within a person to do the right thing, and that by understanding the impact of social norms on our own behaviors, we will be better able to align our values with our actions. So, if our values compel us to take responsibility for the world around us, and we learn that our communities are more likely to share these values than not, then we will feel more empowered to act in a positive way and less likely to commit egregious acts ourselves.

GETTING PEOPLE ON BOARD

Over the years, I have made plenty of mistakes—say, by offering the name of an abortion provider to an eighteen-year-old who, I later learned, was both a practicing Catholic and contentedly pregnant with her second child. Or by snapping at a college freshman after she told the guest speaker from a local LGBTQ+ group that she was opposed to gay parenting, rather than discussing it in a coolheaded way. Or, as a white teacher, by not seeing the role race played in my classroom.

We all make honest mistakes. But these days, I really try to make space for a range of views by saying things like: "I was wrong about that." "Tell me what you think." "I hear you." "You know, I don't have a lot of background in that area." "I'm from a different generation/race/country/ religion than you, so I might not totally get it." "Can you help me understand?" And when I see things differently, I may try to share my viewpoint, often by being up front about my biases from the get-go. I try to make it clear that my identity impacts a lot of how I see the world, just like my students' identities and experiences impact how they see it.

I like to explain to my classes right off the bat that since the topics I teach are dear to me, I don't always hide my views. But neither do I expect them to do so. I tell them that I welcome voices different than my own, and that while I will judge work or claims based on unsubstantiated sources, I won't judge them as people for disagreeing with me.

That's a hard promise to keep when it comes to polarizing topics. But naming my feelings and acknowledging theirs has fundamentally changed the conversations I'm able to have on everything from abortion to sexual assault.

Ultimately, as an educator, I don't see it as my role to teach any one set of values. But it sure is my job to correct misinformation. Sometimes that correction changes minds. Other times it doesn't. But either way, my goal is to have students leave my classes with the ability to think critically about their own and others' viewpoints.

Of course, talking about tough issues isn't only about setting the record straight and acknowledging differences of opinion. It is also about getting people to care about those issues, and then to believe that they can actually have an impact in areas that they determine need change.

When taking on behemoths like sexual assault and sexual harassment, whether in the classroom or out in the world, it's important to remember that not everyone is coming from the same place and not everyone has the same investment in the issues. If people don't care about the hostile sexual climate that you're discussing, or don't believe that rape is a real problem, or think that sexism is a thing of the past, then you aren't going to have a lot of success weaving folks into your efforts at tackling those issues.

In the 1970s, many second-wave feminists tried using consciousness-raising groups as a tool to increase understanding of personal or political issues. Today, a range of voices has helped raise awareness about the extent and impact of sexual hostility. However, even if they are aware, when people are new to an exhausting and demoralizing issue, tackling it can seem daunting. So you need to offer hope. And there is hope! Yes, there are indeed dark tides and deep fractures that continue to thwart progress. But we also know that we can effect change moving forward, and that we have witnessed huge cultural shifts in our history.

I think about this when I remember the experience of a girl from my high school. Dawn was the subject of much gossip after a party where she passed out drunk and a bunch of boys had sex with her. For the next year, kids would give Dawn the side-eye and gossip about her sluttiness. She spent most lunches eating alone.

Did it cross my mind that this was rape? That I should show her compassion and hold the boys accountable? Maybe. But *rape* sure wasn't a word we used in that context in the early '90s at my school. Dawn was a cautionary tale. Maybe she kind of wanted it? Or got what she deserved for drinking? Or for being pretty or flirty or something? Maybe we should just be grateful that it wasn't us being talked about in this way?

I may have puzzled over these questions, but I certainly didn't leap to Dawn's defense. Sure, I was trying out feminism as I understood it at the time—spelling *women* with a *y*, listening to riot grrl bands, and seeing what it was like to stop shaving my armpits for a few weeks. But translating these nascent attempts at politicization into how I treated other girls at school was still a ways away.

In a lot of communities, things have changed significantly since then. Many children grow up learning about consent, sometimes even of the enthusiastic and affirmative variety. Phrases like *slut shaming*, *rape culture*, *toxic masculinity*, and *victim blaming* are becoming common parlance in some places. Schools have become more vigilant about sexual harassment, and mainstream media has been compelled to cover the existence of sexual violence beyond the attack of a virgin in a dark alley by a stranger. I think about these advances when I become disheartened. While there are still plenty of Dawns in the world, there is also real reason to hope.

TALKING ABOUT ABORTION

Some time back, a woman I knew who considered herself pro-choice referred to abortion as "the most upsetting thing a woman could ever experience."

I didn't see it like that, and when I said something to that effect, the tone of the conversation shifted from commiserative to combative.

Thinking about that conversation reminded me: if it's that hard to talk about abortion with people who are fundamentally coming from the same place, then how are we supposed to discuss this with folks who have a totally different point of view? Over the years, this has come up regularly in the college classes I teach. These are generally night classes at one of New York City's public universities, and the students range from traditional undergrads to those supporting families, working full-time, or returning to school after living every type of life you can imagine. And they represent every single demographic the city has to offer.

So it is little wonder that when it comes to one of the most polarizing topics in America today, every single view is also represented.

And some of those views include the opposition to abortion. Those students often cite religious beliefs or explain that they see abortion as murder. Some reference membership in historically disenfranchised communities that carry the legacy of eugenics and forced sterilization. Others say they think if you got yourself into this situation then you need to deal with the consequences, and that if a pregnancy is the result of rape then a baby should be adopted out. Many worry about safety and health risks.

Those are all complicated issues to tackle. So these days, before I think the issue will arise, I try to say something along the lines of:

Abortion is a really hard topic to talk about and one without a universal truth. What is true for you might not be true for me, and our truths might coexist and contradict each other. Just like we might both look at the same sunset and I might see it as red and you might see it as orange, we might also just see abortion in totally different ways.

I will share that I believe that keeping abortion legal and accessible benefits everyone, even those who believe they would never get the procedure themselves. So I will continue to support that right even as I try to support your right to your very different beliefs.

I am not going to try to convince you to see abortion like I do. But I am going to challenge myths about abortion, and I am going to try to correct misinformation about the procedure, about who gets abortions, and about why they do.

I don't think it's my place to try to change someone's core views on this or any matter in the classroom. But when some of those views have been shaped, not by a personal moral code, but rather by propaganda or factual distortion, I do believe that once I have owned my perspective, it *is* my place to set the record straight and then to let folks decide for themselves where they actually stand.

NAVIGATING A WORLD THAT INCLUDES PERPETRATORS OF SEXUAL OFFENSES

Back when Dawn and I were in high school, there was no option but to interact with boys who we knew had crossed lines, even if we weren't calling their actions *rape*. Today, things are a little different, and many of us are now trying to figure out how to navigate a world in which perpetrators of sexual violence and harassment have been named in ways like never before, and in which actions that were sometimes tolerated have now been called out as intolerable.

This can be tricky stuff that brings up a lot of questions. For example, while many of us are learning to feel compassion for victims of sexual violence, should we also consider the impact that a lifetime of hostile messages about sexuality has on perpetrators?

Writer Ijeoma Oluo tackles this conflict in *The Estab-lishment*, saying, "I do know this: every single sexual abuser is 100 percent responsible for their actions and there is nobody else to blame than the person who is choosing to violate another person.

"And I also know this: this entire patriarchal society is responsible for every single sexual assault that occurs.

"Both of these things are 100 percent true at the same time, and if we want to battle rape culture—if we want to finally end the brutality that so many women have faced for pretty much the entirety of history—we have to start addressing both of these realities at once."[12]

And they are two realities. Poisonous environments create poisonous humans. The harm caused by those individuals is not lessened because of the harm they may have themselves suffered. But if we don't look at the larger cultural roots of the initial harm done to perpetrators, then we will just be perpetuating a cycle of abuse and pain.

Many have asked, for example, whether those accused of sexual misconduct should be "allowed" to return to their previous positions of prominence. Or even back to any position at all. Is the answer always a hard no? A qualified yes in some cases? Say, if they truly show change and repentance? Or if their original offense didn't rise to a certain level?

It's a tough question, and one a lot of people shy away from answering for a range of reasons, saying they consider themselves "apolitical," or claiming that they don't have opinions about *other people's* issues. I have to admit, I see that as a bit of a dodge. But what I worry about more are the folks who don't take a stance because they feel unqualified to do so, or because they fear public backlash.

Of course, so many women and gender minorities and so many LGBTQ+ folks have been victimized for so long that there is a place for righteous anger, and many of us have run out of passes for unacceptable actions. While that anger is completely warranted and expected, severe punishment isn't the only possible answer. In recent years, more and more schools, and even some criminal justice facilities, are now practicing restorative justice. The goal of restorative justice is to work with the victims and those who have caused the harm to come to a solution, rather than simply handing down punishment. Restorative justice seeks to fix the problem, impose fair punishment, foster understanding, adjust future behavior, and promote healing.

It's also something that a lot more people want than we often imagine. Michelle Alexander, the author of *The New Jim Crow: Mass Incarceration in the Age of Color-blindness*, explained in a 2019 op-ed that when survivors of violence in New York City were given the opportunity to decide if they wanted the person who harmed them incarcerated or in a restorative justice process, 90 percent chose the restorative justice program. She writes, "Ninety percent is a stunning figure considering everything we've been led to believe that survivors actually want. For years, we've been told that victims of violence want nothing more than for the people who hurt them to be locked up and treated harshly . . . The number of people who are interested only in revenge or punishment is greatly exaggerated. After all, survivors are almost never offered real choices. Usually when we ask victims 'Do you want incarceration?' what we're really asking is 'Do you want something or nothing?'"[13]

It can be hard to imagine restorative justice out of an institutional context, but there are examples of people who have harmed others who are attempting to make amends, some by creating accountability circles within their communities, and I believe it is a model that can and should be expanded.

Whatever model we turn to, in order for these discussions to move forward, we need to acknowledge that there isn't an easy answer, and to make room for open and nuanced dialogue about ways to move forward. As egregious as the forces supporting sexual violence are, it should also be possible to speak up on issues like toxic masculinity, rape culture, and gender stereotypes without always taking a hard line that leaves no room for error or empathy. And it should be possible to discuss issues like this publicly without the fear of public shaming.

MOVING PAST HARM

Can people change? A lot of people find this idea suspect. *A tiger can't change its stripes*, after all.

Yet the research doesn't always support such beliefs. Psychologists report that as people become more mature, they often become more conscientious and develop greater emotional stability. Social scientists remind us that life experiences, trauma, and social supports can affect how individuals act in any range of situations. We also know that there are effective psychological and educational interventions that can change behaviors and impact attitudes and beliefs.

Indeed, how could anyone argue against our inhumane prison system of mandatory minimums and draconian sentencing, which favors punishment over rehabilitation, if they didn't think there was any hope for change?

But when it comes to how we respond to abusers and to those who perpetuate hostile sexual climates, it can be very hard to remember this. First off, we are rightly angry and suffering due to the actions of those abusers. Who has the time, energy, or emotional space to do the heavy lifting required to determine which abusers we absolve and which we condemn?

Personally, I have no interest in any redemption story from the boy who forced himself on me at a high school party despite my protests, or from the stranger who put his hand up my skirt as I stood stuck in the middle of a crowd at a concert. I don't care much about the current state of the upstairs neighbor who yelled obscenities at me and my friends daily before raping a girl in the building, or the man who pulled down his pants and asked, "Wanna watch me get off?" as I walked home from a classmate's house one day in middle school. Or of the countless other incidents that are just too numerous to list.

But I also have decided that there can be space for forgiveness when space is warranted. In particular, I found space for a high school ex, who at the time really wasn't all that good to me. He would have gotten a lot of checks on the survey about unhealthy relationships that I now give to my teen students in health class. But he reached out to me years later. It was during a bleak time, shortly after my partner's sudden death, and I was deep in grief and trying to figure out how I would move forward and raise our children alone. My ex wrote, "If it gives any semblance of order to the universe for you, please know that remorse and shame about acting like such a jerk during that period of time has formed the basis of my adult life, which I have tried to spend being a decent human being."

And you know what? It did give a semblance of order.

What I knew about his life back then, a dark history of abandonment and abuse and alcoholism, and what I knew about his life now, as a father of two, a foster parent, and a social worker who is active in a range of communities, meant something. It felt like he was, in fact, the decent human being he was trying to be.

I decided that making space for him was a way to heal, to move forward, to let go of an identity that no longer fit—a way to acknowledge that people are not always who they once were, and that many who harm have been deeply harmed themselves. His acknowledgment and taking responsibility for his actions felt authentic, and that counted for something with me.

I'm not suggesting anyone else offer exoneration when doing so feels onerous, when words seem hollow, when actions seem insincere. But I am suggesting that we make it possible to find forgiveness when this is the right path, and when doing so embodies the kind of person that we want to be and the kind of world that we want to create.

THE PROBLEM WITH PUBLIC SHAMING

There is a reason so many people fear public shaming. Shame can be an incredibly powerful motivator, and it is something many people respond strongly to, especially if they grew up hearing *you should be ashamed of yourself* or *shame on you*, or if they fear criticism and social rejection.

According to professor and self-help icon Brené Brown, shame is also closely linked to perfectionism, since people believe that if they are perfect, they can avoid being targeted over perceived missteps. So plenty of folks try to avoid shame by presenting an impossibly curated version of themselves in the hopes that doing so will deflect criticism.[14]

That's bad enough. But what happens when we impose such notions on others? What happens when we expect our allies to meet our own impossible standards, and then they fail? One common result is that we reduce people to their real or perceived missteps.

While shame has been used as a tool to police societal norms, particularly around sexual behavior, for millennia, contemporary methods for public humiliation often look different and can happen more quickly and universally online. "Doxing," the practice of exposing people's private information online or rallying online "vigilantism" against someone, has been used with increasing frequency as a way to punish people, often in ways disproportionate to the original offense. Or, more accurately, to the *perceived* offense, since there are plenty of instances where the wrong person is targeted or people are targeted for things they never actually did. And, of course, these methods can be used against people whose only "offense" is crossing some perceived sexual boundary, such as women and girls who are deemed too "slutty," men whose masculinity is questioned, or anyone known or perceived to be LGBTQ+.

So how do we reconcile our need to speak up when we see wrongdoing with the need to temper a culture of public shaming, particularly of those who could be potential allies?

In many cases, taking criticisms out of the public eye could go a long way toward helping the situation. That might mean messaging someone privately online or, in person, cutting someone off mid–offensive joke, but saving the real task taking for a private moment. We might also pause before condemning those who choose to forgive, and examine whether we're confusing forgiveness with acceptance of harmful behavior. Could forgiveness also be a form of personal recovery?

Of course, a lot of what prevents us from forgiving is a sense that if we forgive we have somehow "lost." Many of us feel extremely competitive, even in our interpersonal relationships. The result is that when disagreements arise, our response is to look for weak spots in an argument and then strategize for our "win," rather than actually listening to what the other person is saying. This, combined with the defensiveness so many people exhibit when they feel under attack, makes it almost impossible to really hear other people in an argument. But in order to build bridges and move forward, listening is crucial.

This formula—talking to people individually, listening to them without attacking, and avoiding public humiliation—isn't intended to keep people from naming offenders who need to be named. Rather, it's meant to provide a way for us to distinguish between public shaming and naming someone as a matter of public safety. The former is often designed to do nothing more than humiliate for sport, or deflect attention from our own missteps. Just think of a time you misspoke and had someone call you out on it in front of a room full of people, compared to a time you later got a private text or email about something you had said. Which context gave you greater space to acknowledge your mistakes and learn from them?

There are myriad studies demonstrating that to increase happiness, we should practice gratitude and forgiveness and work to develop a growth mind-set, a term that refers to the ability to see beyond absolutes and to allow for the possibility of human growth and change. It seems to me that we must hold people and systems accountable for unacceptable actions, but if we present outrage and calls for punishment as the only acceptable responses, especially in a racially unfair judicial system, then we risk denying the very people who have been harmed the possibility of finding peace, and we hinder our ability to learn and teach others along the way.

SEXUALITY SPOTLIGHT: FEELING SAFE IN THE WORLD

Depending on their identities or experiences, people will feel sexually safe in the world to different degrees. Cishet men simply tend to feel the most sexually safe in the world. Cis women and sexual and gender minority folks tend to feel less so. Then, regardless of their gender identities or sexual orientations, survivors of sexual violence often feel the least safe. And when you factor in a person's race, it is crucial to understand that safety of all kinds is just a different thing for white people, who often experience a greater sense of safety in everyday life, overall, than do people of color. Measures intended to help people feel safe are often only conceived of with one target group, say, women, in mind, without considering the impact of factors like sexual orientation, race, or ability. So it is important to view the concept of safety through an intersectional lens.

But what does it mean to be sexually safe? For a lot of people, what makes us feel protected and comfortable, versus what seems like a threat, is often off base, since it can be really hard to separate which of our feelings of risk are the result of stepping out of our comfort zones and which are directly related to actual danger.

In large part that is because of how safety, and particularly sexual safety, is taught. Lisa Factora-Borchers, the author of *Dear Sister: Letters From Survivors of Sexual Violence*, explains that when people discuss how to achieve more sexual safety, they aren't usually talking about challenging hostile climates. Rather, they're generally focused on a state of "not-being." Not being harassed. Not being assaulted. Not being raped. As she writes in an article for *Bitch* magazine, safety is often understood as the absence of a violent or "terrible" experience.[15]

However, like so much else, this messaging shifts our focus from real risks (like getting raped at a party by an acquaintance) to perceived risks (like being raped by a stranger as you walk home after dark). When we focus so much on the state of "not being violated" and then emphasize that danger lurks any time you leave your comfort zone (for example, your school, workplace, or community where members are known to you), it makes it easier to blame both survivors and perpetrators for some personal failure than to challenge the larger, more complicated forces at play.

What's the Background?

Traditionally, potential victims of sexual violence have been told that they are responsible for preventing attacks. Women have often heard things like: don't go out too late, have a buddy system, carry a rape whistle, carry mace, avoid this neighborhood or that, learn self-defense. Don't get drunk, flirt, or invite men home unless you plan on having sex with them. Folks in the LGBTQ+ community have long been warned to hide their identities, their relationships, and basically, any evidence of who they are, and are advised that simply by being visibly queer they are inviting attacks.

Starting in the 1960s, activists began to challenge some of this logic, and by the next decade, a series of events began to emerge, like antiviolence marches in the early 1970s, a 1973 protest in San Francisco against pornography, and a 1975 Philadelphia rally following the late-night murder of a woman who had been walking home alone. These came to be known as "Take Back the Night" gatherings, and events under this name continue to this day.

However, the Take Back the Night model has been criticized over the years for a range of reasons, including that it historically excluded men and trans women, and that it focused on the classic "stranger danger" rape scenario while ignoring many more common forms of sexual violence. In recent years, some branches of the organization have addressed these issues. Others remain "women only," for example.

Of course, Take Back the Night was not the only movement dealing with sexual safety. Self-defense classes have been around since the turn of the last century, when women began working more in the public sector. And for many decades, college campuses, and an increasing number of communities, have offered safe-ride or safe-walk programs to accompany women and LGBTQ+ folks home after dark.

Why It's a Problem

It's a huge burden to ask potential victims of sexual violence to protect themselves from assaults. Rather, the onus for protection should be a collective endeavor, not just the responsibility of the women and gender and sexual minorities who are most often the victims. Groups like Men Can Stop Rape were at the forefront of addressing this issue, and today more and more people are raising a call to action for men. For example, Melissa Batchelor Warnke suggests at Refinery29 that in the quest to be allies, men should begin by asking themselves some complicated questions about sexual violence. Among the questions she suggests are:

- ▸ Growing up, what did you learn about rape, sexual violence, and sexual harassment?
- ▸ How were those topics discussed among your friends when you were a teen? How have those conversations stayed the same or changed over the years?
- ▸ Have there been times when you were uncomfortable with a sexual situation?
- ▸ Have there been times when you could have

made someone else uncomfortable in a sexual situation?

▸ Do you think people should ask for sexual consent?

▸ Do you have people in your world who have crossed sexual boundaries or committed sexual offenses?

▸ If so, how has that impacted your interactions or relationship?[16]

Men can also work to be empathetic toward victims and to speak out against harmful behavior. Plus, they can fight for policies that support women who are survivors of sexual assault, and they can vote for politicians who work toward promoting a sexually safe climate.

Nevertheless, we must also remember that one person's notion of safety is often not another's. Our understanding of what is safe is rarely defined by those who are most marginalized. What is considered *safe* is typically safe for a very specific audience. For example, when white people wonder if a neighborhood is "safe," this can really be code for wondering if the neighborhood is predominantly Black or Latinx. Yet when white people gentrify neighborhoods that have historically been home to people of color, their presence can make the original residents feel less safe, since white newcomers are known to call the cops over things like loud music or teens hanging out in front of their buildings. Recently, this has happened for a list of "offenses" that includes, but is by no means limited to, a little girl selling cookies, a family barbecuing, a man entering his own home, a boy walking through a deli wearing his school backpack, friends sitting at Starbucks, and a college student sleeping on a lounge couch. Whatever the motivation, in addition to the trauma this causes, the result can be disastrously dangerous confrontations.

That whole idea of involving authorities can be fraught on many levels. For some people, involving authorities is an automatic default and something they feel comfortable doing. For others, it is nothing they would ever invoke. This came up for me once while volunteering at an event for my preteen daughter. At some point that morning, I'd noticed a man standing in a hallway by the kitchen where another mom and I were preparing food with some of the kids. After a little time passed, the other mom politely asked him if he was with our group. He mumbled something in reply. So I interjected and said firmly, "Excuse me, who are you here with?"

He then walked into the kitchen and picked up the other mom's bag from a chair where it had been perched. "Where did you get this?" he asked her, ignoring my previous question.

"Oh, online," she answered.

"Okay," I said, "I think it's time for you to leave."

He kept asking about the bag. "Where online? How much was it?"

"Not very much," she said. "Can I have my bag, please?"

He kept holding it.

At that point, I said to him loudly, "It doesn't sound like you're here with the event, so you really need to leave." He stayed put. So I said, "If you don't leave, I'm going to have to ask the security guard to walk you out."

He stroked the bag a few times, put it down, and then made his way to the door. In that moment I felt good. I had showed my daughter that she didn't have to let creepy men intimidate her, that she could speak up in uncomfortable situations, and that she didn't always have to be nice.

Score one for mom's empowering life lesson.

Then the other mom turned to me. "You know we get people with mental illness in here a lot. They just wander in, and I think we really need to be compassionate. I never like to threaten someone who may be unstable with security guards or police. Usually people just need a bit of time to leave."

Right. My life lesson didn't feel so good after that. But I was torn, because in the moment when we're dealing with threatening situations, our first job is to take care of ourselves and those around us. What if there isn't time to assess whether bias is causing our reaction?

So I would say, use moments when you're feeling perfectly secure (like now, reading this book) to consider the long history of judgment and myth that can color some of our gut reactions and to ask where you might project cultural biases onto situations that are unlikely to be risky, while ignoring the actual risks presented by actions that are dangerous but normalized. For white people in particular, it can be incredibly helpful to consider doing some antiracism training and to read up on racial bias. Sociologist Robin DiAngelo has done some really important work on this subject, and her recent book, *White Fragility: Why It's So Hard for White People to Talk About Racism,* is a great place to start. The more you do this work out of the moment, the more you will have a better perspective in the moment.

Where We're at Now

Women and LGBTQ+ folks of all genders tend to grow up with the threat of sexual violence hanging over them at every turn. So it's understandable that people who have lived under a cloud of danger will try to employ different strategies to feel secure.

For some, that means walking a different route than you might otherwise take, faking a phone call to a friend when feeling uncomfortable, jogging outdoors without headphones, paying for a taxi, or not traveling alone.

That being said, we also need to ask ourselves if our perception of a threat is based on our own biases, and if it is, what could be the outcomes of our actions. Because it is one thing to jog without music so you feel alert, but it's a whole different story if you're a white person calling the cops simply based on the presence of a person of color in a space where you didn't expect them, while writing off increasingly hostile texts to your daughter's cell phone from a boy at school because you see that behavior as normal crush stuff.

This is a conflict with no easy answer. On the one hand, we want to intervene when need be. On the other, there are plenty of people who do jump in to "help" as bystanders, trying to do the right thing and stand up in what feels like a dangerous situation . . . but actually they *do* make things worse by acting out of prejudiced or faulty information.

So while I want people to feel empowered and secure enough to stand up for others as a bystander, this should not be done at the expense of another person's safety. Though it might be tempting to pretend that racial or other bias doesn't affect our perceptions of risk and when to intervene, clearly this is an issue that many people face. Addressing implicit biases is not something anyone can do overnight, but beginning this work will better equip folks to identify *real* risks and to intervene in these instances, instead of in those where danger is imagined and based on stereotypes.

WHAT IT ALL COMES DOWN TO

Contemplating past actions with a fresh eye and a new viewpoint can bring up a lot of emotions, and you may feel embarrassed, guilty, and scared by a new understanding of your conduct.

Or doing so can cause you to realize that you were the target of behaviors that you haven't before seen as problematic, and it's common to go through phases of rationalizing and self-doubt.

Reconciling these things isn't straightforward. Healing your wounds or changing your behavior won't happen in one easy step. Neither will tackling a hostile culture. But know that if you choose to tackle that culture, you won't be alone.

The journey to good sexual citizenship starts on the individual level, but it then extends to our communities, and from there it can use our collective strength to continue on a national level to take down the structures that have so long supported harmful expressions of sexuality. Because while these structures are enduring and might seem indestructible, like so much of the motivation that drives harm, at their base, they are really quite fragile.

BECOMING A GOOD SEXUAL CITIZEN

After you have a better sense of your own views and values, you can break down your behaviors into four distinct areas: those you want to tackle or change, those you want to strive for, those that you are still trying to figure out, and those you have mastered.

Here are some examples of what that might that look.

TACKLE:

▸ How you contribute to, or perpetuate, a hostile sexual environment.
▸ What gender stereotypes you hold.
▸ Your instinct to blame or shame others for their experiences and choices.
▸ Your use of pressure or coercion for sex.
▸ Your ability to be truthful about your desires.
▸ Internalized and externalized trans- and homophobia, sexism, and misogyny.

STRIVE FOR:

▸ Consent in all your sexual encounters.
▸ Pleasure for both (all) partners.
▸ Safer sex.
▸ Mutuality in all sexual encounters.
▸ Working to actively intervene when you see something that deserves action.

> ▸ Sex that is always wanted by all parties and enjoyed by all parties.

EXAMINE:

- ▸ What happens before, during, and after your sexual encounters.
- ▸ Whether your treatment of partners differs if they are casual or committed.
- ▸ How substances affect your sexual experiences.
- ▸ Your gendered interactions.
- ▸ Your communication style.
- ▸ Whether you are repeating patterns you'd rather break.
- ▸ How your past experiences may impact your current sexual expression.

MASTERED:

- ▸ Where do you already feel confident?
- ▸ Are there ways in which you can use what you're naturally good at to help improve your behavior in other areas of your life?
- ▸ Are any of your current skills things you had to work hard to develop?
- ▸ How did you develop those skills? Can you imagine developing them in other areas as well?

Now try to fill that out for yourself.

Behaviors and beliefs I want to:

Tackle: ....

....

....

Strive for: ....

....

....

Examine: ....

....

....

Have mastered: ....

....

....

Consider which areas stand out, which you think will be easiest to address, and which will be hardest. Are there any you can work on alone? Are there some you will need to work on with others? Which areas are you least eager to address? Why? Which do you think will just take minor changes? Where are you excelling? Why is that easy for you?

If, for example, you are consistent in practicing safer sex but can't communicate honestly with a partner about pleasure, is there a way to transfer that first skill to the second area? Or, if you think you might contribute to victim blaming in your community, but you have positive sexual experiences yourself, what could drive your need to judge others so harshly when they have negative experiences?

Identifying your strengths, weaknesses, and inconsistencies can be eye-opening and can also help you live in a manner that feels more authentic and ethical.

When we work toward healthier interpersonal experiences, we will also see demonstrable changes in our larger communities.

BUILDING
SOMETHING BETTER

Sometimes when I am feeling demoralized about the state of the world, I look at those charts demonstrating how many more people globally have access to clean water or are no longer living in abject poverty than were in the not-too-distant past. I often find myself searching for similar reassurances of progress when I'm worried about the current sexual climate and fear for the future.

In moments like these it is helpful for me to remember how far we've come since I was a kid. I was reminded of that not too long ago when I tried to watch the 1984 movie *Sixteen Candles* with my then twelve-year-old daughter. *Sixteen Candles* tells the story of an awkward teen girl in love with a popular older boy who has no idea she exists. I saw it maybe five years after it came out, and I had remembered it as a classic '80s comedy. So one evening I put it on. But as we sat watching together, a lot of things came into focus. Blatant racism was traded for laughs. Girls' bodies were alternately mocked and sexualized. Rape was presented as a lucky score for a boy fortunate enough to land a girl so drunk she didn't even know what was happening. Boys will be boys and girls will be dispensable and all.

I kept pausing the movie to dissect whatever problematic scene was playing out, but I hardly had to do that. My daughter could clearly see for herself why the movie was so problematic, and at one point when I paused the movie to ask if she understood what was going on, she said, "Well, he can't really touch her if she's drunk." My daughter was in middle school at the time, and this was clear to her. I'm pretty sure that's not only because she got that message at home. It really feels like culture has changed on this front. For one thing, I don't think I formally learned about consent as a concept until my graduate school human sexuality program—and I had been a women's studies major in college, not to mention a regular attendee at antirape rallies!

Needless to say, it's not only my own children who remind me how far we've come. I feel encouraged every time I see people actively dismantling rape culture and challenging toxic masculinity. And I am emboldened daily by the fights for comprehensive sexuality education, reproductive rights, sexual freedom, and expressions of identity that so many brave folks are undertaking.

I need to hold on to these reminders every time yet another revelation of sexual cruelty or contempt or even just clumsiness emerges. I mean, how can we not be angry over our ongoing culture of sexual violence, or disillusioned by political inaction on the matter, or overwhelmingly sad that so many people still have to navigate so much hostility and so many dangerous spaces? While we may be in a one step forward, two steps back era, those forward steps? Well, they count for a lot.

There is no doubt that things have changed. There is also no doubt that there is still room for so much growth. But with this book, I hope that I have given you a clear idea of where we are coming from, what we are up against, and how we can best direct our energies to help build a healthier sexual world for us all.

Because really, whether you have been the target of sexual aggression and violence or have perpetuated it yourself, whether you have played both roles at different times, or whether you have miraculously managed to avoid being significantly impacted by this climate altogether, it is possible for all of us to heal wounds, to grow better communities, and to be and to raise good sexual citizens in the world.

So with that, here's to a safer sexual landscape for us all!

ACKNOWLEDGMENTS

This project would not have been possible without everyone at Cleis Press, particularly Hannah Bennett, who edited my work so skillfully, and Allyson Fields and Meghan Kilduff, who helped make this book a reality. I am so fortunate to have a friend like Emily Mahon who designed my amazing cover. I am deeply thankful to the many sides of my extended family for their endless support, encouragement, and babysitting (and to my kids for letting themselves be sat when I wrote!), and to my parents, who allowed me to follow my own winding path. I am incredibly grateful to the early (and not so early) readers of the manuscript, including my partner Joshua Mendelsohn, as well as Anne Conway, Jonathan Friedrichs, and Renee Harleston. I am also so honored to have been able to work professionally with such inspiring colleagues and students. Finally, credit also has to go to the public schools of Vancouver, BC, and the solid sex education I got there growing up.

NOTES

INTRODUCTION

1 Chauncey, George. *Gay New York: Gender, Urban Culture, and the Makings of the Gay Male World, 1890–1940*. New York: Basic Books, 1994.

CHAPTER 1

1 Fine, Cordelia. *Testosterone Rex: Myths of Sex, Science, and Society*. New York: W. W. Norton, 2018.

2 APA Task Force on Gender Identity, Gender Variance, and Intersex Conditions. "Answers to Your Questions About Individuals With Intersex Conditions." American Psychological Association. 2006. Accessed February 12, 2019. https://www.apa.org/topics/lgbt/intersex.pdf.

3 Wanamaker, Lynne Marie. "Say Something Superhero Field Guide: A Manual for Eliminating Interpersonal Violence." 2015. Accessed February 12, 2019. https://safepass.org/wp-content/uploads/2018/09/SS-FieldGuide-2015.pdf.

4 Penny, Laurie. *Unspeakable Things: Sex, Lies and Revolution*. London: Bloomsbury, 2015.

5 Jost, John T., and Aaron C. Kay. "Exposure to Benevolent Sexism and Complementary Gender Stereotypes: Consequences

for Specific and Diffuse Forms of System Justification." *Journal of Personality and Social Psychology* 88, no. 3 (March 2005): 498–509. Accessed February 12, 2019. doi:10.2139/ssrn. 386981.

6   Becker, Julia C., and Stephen C. Wright. "Yet Another Dark Side of Chivalry: Benevolent Sexism Undermines and Hostile Sexism Motivates Collective Action for Social Change." *Journal of Personality and Social Psychology* 101, no. 1 (July 2011): 62–77. Accessed February 12, 2019. doi:10.1037/a0022615.

7   United States. United States Department of Justice. Office of Justice Programs. "Practical Implications of Current Domestic Violence Research." By Andrew R. Klein. Washington, D.C.: U.S. Department of Justice, 2009.

8   Valenti, Jessica. "'Rejection Killings' Need to Be Tracked." Medium.com. November 21, 2018. Accessed March 5, 2019. https://medium.com/s/jessica-valenti/revenge-killings-need-to-be-tracked-37e78a1cf6ce.

9   Thériault, Anne. "Why the Men's Rights Movement Is Garbage." *HuffPost Canada*. May 28, 2014. Accessed February 12, 2019. https://www.huffingtonpost.ca/anne-theriault-/mens-rights-movement_b_5049999.html.

10 Masters, N. Tatiana, Erin Casey, Elizabeth A. Wells, and Diane M. Morrison. "Sexual Scripts Among Young Heterosexually Active Men and Women: Continuity and Change." *Journal of Sex Research* 50, no. 5 (July 2013): 409–20. Accessed February 12, 2019. doi:10.1080/00224499.2012.661102.

11 Struckman Johnson, Cindy, David Struckman Johnson, and Peter B. Anderson. "Tactics of Sexual Coercion: When Men and Women Won't Take No for an Answer." *Journal of Sex Research* 40, no. 1 (2003): 76–86. doi:10.1080/00224490309552168.

12 Gruber, James E., and Susan Fineran. "Comparing the Impact of Bullying and Sexual Harassment Victimization on the Mental and Physical Health of Adolescents." *Sex Roles* 59, no. 1–2 (2008): 1–13. doi:10.1007/s11199-008-9431-5.

13 Spector, Nicole. "How Sexual Harassment Damages a Woman's Health." NBCNews.com. October 13, 2017. Accessed February

15, 2019. https://www.nbcnews.com/better/health/hidden-health-effects-sexual-harassment-ncna810416.

CHAPTER 2

1   Coontz, Stephanie. "The Nostalgia Trap." *Harvard Business Review*. April 11, 2018. Accessed February 12, 2019. https://hbr.org/2018/04/the-nostalgia-trap.

2   "Residential Schools in Canada." *The Canadian Encyclopedia*. Accessed April 28, 2019. https://www.thecanadianencyclopedia.ca/en/article/residential-schools.

3   Ko, Lisa. "Unwanted Sterilization and Eugenics Programs in the United States." PBS. January 29, 2016. Accessed April 28, 2019. http://www.pbs.org/independentlens/blog/unwanted-sterilization-and-eugenics-programs-in-the-united-states/.

4   Pasko, Lisa. "Damaged Daughters: The History of Girls' Sexuality and the Juvenile Justice System." *Journal of Criminal Law & Criminology* 100, no. 3 (Summer 2010): 1099–130. Accessed February 12, 2019. https://scholarlycommons.law.northwestern.edu/cgi/viewcontent.cgi?referer=https://www.google.com/&httpsredir=1&article=7370&context=jclc.

5   Almog, Shulamit, and Karin Carmit Yefet. "Sexuality, Gender and Law—Part I: Regulating Sexual Economics." *The Hebrew University Law Journal* 43, no. 2 (November 2015): 385–437. Accessed February 12, 2019. https://www.researchgate.net/publication/290607399_mynywt_mgdr_wmspt_-_hlq_m'qlqlt_myn'_l'klklt_myn'_Sexuality_Gender_and_Law-_Part_I_From_Dyseconomic's_to_Sexual_Economics.

6   Hare, Breeanna, and Lisa Rose. "Where Rapists Can Gain Parental Rights." CNN. November 17, 2016. Accessed February 12, 2019. https://www.cnn.com/2016/11/17/health/parental-rights-rapists-explainer/index.html.

7   Martindale, Mike. "Michigan Rapist Gets Joint Custody." *Detroit News*. October 10, 2017. Accessed February 12, 2019. https://www.detroitnews.com/story/news/local/michigan/2017/10/06/rape-victim-attacker-joint-child-custody/106374256/.

8   United States. Centers for Disease Control and Prevention. Division of Vital Statistics. *Contraceptive Methods Women Have Ever Used: United States, 1982–2010*. By Kimberly Daniels, William Mosher, and Jo Jones. February 14, 2013. Accessed February 12, 2019. https://www.cdc.gov/nchs/data/nhsr/nhsr062.pdf.

9   "Louisiana: Repeal 'Crime Against Nature' Laws." Human Rights Watch. April 24, 2014. Accessed February 15, 2019. https://www.hrw.org/news/2014/04/22/louisiana-repeal-crime-against-nature-laws.

10 Savage, Lisa L. "Change in Sexual Behavior With Provision of No-Cost Contraception." *Obstetrics & Gynecology* 124, no. 1 (2014): 163–64. doi:10.1097/aog.0000000000000359.

11 Hill, Catherine, and Holly Kearl. *Crossing the Line: Sexual Harassment at School*. Report. American Association of University Women. November 2011. Accessed February 12, 2019. https://www.aauw.org/files/2013/02/Crossing-the-Line-Sexual-Harassment-at-School.pdf.

12 Vrangalova, Zhana, Rachel E. Bukberg, and Gerulf Rieger. "Birds of a Feather? Not When It Comes to Sexual Permissiveness." *Journal of Social and Personal Relationships* 31, no. 1 (2013): 93–113. Accessed February 12, 2019. doi:10.1177/0265407513487638.

13 Kreager, Derek A., and Jeremy Staff. "The Sexual Double Standard and Adolescent Peer Acceptance." *Social Psychology Quarterly* 72, no. 2 (2009): 143–64. doi:10.1177/019027250907200205.

14 Sewell, Kelsey K., Larissa A. McGarrity, and Donald S. Strassberg. "Sexual Behavior, Definitions of Sex, and the Role of Self-Partner Context Among Lesbian, Gay, and Bisexual Adults." *The Journal of Sex Research* 54, no. 7 (2016): 825–31. doi:10.1080/00224499.2016.1249331.

15 Herbenick, Debby, Jessamyn Bowling, Tsung-Chieh (Jane) Fu, Brian Dodge, Lucia Guerra-Reyes, and Stephanie Sanders. "Sexual Diversity in the United States: Results From a Nationally Representative Probability Sample of Adult Women and Men." *PLOS One* 12, no. 7 (2017). doi:10.1371/journal.pone.0181198.

16 Sewell, Kelsey K., and Donald S. Strassberg. "How Do Heterosexual Undergraduate Students Define Having Sex? A New

Approach to an Old Question." *The Journal of Sex Research* 52, no. 5 (2014): 507–16. doi:10.1080/00224499.2014.888389.

17 Kettrey, Heather Hensman. "'Bad Girls' Say No and 'Good Girls' Say Yes: Sexual Subjectivity and Participation in Undesired Sex During Heterosexual College Hookups." *Sexuality & Culture* 22, no. 3 (2018): 685–705. doi:10.1007/s12119-018-9498-2.

18 Wood, Jessica R., Alexander McKay, Tina Komarnicky, and Robin R. Milhausen. "Was It Good for You Too?: An Analysis of Gender Differences in Oral Sex Practices and Pleasure Ratings Among Heterosexual Canadian University Students." *The Canadian Journal of Human Sexuality* 25, no. 1 (2016): 21–29. doi:10.3138/cjhs.251-a2.

19 Lewis, Ruth, and Cicely Marston. "Oral Sex, Young People, and Gendered Narratives of Reciprocity." *The Journal of Sex Research* 53, no. 7 (2016): 776–87. doi:10.1080/00224499.2015.1117564.

20 Traister, Rebecca. "Why Sex That's Consensual Can Still Be Bad. And Why We're Not Talking About It." *The Cut.* October 20, 2015. Accessed February 12, 2019. https://www.thecut.com/2015/10/why-consensual-sex-can-still-be-bad.html.

21 Garcia, Justin R., Elisabeth A. Lloyd, Kim Wallen, and Helen E. Fisher. "Variation in Orgasm Occurrence by Sexual Orientation in a Sample of U.S. Singles." *The Journal of Sexual Medicine* 11, no. 11 (2014): 2645–652. doi:10.1111/jsm.12669.

22 Ghodsee, Kristen Rogheh. *Why Women Have Better Sex Under Socialism: And Other Arguments for Economic Independence.* New York: Nation Books, 2018.

23 Orenstein, Peggy. *Girls & Sex: Navigating the Complicated New Landscape.* New York: Harper, 2017.

24 Lofrisco, Barbara M. "Female Sexual Pain Disorders and Cognitive Behavioral Therapy." *Journal of Sex Research* 48, no. 6 (2011): 573–79. doi:10.1080/00224499.2010.540682.

25 Herbenick, Debby, Vanessa Schick, Stephanie A. Sanders, Michael Reece, and J. Dennis Fortenberry. "Pain Experienced During Vaginal and Anal Intercourse With Other Sex Partners: Findings From a Nationally Representative Probability Study in the United

States." *The Journal of Sexual Medicine* 12, no. 4 (2015): 1040–051. doi:10.1111/jsm.12841.

26 "When Sex Is Painful." American College of Obstetricians and Gynecologists. September 2017. Accessed February 12, 2019. https://www.acog.org/Patients/FAQs/When-Sex-Is-Painful.

27 Reed, Barbara D., Hope K. Haefner, Siobán D. Harlow, Daniel W. Gorenflo, and Ananda Sen. "Reliability and Validity of Self-Reported Symptoms for Predicting Vulvodynia." *Obstetrics & Gynecology* 108, no. 4 (2006): 906–13. doi:10.1097/01. aog.0000237102.70485.5d.

28 "Pain With Penetration." The North American Menopause Society. Accessed February 12, 2019. http://www.menopause.org/ for-women/sexual-health-menopause-online/sexual-problems-at-midlife/pain-with-penetration.

29 Bober, Sharon L., and Veronica Sanchez Varela. "Sexuality in Adult Cancer Survivors: Challenges and Intervention." *Journal of Clinical Oncology* 30, no. 30 (2012): 3712–719. doi:10.1200/ jco.2012.41.7915.

30 Weinberger, James M., Justin Houman, Ashley T. Caron, and Jennifer Anger. "Female Sexual Dysfunction: A Systematic Review of Outcomes Across Various Treatment Modalities." *Sexual Medicine Reviews*, 2018. doi:10.1016/j.sxmr.2017.12.004.

31 Weinberger, James M., Justin Houman, Ashley T. Caron, Devin N. Patel, Avi S. Baskin, A. Lenore Ackerman, Karyn S. Eilber, and Jennifer T. Anger. "Female Sexual Dysfunction and the Placebo Effect." *Obstetrics & Gynecology* 132, no. 2 (2018): 453–58. doi:10.1097/aog.0000000000002733.

32 Cook, Hera. *The Long Sexual Revolution: English Women, Sex, and Contraception, 1800–1975*. Oxford: Oxford University Press, 2007.

33 Zakaria, Rafia. "Did the Sexual Revolution Liberate Women?" *Dame*. December 9, 2017. Accessed February 12, 2019. https:// www.damemagazine.com/2016/11/07/did-sexual-revolution-liberate-women/.

34 "GSS General Social Survey." GSS General Social Survey. Accessed February 12, 2019. http://gss.norc.org/.

35 Twenge, Jean M., Ryne A. Sherman, and Brooke E. Wells. "Changes in American Adults' Sexual Behavior and Attitudes, 1972–2012." *Archives of Sexual Behavior* 44, no. 8 (2015): 2273–285. doi:10.1007/s10508-015-0540-2.

36 Conroy, Scott. "Premarital Sex: Almost Everyone's Doing It." CBS News. December 20, 2006. Accessed February 12, 2019. https://www.cbsnews.com/news/premarital-sex-almost-everyones-doing-it/.

37 Fisher, Maryanne L., Kerry Worth, Justin R. Garcia, and Tami Meredith. "Feelings of Regret Following Uncommitted Sexual Encounters in Canadian University Students." *Culture, Health & Sexuality* 14, no. 1 (2012): 45–57. doi:10.1080/13691058.2011.619579.

38 Campbell, Anne. "The Morning After the Night Before." *Human Nature* 19, no. 2 (2008): 157–73. doi:10.1007/s12110-008-9036-2.

39 "Women Have Not Adapted to Casual Sex, Research Shows." *ScienceDaily*. June 26, 2008. Accessed February 12, 2019. https://www.sciencedaily.com/releases/2008/06/080625092023.htm.

40 Fisher, Maryanne L., Kerry Worth, Justin R. Garcia, and Tami Meredith. "Feelings of Regret Following Uncommitted Sexual Encounters in Canadian University Students." *Culture, Health & Sexuality* 14, no. 1 (2012): 45–57. doi:10.1080/13691058.2011.619579.

41 Armstrong, Elizabeth A., Paula England, and Alison C. K. Fogarty. "Accounting for Women's Orgasm and Sexual Enjoyment in College Hookups and Relationships." *American Sociological Review* 77, no. 3 (2012): 435–62. doi:10.1177/0003122412445802.

42 Churchland, Patricia S., and Piotr Winkielman. "Modulating Social Behavior With Oxytocin: How Does It Work? What Does It Mean?" *Hormones and Behavior* 61, no. 3 (2012): 392–99. doi:10.1016/j.yhbeh.2011.12.003.

43 Bersamin, Melina M., Byron L. Zamboanga, Seth J. Schwartz, M. Brent Donnellan, Monika Hudson, Robert S. Weisskirch, Su Yeong Kim, V. Bede Agocha, Susan Krauss Whitbourne, and S. Jean Caraway. "Risky Business: Is There an Association Between Casual Sex and Mental Health Among Emerging Adults?" *The Journal of Sex Research* 51, no. 1 (2013): 43–51. doi:10.1080/00224499.2013.772088.

44 Twenge, Jean M., Ryne A. Sherman, and Brooke E. Wells. "Declines in Sexual Frequency Among American Adults, 1989–2014." *Archives of Sexual Behavior* 46, no. 8 (2017): 2389–401. doi:10.1007/s10508-017-0953-1.

45 United States. Centers for Disease Control and Prevention. Division of Adolescent and School Health. "Trends in the Prevalence of Sexual Behaviors and HIV Testing National YRBS: 1991–2017." Accessed February 12, 2019. https://www.cdc.gov/healthyyouth/data/yrbs/pdf/trends/2017_sexual_trend_yrbs.pdf.

CHAPTER 3

1 Gay, Roxane. *Not That Bad: Dispatches From Rape Culture.* New York: Harper Perennial, 2018.

2 Gross, Jane. "Combating Rape on Campus in a Class on Sexual Consent." *The New York Times.* September 25, 1993. Accessed February 12, 2019. https://www.nytimes.com/1993/09/25/us/combating-rape-on-campus-in-a-class-on-sexual-consent.html?pagewanted=all.

3 Saltman, Bethany, on Michael Barbaro's podcast (interview). "Sexual Harassment's Toll on Careers." *The Daily.* May 3, 2018.

4 "Dear Colleague letter." Russlynn Ali. April 4, 2011. Office of the Assistant Secretary, U.S. Department of Education, Washington, DC.

5 SB-967 Student safety: Sexual assault., § California Senate Bill No. 967 (2013–2014).

6 "Scope of the Problem: Statistics." RAINN. Accessed February 12, 2019. https://www.rainn.org/statistics/scope-problem.

7 Morgan, Rachel E., and Grace Kena. "Criminal Victimization, 2016: Revised." U.S. Department of Justice. October 2018. Accessed February 13, 2019. https://www.bjs.gov/content/pub/pdf/cv16re.pdf.

8 "Sexual Offences in England and Wales: Year Ending March 2017." Office for National Statistics. Accessed February 13, 2019. https://www.ons.gov.uk/peoplepopulationandcommunity/

crimeandjustice/articles/sexualoffencesinenglandandwales/
yearendingmarch2017.

9   Foubert, John, and Johnathan T. Newberry. "Effects of Two
    Versions of an Empathy-Based Rape Prevention Program on
    Fraternity Men's Survivor Empathy, Attitudes, and Behavioral
    Intent to Commit Rape or Sexual Assault." *Journal of College
    Student Development* 47, no. 2 (2006): 133–48. doi:10.1353/
    csd.2006.0016.

10 Suarez, Eliana, and Tahany M. Gadalla. "Stop Blaming the Victim: A
    Meta-Analysis on Rape Myths." *Journal of Interpersonal Violence*
    25, no. 11 (2010): 2010–035. doi:10.1177/0886260509354503.

11 Taschler, Miriam, and Keon West. "Contact With Counter-
    Stereotypical Women Predicts Less Sexism, Less Rape Myth
    Acceptance, Less Intention to Rape (in Men) and Less Projected
    Enjoyment of Rape (in Women)." *Sex Roles* 76, no. 7–8 (2016):
    473–84. doi:10.1007/s11199-016-0679-x.

12 McClelland, Sara I. "Intimate Justice: A Critical Analysis of
    Sexual Satisfaction." *Social and Personality Psychology Compass*
    4, no. 9 (2010): 663–80. doi:10.1111/j.1751-9004.2010.00293.x.

13 Diamond, Lisa M., and Sarah Lucas. "Sexual-Minority and
    Heterosexual Youths' Peer Relationships: Experiences, Expec-
    tations, and Implications for Well-Being." *Journal of Research
    on Adolescence* 14, no. 3 (2004): 313–40. doi:10.1111/j.1532-
    7795.2004.00077.x.

14 "Statistics About Sexual Violence." National Sexual Violence
    Resource Center. Accessed February 12, 2019. http://www.
    nsvrc.org/sites/default/files/publications_nsvrc_factsheet_media-
    packet_statistics-about-sexual-violence_0.pdf.

15 Alptraum, Lux. *Faking It: The Lies Women Tell about Sex—and
    the Truths They Reveal.* New York: Seal Press, 2018.

16 "Rape Addendum." FBI. October 27, 2014. Accessed February
    13, 2019. https://ucr.fbi.gov/crime-in-the.u.s/2013/crime-in-the-
    u.s.-2013/rape-addendum/rape_addendum_final.

17 Du Mont, Janice, Karen-Lee Miller, and Terri L. Myhr. "The Role
    of 'Real Rape' and 'Real Victim' Stereotypes in the Police Reporting

Practices of Sexually Assaulted Women." *Violence Against Women* 9, no. 4 (2003): 466–86. doi:10.1177/1077801202250960.

18 McKinley, James C. "Gang Rape of Schoolgirl, and Arrests, Shake Texas Town." *The New York Times.* March 8, 2011. Accessed February 13, 2019. https://www.nytimes.com/2011/03/09/us/09assault.html?_r=0.

19 "Girlhood Interrupted: The Erasure of Black Girls' Childhood." Report. The Georgetown Law Center on Poverty and Inequality. August 14, 2017. Accessed April 27, 2019. https://www.law.georgetown.edu/poverty-inequality-center/wp-content/uploads/sites/14/2017/08/girlhood-interrupted.pdf.

20 "Victim's and Father's Statements in Campus Sexual Assault Case Draw Strong Reactions Online." *Women in the World.* June 6, 2016. Accessed February 13, 2019. https://womenintheworld.com/2016/06/06/victims-and-fathers-statements-in-campus-sexual-assault-case-draw-strong-reactions-online/.

21 Grinberg, Emanuella. "Mad About Brock Turner's Sentence? It's Not Uncommon." CNN. September 4, 2016. Accessed February 13, 2019. https://www.cnn.com/2016/09/02/us/brock-turner-college-athletes-sentence/index.html.

22 Freedman, Estelle B. *Redefining Rape: Sexual Violence in the Era of Suffrage and Segregation.* Cambridge, MA: Harvard University Press, 2015.

23 Letzter, Rafi. "Here's How Bad Government Math Spawned a Racist Lie About Sexual Assault." *Business Insider.* October 18, 2016. Accessed February 13, 2019. https://www.businessinsider.com/stupid-racist-meme-rape-black-men-2016-10.

24 Michelle Eddy, and Stephanie Sandor. "Perceptions of Rape Perpetrators Based on Skin Tone, Attire, and Relationship to Victim." *Journal of Undergraduate Research* XIV (2011): 1–9. Accessed February 13, 2019. https://www.uwlax.edu/urc/jur-online/PDF/2011/eddy.sandor.PSY.pdf.

25 Hauser, Christine. "Gunman Quoted as Saying: 'I Have to Do It.'" *The New York Times.* June 18, 2015. Accessed February 13, 2019. https://www.nytimes.com/live/updates-on-charleston-church-shooting/gunman-was-quoted-as-saying-i-have-to-do-it/.

26 "Perpetrators of Sexual Violence: Statistics." RAINN. Accessed February 13, 2019. https://www.rainn.org/statistics/perpetrators -sexual-violence.

27 finoh, maya, and jasmine Sankofa. "The Legal System Has Failed Black Girls, Women, and Non-Binary Survivors of Violence." American Civil Liberties Union. Accessed April 27, 2019. https:// www.aclu.org/blog/racial-justice/race-and-criminal-justice/legal-system-has-failed-black-girls-women-and-non.

28 Korbel, Marissa. "Sometimes You Make Your Rapist Breakfast." *Harper's Bazaar.* April 25, 2018. Accessed February 13, 2019. https://www.harpersbazaar.com/culture/features/a19158567/ what-is-rape/.

29 Marcello, Maria. "My Rape Was Unacceptable. It Wasn't Trau- matising." Medium.com. September 8, 2014. Accessed February 13, 2019. https://medium.com/@missmarcello/my-rape-was -unacceptable-it-wasnt-traumatising-f9cb99a6b012.

30 McGee, Hannah, Madeleine O'Higgins, Rebecca Garavan, and Ronán Conroy. "Rape and Child Sexual Abuse: What Beliefs Persist About Motives, Perpetrators, and Survivors?" *Journal of Interpersonal Violence* 26, no. 17 (2011): 3580–593. doi:10.1177/0886260511403762.

31 Iconis, Rosemary. "Rape Myth Acceptance in College Students: A Literature Review." *Contemporary Issues in Education Research (CIER)* 1, no. 2 (2011): 47. doi:10.19030/cier.v1i2.1201.

32 Ferguson, Claire E., and John M. Malouff. "Assessing Police Clas- sifications of Sexual Assault Reports: A Meta-Analysis of False Reporting Rates." *Archives of Sexual Behavior* 45, no. 5 (2015): 1185–193. doi:10.1007/s10508-015-0666-2.

33 Spohn, Cassia, Clair White, and Katharine Tellis. "Unfounding Sexual Assault: Examining the Decision to Unfound and Identi- fying False Reports." *Law & Society Review* 48, no. 1 (2014): 161–92. doi:10.1111/lasr.12060.

34 Lind, Dara. "What We Know About False Rape Allegations." Vox.com. June 1, 2015. Accessed February 13, 2019. https://www. vox.com/2015/6/1/8687479/lie-rape-statistics.

35 Spohn, Cassia, Clair White, and Katharine Tellis. "Unfounding Sexual Assault: Examining the Decision to Unfound and Identifying False Reports." *Law & Society Review* 48, no. 1 (2014): 161–92. doi:10.1111/lasr.12060.

36 "The Criminal Justice System: Statistics." RAINN. Accessed February 13, 2019. https://rainn.org/statistics/criminal-justice-system.

37 Ibid.

38 Armstrong, Ken, and T. Christian Miller. *A False Report: A True Story of Rape in America*. New York: Crown Publishers, 2018.

39 Green, Erica L., and Sheryl Gay Stolberg. "Campus Rape Policies Get a New Look as the Accused Get DeVos's Ear." *The New York Times*. July 12, 2017. Accessed February 13, 2019. https://www.nytimes.com/2017/07/12/us/politics/campus-rape-betsy-devos-title-iv-education-trump-candice-jackson.html.

CHAPTER 4

1   "Parents Ratings Advisory Study—2015." Motion Picture Association of America. 2015. Accessed February 13, 2019. https://www.mpaa.org/wp-content/uploads/2015/11/Parents-Rating-Advisory-Study-2015.pdf.

2   Silverberg, Cory, and Fiona Smyth. *Sex Is a Funny Word*. New York: Seven Stories Press, 2015.

3   Fine, Cordelia. *Testosterone Rex: Myths of Sex, Science, and Society*. New York: W. W. Norton, 2018.

4   Meyer, Elizabeth J. "The Danger of 'Boys Will Be Boys.'" *Psychology Today*. March 14, 2014. Accessed February 13, 2019. https://www.psychologytoday.com/us/blog/gender-and-schooling/201403/the-danger-boys-will-be-boys.

5   Chaplin, Tara M., and Amelia Aldao. "Gender Differences in Emotion Expression in Children: A Meta-Analytic Review." *Psychological Bulletin* 139, no. 4 (2013): 735–65. doi:10.1037/a0030737.

6 "APA Guidelines for Psychological Practice With Boys and Men."
   American Psychological Association. August 2018. Accessed
   February 13, 2019. https://www.apa.org/about/policy/boys-men-
   practice-guidelines.pdf.

7 "Morbidity and Mortality Weekly Report (MMWR)." Centers for
   Disease Control and Prevention. June 7, 2018. Accessed February
   15, 2019. https://www.cdc.gov/mmwr/volumes/67/wr/mm6722a1.
   htm?s_cid=mm6722a1_w.

8 Scheller, Alissa. "At Least a Third of All Women Murdered in the
   U.S. Are Killed by Male Partners." *HuffPost Canada*. December
   6, 2017. Accessed February 13, 2019. https://www.huffingtonpost.
   ca/entry/men-killing-women-domesti_n_5927140.

9 Berkowitz, Bonnie, Denise Lu, and Chris Alcantara. "The Terrible
   Numbers That Grow With Each Mass Shooting." *The Washington
   Post*. January 24, 2019. Accessed February 13, 2019. https://www.
   washingtonpost.com/graphics/2018/national/mass-shootings-in-
   america/?noredirect=on&utm_term=.f3b0db084ea7.

10 Whitton, Sarah W., Christina Dyar, Michael E. Newcomb, and
   Brian Mustanski. "Romantic Involvement: A Protective Factor for
   Psychological Health in Racially Diverse Young Sexual Minorities." *Journal of Abnormal Psychology* 127, no. 3 (2018): 265–75.
   doi:10.1037/abn0000332.

11 "Report of the APA Task Force on Appropriate Therapeutic
   Responses to Sexual Orientation." American Psychological Association. Accessed February 15, 2019. https://www.apa.org/pi/lgbt/
   resources/sexual-orientation.

12 "Parent Tips for Preventing and Identifying Child Sexual Abuse."
   American Academy of Pediatrics. Accessed February 15, 2019.
   https://www.aap.org/en-us/about-the-aap/aap-press-room/news-
   features-and-safety-tips/Pages/Parent-Tips-for-Preventing-and-
   Identifying-Child-Sexual-Abuse.aspx.

13 Savage, Elayne. *Don't Take It Personally: The Art of Dealing With
   Rejection*. Oakland, CA: New Harbinger Publications, 1997.

14 "Penn GSE Report Offers District-by-District Look at How
   Black Students Are Disciplined at Highest Rates in Southern
   Schools." Penn GSE. August 25, 2015. Accessed February

13, 2019. https://www.gse.upenn.edu/news/press-releases/penn-gse-report-offers-district-district-look-how-black-students-are-disciplined.

15 Hurley, Katie. *The Happy Kid Handbook: How to Raise Joyful Children in a Stressful World*. New York: TarcherPerigee, 2015.

16 Ward, L. Monique, and Jennifer Stevens Aubrey. "Watching Gender: How Stereotypes in Movies and on TV Impact Kids' Development." Report. Common Sense Media. 2017. Accessed February 13, 2019. https://www.commonsensemedia.org/sites/default/files/uploads/pdfs/2017_commonsense_watchinggender_executivesummary_0620_1.pdf.

17 Chapman, Rachel. "A Case Study of Gendered Play in Preschools: How Early Childhood Educators' Perceptions of Gender Influence Children's Play." *Early Child Development and Care* 186, no. 8 (2015): 1271–284. doi:10.1080/03004430.2015.1089435.

18 "Girls Feel They Must 'Play Dumb' to Please Boys." University of Warwick. August 5, 2014. Accessed February 13, 2019. https://warwick.ac.uk/newsandevents/pressreleases/girls_feel_they/.

19 Blum, Robert W., Kristin Mmari, and Caroline Moreau. "It Begins at 10: How Gender Expectations Shape Early Adolescence Around the World." *Journal of Adolescent Health* 61, no. 4 (2017). doi:10.1016/j.jadohealth.2017.07.009.

20 "Challenging Gender Stereotypes in the Early Years: The Power of Parents." Report. Our Watch. 2018. Accessed February 13, 2019. https://www.ourwatch.org.au/getmedia/e42fe5ce-8902-4efc-8cd9-799fd2f316d7/OUR0042-Parenting-and-Early-Years-AA.pdf.aspx?ext=.pdf.

21 Myers, Kyl. "Sweet Social Experiment?" *Raising Zoomer*. March 13, 2016. Accessed February 13, 2019. http://www.raisingzoomer.com/article/2016/1/26/sweet-social-experiment.

CHAPTER 5

1 United States. Centers for Disease Control and Prevention. Division of Adolescent and School Health. "Trends in the Prevalence of Sexual Behaviors and HIV Testing National YRBS: 1991–2017."

Accessed February 12, 2019. https://www.cdc.gov/healthyyouth/data/yrbs/pdf/trends/2017_sexual_trend_yrbs.pdf.

2 Ibid.

3 Wade, Lisa. "Sociology and the Culture of Sex on Campus—Sociological Images." *Sociological Images.* February 3, 2017. Accessed February 13, 2019. https://thesocietypages.org/socimages/2017/02/03/sociology-and-the-culture-of-sex-on-campus/.

4 Males, Mike A. *Teenage Sex and Pregnancy: Modern Myths, Unsexy Realities.* Santa Barbara, CA: Praeger, 2010.

5 Shulman, Shmuel, Inge Seiffge-Krenke, and Sophie D. Walsh. "Is Sexual Activity During Adolescence Good for Future Romantic Relationships?" *Journal of Youth and Adolescence* 46, no. 9 (2017): 1867–877. doi:10.1007/s10964-017-0699-z.

6 Furman, Wyndol, and Charlene Collibee. "Sexual Activity With Romantic and Nonromantic Partners and Psychosocial Adjustment in Young Adults." *Archives of Sexual Behavior* 43, no. 7 (2014): 1327–341. doi:10.1007/s10508-014-0293-3.

7 Harden, K. Paige. "True Love Waits? A Sibling-Comparison Study of Age at First Sexual Intercourse and Romantic Relationships in Young Adulthood." *Psychological Science* 23, no. 11 (2012): 1324–336. doi:10.1177/0956797612442550.

8 Di Giacomo, Ester, Michael Krausz, Fabrizia Colmegna, Flora Aspesi, and Massimo Clerici. "Estimating the Risk of Attempted Suicide Among Sexual Minority Youths." *JAMA Pediatrics* 172, no. 12 (2018): 1145. doi:10.1001/jamapediatrics.2018.2731.

9 Mustanski, Brian, and Richard T. Liu. "A Longitudinal Study of Predictors of Suicide Attempts Among Lesbian, Gay, Bisexual, and Transgender Youth." *Archives of Sexual Behavior* 42, no. 3 (2012): 437–48. doi:10.1007/s10508-012-0013-9.

10 Rubin, A. G., M. A. Gold, and B. A. Primack. "Associations Between Depressive Symptoms and Sexual Risk Behavior in a Diverse Sample of Female Adolescents." *Journal of Pediatric and Adolescent Gynecology* 22, no. 5 (2009): 306–12. doi:10.1016/j.jpag.2008.12.011.

11 Schalet, Amy T. *Not Under My Roof: Parents, Teens, and the Culture of Sex*. Chicago: University of Chicago Press, 2011.

12 Sedgh, Gilda, Lawrence B. Finer, Akinrinola Bankole, Michelle A. Eilers, and Susheela Singh. "Adolescent Pregnancy, Birth, and Abortion Rates Across Countries: Levels and Recent Trends." *Journal of Adolescent Health* 56, no. 2 (2015): 223–30. doi:10.1016/j.jadohealth.2014.09.007.

13 "Sex Under the Age of 25." Rutgers. Accessed February 15, 2019. https://www.rutgers.international/how-we-work/research/sex-under-age-25.

14 United States. Centers for Disease Control and Prevention. Division of Adolescent and School Health. "Trends in the Prevalence of Sexual Behaviors and HIV Testing National YRBS: 1991–2017." Accessed February 12, 2019. https://www.cdc.gov/healthyyouth/data/yrbs/pdf/trends/2017_sexual_trend_yrbs.pdf.

15 Planned Parenthood. "Sexual Health Information for Teens." Planned Parenthood. Accessed March 5, 2019. https://www.plannedparenthood.org/learn/teens.

16 Vernacchio, Al. *For Goodness Sex: Changing the Way We Talk to Teens About Sexuality, Values, and Health*. New York: Harper, 2014.

17 Palmer, Melissa J., Lynda Clarke, George B. Ploubidis, and Kaye Wellings. "Prevalence and Correlates of 'Sexual Competence' at First Heterosexual Intercourse Among Young People in Britain." *BMJ Sexual & Reproductive Health*, 2019. doi:10.1136/bmjsrh-2018-200160.

18 Kempner, Martha. "Poverty Causes Teen Parenting, Not the Other Way Around." *Rewire.News*. June 3, 2013. Accessed February 13, 2019. https://rewire.news/article/2013/04/29/poverty-causes-teen-parenting-not-the-other-way-around/.

19 "History of Sex Education in the U.S." Planned Parenthood. November 2016. Accessed February 13, 2019. https://www.plannedparenthood.org/uploads/filer_public/da/67/da67fd5d-631d-438a-85e8-a446d90fd1e3/20170209_sexed_d04_1.pdf.

20 "A History of Federal Funding for Abstinence-Only-Until-Marriage Programs." SIECUS. June 30, 2009. Accessed February

13, 2019. https://siecus.org/wp-content/uploads/2018/07/4-A-Brief-History-of-AOUM-Funding.pdf.

21 United States. Office of Management and Budget. May 23, 2017. Accessed February 13, 2019. https://www.whitehouse.gov/sites/whitehouse.gov/files/omb/budget/fy2018/budget.pdf.

22 Hellmann, Jessie. "Abstinence Education Advocate Named to HHS Post." *The Hill.* June 6, 2017. Accessed February 13, 2019. https://thehill.com/policy/healthcare/336620-abstinence-education-advocate-named-to-hhs-post.

23 "Abstinence-Only-Until-Marriage Policies and Programs: An Updated Position Paper of the Society for Adolescent Health and Medicine." *Journal of Adolescent Health* 61, no. 3 (2017): 400–03. doi:10.1016/j.jadohealth.2017.06.001.

24 Shepherd, Lindsay M., Kaye F. Sly, and Jeffrey M. Girard. "Comparison of Comprehensive and Abstinence-Only Sexuality Education in Young African American Adolescents." *Journal of Adolescence* 61 (2017): 50–63. doi:10.1016/j.adolescence.2017.09.006.

25 Fox, Ashley M., Georgia Himmelstein, Hina Khalid, and Elizabeth A. Howell. "Funding for Abstinence-Only Education and Adolescent Pregnancy Prevention: Does State Ideology Affect Outcomes?" *American Journal of Public Health* 109, no. 3 (2019): 497–504. doi:10.2105/ajph.2018.304896.

26 Breuner, Cora Collette. "Talking About Sex: AAP Recommends Evidence-Based Education, With Pediatricians' Help." AAP Gateway. January 23, 2019. Accessed February 13, 2019. http://www.aappublications.org/news/2016/07/18/SexEd071816.

27 "Abstinence-Only-Until-Marriage Policies and Programs: An Updated Position Paper of the Society for Adolescent Health and Medicine." *Journal of Adolescent Health* 61, no. 3 (2017): 400–03. doi:10.1016/j.jadohealth.2017.06.001.

28 "Separate Program for Abstinence Education." Compilation of the Social Security Laws. February 22, 2018. Accessed February 13, 2019. https://www.ssa.gov/OP_Home/ssact/title05/0510.htm#ft25.

29 US Census Bureau. "Unmarried and Single Americans." Census Bureau QuickFacts. August 3, 2018. Accessed February 13, 2019. https://www.census.gov/newsroom/facts-for-features/2017/single-americans-week.html.

30 "Births: Final Data for 2015." Centers for Disease Control and Prevention. January 5, 2017. Accessed February 13, 2019. https://www.cdc.gov/nchs/data/nvsr/nvsr66/nvsr66_01.pdf.

31 Rebhahn, Peter. "Juneau County District Attorney Loses Re-Election Bid." Wiscnews.com. August 16, 2012. Accessed February 13, 2019. https://www.wiscnews.com/portagedailyregister/news/local/juneau-county-district-attorney-loses-re-election-bid/article_e8e78fbe-e752-11e1-93c8-0019bb2963f4.html.

32 Sclamberg, Alexis, Samantha Kimmey, and Corinna Barnard. "Utah's Feticide Law Puts Miscarriage on Trial." *Women's ENews*. April 19, 2010. Accessed February 13, 2019. https://womensenews.org/2010/04/utahs-feticide-law-puts-miscarriage-trial/.

33 "Sex Education Law Needs a New Look." *Daily Herald*. June 3, 2008. Accessed February 13, 2019. https://www.heraldextra.com/news/opinion/editorial/article_2da39f66-0e87-5560-b69d-120c4d4ddb16.html.

34 "'No Promo Homo' Laws." GLSEN. Accessed February 13, 2019. https://www.glsen.org/learn/policy/issues/nopromohomo.

35 Paik, Anthony, Kenneth J. Sanchagrin, and Karen Heimer. "Broken Promises: Abstinence Pledging and Sexual and Reproductive Health." *Journal of Marriage and Family* 78, no. 2 (2016): 546–61. doi:10.1111/jomf.12279.

36 Wu, Lawrence L., Steven P. Martin, and Paula England. "Reexamining Trends in Premarital Sex in the United States." *Demographic Research* 38 (February 27, 2018): 727–36. Accessed February 25, 2019. https://www.demographic-research.org/Volumes/Vol38/27/.

37 "Sexual Behaviors | Adolescent and School Health | CDC." Centers for Disease Control and Prevention. June 14, 2018. Accessed February 13, 2019. https://www.cdc.gov/healthyyouth/sexualbehaviors/.

38 "Advancing Sex Education." SIECUS. May 2018. Accessed February 13, 2019. https://siecus.org/wp-content/uploads/2018/07/CSE-Federal-Factsheet-May-2018-FINAL.pdf.

39 Jehl, Douglas. "Surgeon General Forced to Resign by While House." *The New York Times.* December 10, 1994. Accessed February 15, 2019. https://www.nytimes.com/1994/12/10/us/surgeon-general-forced-to-resign-by-white-house.html.

40 Stacey, Dawn, and Meredith Shur. "How Does Plan B Work to Prevent Pregnancies?" Verywell Health. November 12, 2018. Accessed February 16, 2019. https://www.verywellhealth.com/how-plan-b-works-906842.

41 Abrams, Abigail. "No, Birth Control Doesn't Make You Have Riskier Sex, Researchers Say." *Time.* October 12, 2017. Accessed April 15, 2019. http://time.com/4975951/donald-trump-birth-control-mandate-sexual-behavior/.

42 Dann, Carrie. "NBC/WSJ Poll: Support for *Roe v. Wade* Hits New High." NBCNews.com. July 23, 2018. Accessed February 13, 2019. https://www.nbcnews.com/politics/first-read/nbc-wsj-poll-support-roe-v-wade-hits-new-high-n893806?smid=nytcore-ios-share.

43 Cartwright, Alice F., Mihiri Karunaratne, Jill Barr-Walker, Nicole E. Johns, and Ushma D. Upadhyay. "Identifying National Availability of Abortion Care and Distance from Major US Cities: Systematic Online Search." *Journal of Medical Internet Research* 20, no. 5 (May 2018). doi:10.2196/preprints.9717.

44 Editorial board. "When Prosecutors Jail a Mother for a Miscarriage." *The New York Times.* December 28, 2018. Accessed February 13, 2019. https://www.nytimes.com/interactive/2018/12/28/opinion/abortion-pregnancy-pro-life.html.

45 "HPV Vaccination Coverage Data." Centers for Disease Control and Prevention. August 23, 2018. Accessed February 13, 2019. https://www.cdc.gov/hpv/hcp/vacc-coverage/index.html?CDC_AA_refVal=https://www.cdc.gov/hpv/hcp/vacc-coverage.html.

46 "An Overview of Minors' Consent Law." Guttmacher Institute. February 5, 2019. Accessed February 13, 2019. https://www.guttmacher.org/state-policy/explore/overview-minors-consent-law.

47 Jerman, Jenna, Tsuyoshi Onda, and Rachel K. Jones. "What Are People Looking for When They Google 'Self-Abortion'?" Guttmacher Institute. February 26, 2018. Accessed February 13, 2019. https://www.guttmacher.org/article/2018/02/what-are-people-looking-when-they-google-self-abortion.

48 Colman, Silvie, Thomas Dee, and Theodore Joyce. "Do Parental Involvement Laws Deter Risky Teen Sex?" *Journal of Health Economics* 32, no. 5 (September 2013): 873–80. doi:10.3386/w18810.

49 Adolescence, Committee on. "The Adolescent's Right to Confidential Care When Considering Abortion." *Pediatrics*. February 1, 2017. Accessed February 13, 2019. http://pediatrics.aappublications.org/content/139/2/e20163861.

50 Chow, Kat. "Walgreens Pharmacist Refuses to Provide Drug for Ariz. Woman With Unviable Pregnancy." NPR. June 25, 2018. Accessed February 13, 2019. https://www.npr.org/2018/06/25/623307762/walgreens-pharmacist-denies-drug-for-woman-with-unviable-pregnancy.

51 Bilton, Nick. "Parenting in the Age of Online Pornography." *The New York Times*. January 7, 2015. Accessed February 13, 2019. https://www.nytimes.com/2015/01/08/style/parenting-in-the-age-of-online-porn.html.

52 "Report of the APA Task Force on the Sexualization of Girls." Report. 2007. Accessed February 13, 2019. https://www.apa.org/pi/women/programs/girls/report-full.pdf.

53 Ibid.

54 McCall, Catherine. "The Sexualization of Women and Girls." *Psychology Today*. March 4, 2012. Accessed February 13, 2019. https://www.psychologytoday.com/us/blog/overcoming-child-abuse/201203/the-sexualization-women-and-girls.

55 Graff, Kaitlin A., Sarah K. Murnen, and Anna K. Krause. "Low-Cut Shirts and High-Heeled Shoes: Increased Sexualization Across Time in Magazine Depictions of Girls." *Sex Roles* 69, no. 11–12 (2013): 571–82. doi:10.1007/s11199-013-0321-0.

56 Ragusa-Salerno, Laura M., and Kristen M. Zgoba. "Taking Stock of 20 Years of Sex Offender Laws and Research: An Examination of Whether Sex Offender Legislation Has Helped or Hindered Our Efforts." *Journal of Crime and Justice* 35, no. 3 (2012): 335–55. doi:10.1080/0735648x.2012.662069.

57 "Raised on the Registry | The Irreparable Harm of Placing Children on Sex Offender Registries in the US." Human Rights Watch. June 23, 2015. Accessed February 13, 2019. https://www.hrw.org/report/2013/05/01/raised-registry/irreparable-harm-placing-children-sex-offender-registries-us.

58 Letourneau, Elizabeth, speaker. "Child Sexual Abuse Is Preventable, Not Inevitable." TEDMED. 2016. Accessed February 13, 2019. https://www.tedmed.com/talks/show?id=620399.

59 Letourneau, Elizabeth J., Andrew J. Harris, Ryan T. Shields, Scott M. Walfield, Amanda E. Ruzicka, Cierra Buckman, Geoffrey D. Kahn, and Reshmi Nair. "Effects of Juvenile Sex Offender Registration on Adolescent Well-Being: An Empirical Examination." *Psychology, Public Policy, and Law* 24, no. 1 (2018): 105–17. doi:10.1037/law0000155.

60 Jennings, Diane. "Some Say List Ruins a Juvenile's 2nd Chance." *Dallas Morning News.* July 19, 2009. Accessed February 13, 2019. https://www.pressreader.com/usa/the-dallas-morning-news/20090719/281629596268593.

61 Schmidt, Samantha. "Cyntoia Brown, Sentenced to Life for Murder as Teen, Is Granted Clemency." *The Washington Post.* January 7, 2019. Accessed February 13, 2019. https://www.washingtonpost.com/local/social-issues/cyntoia-brown-a-16-year-old-sentenced-to-life-for-murder-granted-clemency/2019/01/07/8f4ac71e-12a2-11e9-803c-4ef28312c8b9_story.html.

62 Claiborne, William. "Unwed Mothers Lift Welfare Costs." *The Washington Post.* December 9, 1993. Accessed February 13, 2019. https://www.washingtonpost.com/archive/politics/1993/12/09/unwed-mothers-lift-welfare-costs/5496d986-8c03-47c7-810a-aeb1146b4900/?utm_term=.1d7dc5b16f6a.

63 Hasinoff, Amy Adele. *Sexting Panic: Rethinking Criminalization, Privacy, and Consent.* Urbana, IL: University of Illinois Press, 2015.

64 "Representing Lesbian, Gay, Bisexual, Transgender, Queer, or Questioning (LGBTQ) Youth in Juvenile Court." Office of the Juvenile Defender. Report. April 2011. Accessed February 13, 2019. http://www.ncids.org/JuvenileDefender/Guides/LGBTQ_Guide.pdf.

65 "Sex Offender Laws and Child Offenders." Human Rights Watch. 2007. Accessed February 15, 2019. https://www.hrw.org/reports/2007/us0907/7.htm.

66 Nelson, Teresa. "Minnesota Prosecutor Charges Sexting Teenage Girl With Child Pornography." American Civil Liberties Union. December 3, 2018. Accessed February 13, 2019. https://www.aclu.org/blog/juvenile-justice/minnesota-prosecutor-charges-sexting-teenage-girl-child-pornography.

67 "Victory! Judge Dismisses Charges in Minnesota Teen Sexting Case." ACLU of Minnesota. September 7, 2018. Accessed April 15, 2019. https://www.aclu-mn.org/en/press-releases/victory-judge-dismisses-charges-minnesota-teen-sexting-case.

68 "Pregnancy and Childbearing Among U.S. Teens." Planned Parenthood Federation of America. June 2013. Accessed February 16, 2019. https://www.plannedparenthood.org/files/2013/9611/7570/Pregnancy_And_Childbearing_Among_US_Teens.pdf.

69 "Youth at Disproportionate Risk." American Psychological Association. Accessed February 13, 2019. https://www.apa.org/pi/lgbt/programs/safe-supportive/disproportionate-risk/index.

70 Jones, Jeffrey M. "Americans Hold Record Liberal Views on Most Moral Issues." Gallup.com. May 11, 2017. Accessed February 13, 2019. https://news.gallup.com/poll/210542/americans-hold-record-liberal-views-moral-issues.aspx.

CHAPTER 6

1 "The Determinants of Health." World Health Organization. December 1, 2010. Accessed February 13, 2019. https://www.who.int/hia/evidence/doh/en/.

2 Faludi, Susan. "The Patriarchs Are Falling. The Patriarchy Is Stronger Than Ever." *The New York Times*. December 28, 2017. Accessed February 13, 2019. https://www.nytimes.

com/2017/12/28/opinion/sunday/patriarchy-feminism-metoo.
html.

3   Anti-Defamation League. "The Pyramid of Hate." ADL New
    York/New Jersey. Accessed March 5, 2019. https://nynj.adl.org/
    the-pyramid-of-hate/.

4   "Mentors in Violence Prevention Game Change Curriculum
    Overview." Northeastern University. October 2016. Accessed
    February 13, 2019. https://www.northeastern.edu/sportinsociety/
    wp-content/uploads/2016/10/MVP-for-Game-Change
    -Curriculum-Progression.pdf.

5   Manne, Kate. *Down Girl: The Logic of Misogyny.* Oxford:
    Oxford University Press, 2019.

6   Staub, Ervin. *The Roots of Evil: The Origins of Genocide and
    Other Group Violence.* Cambridge, MA: Cambridge University
    Press, 2007.

7   Barnet, Victoria J. "The Changing View of the 'Bystander' in
    Holocaust Scholarship: Historical, Ethical, and Political Implica-
    tions." *Utah Law Review* 4 (2017): 633–47.

8   Tabachnick, Joan. "Engaging Bystanders in Sexual Violence
    Prevention." National Sexual Violence Resource Center. 2009.
    Accessed February 13, 2019. https://www.nsvrc.org/sites/default/
    files/Publications_NSVRC_Booklets_Engaging-Bystanders-
    in-Sexual-Violence-Prevention.pdf.

9   Ruiz-Grossman, Sarah. "Hundreds of New Yorkers Are Taking
    Classes to Defend Muslim Neighbors." *The Huffington Post.*
    March 2, 2017. Accessed February 25, 2019. https://www.
    huffingtonpost.com/entry/accompany-project-bystander
    -training_us_58b5b19fe4b0a8a9b7868733.

10 Murphy Austin, Megan J., Christina M. Dardis, Milo S. Wilson,
    Christine A. Gidycz, and Alan D. Berkowitz. "Predictors of
    Sexual Assault–Specific Prosocial Bystander Behavior and Inten-
    tions." *Violence Against Women* 22, no. 1 (2015): 90–111.
    doi:10.1177/1077801215597790.

11 Berkowitz, Alan D. "A Grassroots Guide to Fostering Healthy
    Norms to Reduce Violence in Our Communities: Social Norms

Toolkit." New Jersey Coalition Against Sexual Assault. 2017. Accessed February 13, 2019. http://socialnorms.org/wp-content/uploads/2017/03/Social_Norms_Violence_Prevention_Toolkit.pdf.

12 Oluo, Ijeoma. "When You Can't Throw All Men Into the Ocean, What CAN You Do?" Medium.com. November 11, 2017. Accessed February 13, 2019. https://medium.com/the-establishment/when-you-cant-throw-all-men-into-the-ocean-start-over-what-can-you-do-a9e48b040d08.

13 Alexander, Michelle. "Reckoning With Violence." *The New York Times*. March 4, 2019. Accessed March 4, 2019. https://www.nytimes.com/2019/03/03/opinion/violence-criminal-justice.html.

14 Brown, Brené. *Daring Greatly: How the Courage to Be Vulnerable Transforms the Way We Live, Love, Parent, and Lead*. London: Penguin Books, 2016.

15 Factora-Borchers, Lisa. "The Fragility of Safety: Beyond the Promise of #MeToo." Bitch Media. December 28, 2017. Accessed February 13, 2019. https://www.bitchmedia.org/article/fragility-safety/beyond-promise-metoo.

16 Warnke, Melissa Batchelor. "How to Be a Male Ally to Survivors of Sexual Assault & Harassment." Refinery29. October 16, 2017. Accessed February 13, 2019. https://www.refinery29.com/en-us/2017/10/176776/how-to-be-an-ally-sexual-assault.